Between Overs

Between Overs

How Life Gets in the Way of Cricket

Michéle Savidge

A story of love and loss inspired by Sir Viv Richards

First published by Pitch Publishing, 2022

Pitch Publishing
A2 Yeoman Gate
Yeoman Way
Worthing
Sussex
BN13 3QZ
www.pitchpublishing.co.uk
info@pitchpublishing.co.uk

ISBN 978 1 80150 071 5

Typesetting and origination by Pitch Publishing
Printed and bound in Great Britain by TJ Books, Padstow

Contents

In memory of my wonderful father,

Bill Savidge, who opened the door

The End

A Week Before the Funeral

A DESICCATED dead mouse lies on its side on a plate of old, cold chips. One of its eyes is open, completely white and staring at me. I tear open a packet of bright yellow Marigold rubber gloves, put them on with a shudder to pick up the mouse and walk out to the garden, where I lay it gently on a pile of crinkly leaves. Going back into the house, I notice that the edge of the front door is deeply gouged and I realise it must have been scarred by the paramedics when they took my mother out for her journey to the hospital. I know she will be (sorry, would have been) absolutely furious that they had damaged the door. I trip over a pile of newspapers and dozens of tins of food – mostly rice pudding and sliced peaches – as I make my way back into the living room and begin to gather up some damp clothes and put them in a carrier bag. I am crying so much I feel as though I am under water and my chest aches, almost as if I have been punched. I can feel my mum's spirit all around me; she cannot rest yet.

My mother was a world champion hoarder and every inch of carpet is smothered in rubbish. I know that the tiniest morsel of detritus had meant something to her, even the Fruit Pastilles wrappers of which there are dozens. I can hear her voice in my head saying, 'Just leave that, will you?'

I can't leave it but how can I even begin to sort it out?

Among the chaos, my father's slippers are still lined up neatly side by side at the foot of the armchair where he used to sit until his death five years before. On the chair is an open, empty CD case: The Treorchy Male Choir, a favourite of my mother's. (Definitely not of my father, who was passionate about big band jazz and Frank Sinatra.) I switch on the CD player.

Well, that was a big mistake.

If you are already feeling bereft, would hearing a Welsh choir help? And if you then heard them sing:

> Close thine eyes and sleep secure
> Thy soul is safe, thy body sure
> He that guards thee, he thee keeps
> Who never slumbers, never sleeps
> A quiet conscience in a quiet breast
> Has only peace, has only rest
> The music and the mirth of kings
> Are out of tune unless she sings

Then close thine eyes in peace and rest secure
No sleep so sweet as thine, no rest so sure

Would that help you to feel a) better or b) worse?

I am still crying enough tears to fill a Welsh valley and try to focus on a pile of papers next to where my mum, until only last week, had spent her days – and nights. She was an inveterate notetaker all her life; writing down the time when she had turned the immersion on (and off); noting what time she boiled the kettle; a reminder to wash her skirts or dust the skirting board; pages of the exact time all telephone calls were made and received, and of their duration. And every single jotting had been kept. Over the next few weeks, I will find thousands and thousands of these notes, as well as hundreds of letters she wrote and never sent.

But from the middle of the scruffy bits of paper, a menu on thick white card falls on to the threadbare carpet. It is from an *Evening Standard* lunch at the Café Royal held years ago to honour the legendary England cricketer Denis Compton. In my previous life as a cricket journalist, a career that had seemed impossibly out of reach to me when I was a young girl, I had spoken to the great man after lunch and, on the menu, Compton had written to my father, *To Bill, God Bless You, Denis Compton.*

'That was me!' I thought. 'What on earth happened to her?'

The reminder of my other life was the starting pistol to begin my journey through grief. After all, the expedition had to begin somewhere, even if it just meant putting one foot in front of the other. But how did I navigate my way through a world that no longer held my parents, who I had loved with all my heart?

The trouble was, I didn't know how to start. All I knew was that I felt I was no longer anyone's daughter and, if I wasn't that, who was I?

Opening the Batting
A Village in Somerset, Summer 1973

IT WAS the hottest and sunniest of days, as all our childhood summer days undoubtedly become the older we get. The sky was as blue as Paul Newman's eyes (Paul Newman, the Hollywood actor not the former Derbyshire cricketer) and the clouds were as wispy as cotton wool. I could go on but let's just say it was as close to a damn perfect English summer's day as it was possible to be. Well, who is going to contradict me from this distance?

I was sprawled by the boundary, trying to arrange my pre-pubescent giraffe-like legs into something approaching sophistication. Not much chance of that. And, anyway, my legs were (and still are) the very essence of Nottingham-grey: a shade you will struggle to find on any paint chart.

The match on the other side of the rope was trundling along like so many others before and since.

Nothing to see here, move along. I could just wallow in watching the dance in front of me. Men all in white moving in synchronised waves from the boundary ropes each time the bowler ran up to the wicket, then a lethargic walk backwards after the batsman had hit the ball. Slow, slow, quick-quick, slow. After a few overs of the dance and a throaty cry of 'Howzat?' came the quiet applause from perhaps a dozen pairs of hands.

I yawned and looked at my father, prone on the grass. He opened one eye. 'Wicket?' he asked. I nodded and he stirred to prop himself up on one elbow.

I could hear a few murmurs from the pavilion and a cloud briefly appeared before ambling off. The atmosphere changed then: it was as though a divine being somewhere above turned the sunlight to its highest setting. Yards away, the men in white became iridescent. There was a little more chatter and the air itself seemed to quiver. There may even have been a small earth tremor. Well, trust me, I felt it.

The incoming batsman prowled out of the pavilion, wheeling his right arm, then his left, his bat held momentarily above his head, seemingly already in victory. He wasn't especially tall but he seemed to tower over the rest of the men on the field. He carried himself differently too, not in an arrogant way but definitely with some swagger. It was as if a swashbuckler had arrived on a battlefield where most of the men lay dead or dying and was ready to claim he had slain them all.

He took his position at the crease, checked his guard, held his bat as though it were a blade and looked around the field for the gaps he knew he had a God-given right to breach.

First ball: thwack. It even sounded different. His predecessor's style had definitely been more: thud. The ball had no choice other than to speed towards the boundary, the fielders' slow, slow, quick-quick, slow choreography simply not up to chasing it. The next ball went the same way. How did this batsman have more time to see it and then know exactly what to do with it?

A few of the spectators sat a little more upright, my father included, in response to the change in tempo from the man in the middle. It seemed that more people were arriving at the ground by the minute but my memory, even if I have got the weather right, might be playing tricks here. I put an end to my off-field sprawl and sat up, utterly transfixed.

It was a different game now. The leaden ballroom shuffle was still being practised by the fielding side but the batsman was Fred Astaire compared to them. By the tenth ball the batsman struck, my father was on his haunches and just as spellbound as me.

He looked at me and beamed. 'He's a bit good, isn't he? I'll just go and find out his name.'

My father stood up, rubbed the small of his back as was his habit, and I watched him walk towards the pavilion.

I had been watching cricket from early childhood, mostly at Trent Bridge, where my father would drop off my brother and me at Test and county games, our little hands clutching bags of soon-to-be squashed sandwiches, crisps and pop. I had seen plenty of world-class players. But I had never seen one like this. He looked like a Greek god, if a Greek god had ever wielded a cricket bat.

My father returned with his news. 'I think we should keep an eye on that young man, don't you, sweetheart? I've got a feeling we're going to hear a lot more about him.'

And that was the day Vivian Richards changed my life.

Chapter One

Careers For Girls

I was a moody and hyper-anxious teenager (show me the girl and I will show you the woman) and spent most days sobbing in my bedroom, reading *The Cricketer* magazine and listening to David Cassidy singing 'Could It Be Forever?' on my rudimentary stereo. Thinking about it now, it was probably a mono.

MAYBE IT isn't possible to get truly hooked by music, sport, literature or films until you find The One. Then that's it; you're in, nailed on. Oh of course there will be Other Ones you hear, see, read or watch but, however many turn up, they can never replace The One who opens the door to rampant enthusiasm, if not obsession. You start collecting paraphernalia that you proclaim will be valuable memorabilia of the future. All you can talk about is The One, spilling random facts into every family meal and God forbid anyone trying to change the subject because you will just get The Hump. Oh, the joy and the pain of that youthful compulsion.

Years later, with many more summers under your belt and as you start to throw away a few bits and bobs (because, come *on*, why on earth do you need to keep *that* for God's sake?), you might just feel wildly grateful that The One so enriched your little life.

It might also help if you don't have Ones competing in the same category in your younger days. It was fortunate, then, that David Cassidy (my One for music) didn't have to be displaced from my wall by Viv Richards. David just had to be squished up a bit. To be fair, there wasn't a lot of Viv paraphernalia around then, so I don't think David was too put out. And neither of them were disturbed by the poster of Elton John – at head height so I could kiss him every morning – on the inside of my wardrobe door. All was good and peaceful on my walls then, for a while at least. Until more of anything to do with West Indies cricket generally – Viv opened the door to that too – started to be stuck over David's pictures. I'm sorry, David; I feel guilty now about my fickleness, especially when I think about your wretched later life. There is still a sliver of my heart that belongs to you, though, and even now the opening bars of 'How Can I Be Sure' make my knees tremble.

I still wasn't quite a teenager, although my moodiness (I have actually been a slave to my hormones my entire life) and immense height (more gawkiness and gangliness in truth; I just *felt* really tall) gave the lie to that. I was uncomfortable in my skin, completely alarmed by my bodily changes and embarrassed by my (I thought) hideous buck front teeth. I had sucked my thumb until I was eight years old, which had caused my teeth to protrude with a gap into which I could put a twopence piece, had I ever needed to. In my early teens, I used to curl my tongue up and over my teeth to hide them.

My moody behaviour sometimes startled me more than it did my poor parents and little brother, Mark, the only solace for all of us being the countless times I was sent to my room where, in between my hysterical sobbing, I could lie on my bed and read *The Cricketer* magazine usually accompanied by Cassidy's 'Could It Be Forever?' on repeat on my rudimentary stereo. Actually, thinking about it now, it was probably a mono.

Growing up in a Derbyshire village, I was a confused and anxious child (show me the girl and I will show you the woman) and completely ill prepared for all that puberty was about to hurl at me. My mother wasn't ready either; in fact, she was in denial, a safe place she would inhabit on many other occasions in her life. In this instance, she was so far along the road of denial that I had written her a letter, which I left on her bedside table, telling her that I thought I had started my periods. She didn't mention it for a few days until one morning she told me 'not to be so stupid', so I decided to make my own sanitary protection out of folded Izal toilet paper (ouch)[1] which led to many gory incidents (think along the lines of *The Texas Chainsaw Massacre* and you'll get the picture) and secret knicker-washing in the bathroom. There were some nights when I would lie in bed in agony from the heavy bleeding, the cramps and the discomfort from my makeshift non-absorbent, greaseproof sanitary pads. I didn't really know what was happening to my poor body although, for many weeks, I thought I might die and imagined my parents standing around my bed as I lay dead among mountains of discarded bloody paper.

Three months after I had written the note to my mother, I discovered a packet of Libresse (the very name!) sanitary pads in my underwear drawer. They had been put there by my father. I knew he had got them as he was the one who did all the shopping for the household, my mother too afraid of most things (for example, she would hide with us in a cupboard under the stairs if salesmen, who she referred to as gypsies, knocked on our front door) and especially of going into a supermarket. I am not exaggerating when I say that Libresse changed my life and it was another early indicator that my father, the thoughtful purchaser, was a modern man in the 1970s before modern man had even been imagined.

---

1 Younger readers may need to Google.

Neither of my parents, however, were modern enough to properly discuss my bodily changes and there was no mention of it at my all-girls' school either. Indeed, the school had been established in 1799 and seemed to have based its sex education on the practices of that time. Thus, I thought my first period, when I didn't think I was dying, actually signified that I was pregnant. I discussed this with a couple of friends at school during a morning break-time in the playground and they advised me that they didn't think it meant that, although they couldn't be completely sure. This confused me even more and I tried to rehearse telling my parents that I was expecting a baby even though, somewhere at the back of my mind, I thought maybe a boy did need to be involved and I hadn't ever spoken to one of those, apart from my brother, so how could it have happened?

At that stage, I was just trying to get through each day of increasingly volatile mood swings and schoolwork wasn't exactly my priority. There was far too much science and maths and not nearly enough reading and writing for my liking. I had been told at the age of five by a maths teacher to 'go over there and write something, you're quite good at that but not really any good at numbers, are you?' 'Why, thank you Miss,' I should have replied, 'for ensuring that I won't enjoy anything to do with numbers for the rest of my life.' Her legacy would also mean that I would have difficulty remembering cricket scores in the future. But, hey, that's why we have *Wisden*, isn't it?

Maths lessons, for me, were a special form of torture and they induced headaches that often resulted in vomiting. This under-researched condition meant I lost count (obviously) of the number of hand basins I blocked before the realisation that if I threw up in a toilet, I wouldn't have to spend ages trying to force bits of my disgusting school lunch down a plughole. And when I say 'disgusting', I mean just that. Every Thursday, we were served up 'dead bird pie', which the school professed to be chicken. It didn't fool us. I swear that I once spotted in a pie a little yellow beak of a blackbird. And as for the semolina … please, let's not remember that in any great detail.

My frequent nauseous episodes also meant I missed many modules of maths lessons, which only added to my complete confusion about the subject. There would often be a critical piece of information which I had missed, meaning I would never know exactly how I had to justify an answer to some obscure algebraic formula. It was utterly bewildering to me. And, really, what was the point of algebra? Was I ever, ever going to need that in my dreamed-of career as a sports journalist?

To help me overcome my aversion to maths, my mother enlisted the paid help of a young chap called Chris, who would trudge round to our house a couple of times a week to drink beer and sigh when I got yet another calculation wrong. He would explain formulas and methods to show me my mistakes but all I heard was, 'Blah, blah, blah' and nothing at all went in.

After a few weeks of this, when I had made zero (one number I was well acquainted with) progress, I realised that Chris was spending far more time talking to Mum than teaching me how to do equations. I noticed, too, that Mum would be busy applying lipstick every time Chris came to our door. Nothing untoward to report and, looking back, I suppose I can't blame my mother for enjoying a frisson of excitement. I hoped it made up for the fact that I wasn't.

However, even with this extra tuition, my mock O level maths exam paper was, according to poor Mrs Lowe, who marked it, one of the worst she had ever seen in her long career. (I got 17 per cent. That would probably be a decent pass these days.) She did add that some of my answers were correct but she had no idea how I had worked them out, so she couldn't mark them.

Bizarrely, I took this to mean that I was, in fact, a misunderstood and unrecognised mathematical genius who had devised some remarkable methods which the world was not yet ready for. So I ploughed on with my recherché workings-out. My theory was spectacularly debunked, however, in the O level proper, which I failed three times. (I counted that on my fingers.) Meanwhile, my genius little brother took his O level two years early and got an A. Indeed, he even got an A in Advanced Maths before I achieved a pass in the Ordinary.

Maths aside, the main thrust of my school seemed to lie in the compulsory practice of handwriting with an italic fountain pen for what seemed like several hours every day. Woe betide you if you didn't make your dots above an *i* or a *j* into a perfect diamond shape. You might say it was not a school with much space for freedom of expression.

I had to find my solace where I could and my gangly legs and I did find some in running, specifically in the 100 metres and 200 metres, having built up speed over many hours of racing my father round the village cricket ground. He told me that he would stop training me the day I beat him. That day never came (yet the man was 33 years older than me). As I remember, it was while I was ripping up the grass track in a 100 metres race on a school sports day that a Derby Athletics Club coach spotted me and invited me to go for a trial. Success there meant that I spent the next few years getting up early at weekends to travel on coaches to Northampton, Leicester and other glamorous Midlands towns to compete for Derby Ladies Athletic Club.

My father would often follow later to wherever I was running and stand yelling encouragement at the finishing line. It might sound as though he was what would now be termed a pushy parent but I won't allow that. Even then, I realised he was simply helping me to try my best because he knew that would make me feel good about myself. In common with his generation, pushy parenting was not a feature: it was the *trying* that was important.

However, my extreme nerves often threatened to get the better of me in the starting blocks, where if you had given me the choice between running and vomiting I would have taken throwing up every time. That dread also made me a slow starter but, after the first ten metres, I would settle into my stride and run like someone had shoved a firework up my backside. I discovered, for the first time, that I enjoyed winning as well as the mindfulness – although that was not a word we used in that decade – that sprinting gave me. I could literally run away from all my angst and not think about anything else other than being the first to the tape. It might have been only a few seconds' respite from my brain but at least it was some. Maybe that is why some people take illegal drugs but I'll take running, thanks. Or I did for a while.

Glory years don't last forever, though, and as I began to throw myself into full-blown and thoroughly revolting adolescence, I realised that boys and cigarettes (preferably combined) were much more exciting than multiple training sessions in cold, wet weather. And thus my dreams of competing in the Olympics disappeared in a puff of smoke.

* * *

At my – and perhaps at most – all-girls' school in the late 1970s, there was only a rudimentary nod to discussions about our future professions. It may be hard to imagine now but in those pre-Thatcher days not much was expected of many young girls, unless you were very brainy (I wasn't). If you were interested in reading or writing, like me, you might aspire to become a librarian or a teacher. If you were more scientifically-minded, you could become a dental assistant or a doctor's receptionist. The thought of being an actual dentist or doctor didn't have much traction. Or maybe that was just me.

The same year that I saw Viv Richards bat for the first time, I was given a book entitled *Careers for Girls*, which had first been published in 1966; my copy published in 1973 was the third edition. I am not sure whether there were any more but I certainly hope not. I still have the book or, more accurately, I discovered it while I was clearing out my mother's house. (You see, there can be advantages to having had a hoarder mother.) the *Daily Mirror*, some distance perhaps from its future as a self-professed beacon for feminism, reviewed it as 'an admirable new reference book which should be in every school library'. Meanwhile, the *Times Educational Supplement* in its review of the book said, 'Great care has been taken to make this information accurate, yet readable by the average girl in search of ideas.'

As we have already established, I was certainly an average girl. Exceedingly average by any standards. Thus

I was able to cross out a number of potential careers: accountancy; air stewardess – helpfully the book actually pointed out that 'an attractive appearance (not too tall or heavy)' was a positive attribute; beautician (some of the personal qualities listed are 'a liking for women of all ages' and for *naturally* – their italics – good skin'), and it was a 'no' from me for becoming a florist, for which one of the personal characteristics advised was 'good health (no tendency to chilblains)'. The next time I go into a florist, I must remember to ask them about their circulation.

I could also rule out on many grounds (i.e. aforementioned mathematical inability) a career as a quantity surveyor, although I could agree with their advice that potential candidates should show 'indifference to working in an almost all-male world'.

I had even marked a cross in thick black pen on the chapter devoted to publishing, a career you might have thought would appeal to my literary bent. However, the book pointed out that there were limited opportunities to be had in this industry, although 'women do well in children's and educational publishing. There is no prejudice against women in publishing as a whole but this is a very overcrowded field. However, women have the advantage in that they can use the back door closed to men – they can come in as secretaries.' Fantastic news!

A few careers had 'excellent' prospects, including chiropody, which didn't really attract me though perhaps I might find myself having to earn my money where I could? But, no, they needed an O level in one science subject or mathematics, so I would probably fall short. A shame, though, as I might have been able to fulfil the personal attributes outlined: 'Unlike many other careers with patients, the shy, retiring girl may get on well, providing she is polite and even-tempered with patients.' I lived in hope that, one day, I might, if my hormones ever achieved some equilibrium, become even-tempered, so perhaps if I also passed a maths exam (a combination that admittedly seemed very unlikely), looking after people's feet could become an option.

More tempting could have been a career as a press photographer but any thoughts in that direction could be swiftly dispatched with the warning that 'prejudice against girls is understandable, as editors send out press photographers on stories which may involve roughing it, and on assignments where girls would be unwelcome'. In the callowness of youth, I had no idea what 'roughing it' could possibly mean and the book didn't give examples of what assignments might involve girls being unwelcome but, many years on, perhaps we could all take a few moments together just to imagine some?

No? Me neither.

The only career I had marked with three forceful ticks in pen (as opposed to the pencilled crosses I had written next to almost everything else) was journalism.

However, I had written question marks in Biro under some of the personal attributes listed for journalists: 'resourcefulness, resilience, tact, willingness to work very hard, punctuality'. I had enclosed this last requirement on the list into my own Biro brackets as though my 12-year-old self had perhaps thought this was an optional characteristic.

The book advised that in choosing a career in journalism, 'there are no special difficulties for women. Many section editors are women but few are sub-editors and editors-in-chief.' But, it warned, 'there are more applicants for jobs than vacancies in big cities'. In fact, with a klaxon seemingly erupting from the page, it went on, 'On newspapers: Journalism is a highly competitive profession and only the good *and* [their italics] the tough have much chance on London papers – in the provinces it is not so difficult.' That'll be the provinces for me then.

No mention at all in this 1973 updated edition of *Careers for Girls* of prospects for a girl in sports journalism. I imagine that the writer of The Guide prepared something along the lines of, 'There are no prospects for a girl in sports journalism regardless of her academic ability. The men would have a tendency to look down on her and not encourage her as it is very much their domain and they would rather it wasn't infiltrated by a mere girl,' but the editor struck it out as irrelevant and taking up too much space in the book.

So it looked as though I would have to devise my own plan, daunting though that was.

When I wasn't listening to David Cassidy or thinking about Viv Richards, I spent a disproportionate amount of my time watching sport on television and started to write a few dummy reports of cricket and football matches. I screwed up most of them into paper balls and threw them in the bin or to our black and white cat, Bosie, for her to play with. She had been a stray who adopted my father (it was definitely that way round) at his office and he had no option but to bring her home. She was stunningly beautiful, with a touch of Sophia Loren about her, and I was heartbroken when she died during the Edgbaston Test of Botham's Ashes series in 1981; but I am getting ahead of myself.

The practice of writing those reports emboldened me enough to write an account of an actual village football match in the dizzying Derby and District Combination League Division 2. I sent it to the sports editor of the *Derby Evening Telegraph*. Luckily, my mother had saved his reply. He wrote, 'I was interested to read your football report, not least because we do not receive many from young ladies.' Did you feel that pat on the head there?

He was faintly encouraging, or at least offered enough for me ('all round, it was a very good effort') to continue with my dream of becoming a sports journalist, even though I had no idea how I was going to turn it into reality, because I continued to blaze a trail of mediocrity during my schooldays. I dreaded exams; had pneumonia during my O levels and spent two A level exams in the sickroom throwing up into a Dettol-smelling bowl under the unsympathetic eye of the school matron who made Miss Trunchbull in *Matilda* appear to have the compassion of a saint.

For my A levels, and prior to throwing up in those exams, I attended a boys' school, which had just started admitting girls into the sixth form. The move had been a bold decision on my father's part – not least because of the financial sacrifice – but he was determined that I should learn to compete with the male gender if I was to pursue my dream career. However, even with his undoubted wisdom, my father had not accounted for the melting pot of oestrogen and testosterone in a school of just 12 girls and 550 boys.

I spent the first couple of terms in a dogfight with my hormones, losing all sense of reason and decorum in the pursuit of a very unsuitable boy, John (the problem being that he wasn't in pursuit of me and much preferred one of my friends). It took me some time to get over the shame of throwing myself at his feet (as well as a characteristically pathetic experiment with an attempted overdose of paracetamol, which was the first of several depression-related episodes in my life) but the little resilience I had soon saw me back on the hunt and I started going out with Gord from the year above.

With no thought for my feelings, this was the exact time that singer-songwriter-actor Graham Fellows chose to issue the single 'Jilted John' by Jilted John with its chorus of *Gordon Is A Moron* which, of course, caused much hilarity at school. It was well worth the *Schadenfreude* to be had, however, while singing one of the song's best lines *He's more of a man than you'll ever be* whenever John walked past me in a corridor.

It didn't take me long to fall hook, line and sinker for Gord, who had the added attraction of returning to his family home in Zambia for school holidays, meaning he didn't clash with my cricket-watching. Last year, I discovered that my mother had kept, in a damp sideboard, several shoeboxes of letters[2] exchanged between Gord and me (I only hope she never read them). I was reminded that we often wrote to each other more than once a day, sometimes three times, such was the intensity of our relationship which, in fact, lasted for more than four years. I can't report that the letters contained much of substance other than teenage cooings, where we had been for drinks and how we couldn't wait to see each other again. What was very clear was that my poor heart ached for Gord when he was away.

Perhaps under Gord's influence (he was naturally clever), I also began to settle down to my school work, revelling in longer A level English Literature lessons.

---

2   Younger readers again please Google.

W.H. Auden became my One for poetry and my obsession means that I can still recite huge chunks of his work today. To be honest, it's a pretty useless 'skill'. In fact, my daughters are sick of me quoting from WH Auden's 'As I Walked Out One Evening' which I recite in my bleaker moments while trying to alleviate theirs. There is much in the poem about regret and how time will defeat us all. Admittedly, it is not very cheery.

However, I really didn't like looking at Auden's face on the front of his *Selected Poems* (it is worth pointing out that even the poet himself described his face as looking 'like a wedding cake left out in the rain'). Instead, I stuck over it a photograph of Formula One racing driver James Hunt, which gave me, as it might have given you, infinitely more joy.

I had my English teacher, Mr Edmonds, to thank for my passion for Auden. I'd seen him as inspirational, until one of his lessons gave an insight into what lay beneath his thin veneer of respectability. He leant suggestively across a desk to ask me, 'Has anyone ever told you that you have got bedroom eyes?' It was totally inappropriate and I stormed out of the classroom. I thought little of it until a few years later, when he was convicted of paedophilia and thankfully would never teach again.

Another of my sixth form teachers – take a bow Mr Pete Cash wherever you may be – had written in a report that 'Michéle is a remarkably intelligent young lady'.

To be fair, Mr Cash's lessons mostly involved listening to Leonard Cohen and Bob Dylan, so perhaps I hadn't needed to use too much of my remarkable intellect. Mr Cash's glowing praise, you will be unsurprised to hear, was not reflected in any actual results and I missed out on going to my first-choice university to read philosophy. What, in any case, had I been thinking in applying for *that*? During one of my interviews, possibly at Essex, a lecturer asked me what I would think if an elephant started to come through the walls of the interview room. I replied, 'I would think I was drunk.' It must have been pretty clear to them that philosophy was not my natural calling but I recently found their offer letter at the bottom of a wardrobe (thanks, again, Mum, although I think now that she must have opened it and never told me). They wrote that they would consider me even if I didn't get the required grades. To think just how close I came to joining Plato, Socrates, Kant, Aristotle et al.

Instead, I ended up studying for one of the first BA degree courses in English and Media which, like all the later degrees in that conjoined subject, was merely an arrangement of words in any order that added up to nothing much. It did cement my passions for Auden and also Thomas Hardy (definitely my One in the novelist category) but that was about it. Hardy is seemingly out of favour now and will probably be on the cancelled list soon. It is surely a tragedy worthy of Hardy himself that a whole generation (or more) may have chosen not to expose themselves to such prose as:

'To her he was, as of old, all that was perfection, personally and mentally. He was still her Antinous, her Apollo even; his sickly face was beautiful as the morning to her affectionate regard on this day no less than when she first beheld him; for was it not the face of the one man on earth who had loved her purely, and who had believed in her as pure.'[3]

I immersed myself in Hardy's novels, walked the walks he had walked in Dorset and even made a short film (it remains unreleased but my mother kept it in the bottom of my bedroom cupboard) called *A Journey Through The Mayor of Casterbridge*. One of my fellow undergrads asked me whether I had made it as far as The Mayor's alimentary canal. Well, he thought it was witty.

Hardy apart, the real upside of my 'degree' was that the lack of intense application to my studies allowed me to further deepen my obsession with cricket. When my parents moved from the East Midlands to my mother's county of birth, Somerset, in 1980, I joined Somerset CCC to watch more of Viv and also Joel Garner, who became The One to ignite my passion for West Indies fast bowling. I became a committed Somerset fan; my maroon Triumph Dolomite later

---

3   *Tess of the D'Urbervilles*, Thomas Hardy, 1891.

sporting a sunstrip (again, younger readers may have to Google those) announcing *Somerset Do It On Grass*, which *might* have been an ironic reference to some players enjoying cannabis as well as to cricket. Being vehemently anti-drugs, I refused to believe any rumours about *that*.

But it was all well and good being wrapped up in cricket, whether watching at a ground, on TV or listening to the radio. How was I actually going to get a job? Ludicrously, I had applied for the job as the secretary – which was actually a senior administrative post rather than clerical – at Derbyshire County Cricket Club while completely ignoring the advice in *Careers for Girls* that 'nothing can be more disappointing than aiming too high and failing'. I don't think I got a reply (or my mother didn't keep it). I did find, though, a reply from Somerset CCC dated 13 August 1982 in response to my enquiry about the post of club secretary there. It pointed out that the secretary was the club's principal paid employee and addressed the letter to me as 'Dear Sir'.

There was only one thing for it. I was going to have to take my car on the road and find my dream cricket job, wherever it might be. By this stage in the Dolomite's life, I was always accompanied on the Bri-Nylon-upholstered (I kid you not, that was the standard fabric) passenger seat by my *Haynes Motor Manual*. That book was my guide to once removing the battery and carrying it two miles to a repair garage. It hadn't warned me, though, how heavy a car battery was and I couldn't lift my arms for the next few days. But even Haynes hadn't been much use on one of my regular journeys along the Fosse Way. On that trip, I heard a deafening, clanking rattle around my rear end while driving up a steep hill near Stow-on-the-Wold in Gloucestershire. I managed to pull into a lay-by and was just getting out of the car when I heard the beep of a horn. With both of us a hundred miles or so from home, there was my dear dad, in his pale yellow Triumph 2.5 PI[4], by chance driving along the same road.

'Are you all right, sweetheart?' he asked, screeching to a halt, saying just the right words from just the right mouth at just the right moment. We walked round to the back of my car to find the rusty exhaust hanging by a thread. My father thought there was only one thing for it: I put on a pair of old gloves to pull the exhaust off and continued on my way for a very noisy drive home.

I got the Dolomite into as roadworthy a state as possible after graduating, working in a pub to pay for car repairs as well as to earn enough money to follow much of Pakistan's summer tour of England. I fully intended to try to make a contact who would give me a proper job in cricket but first was distracted by the sublime spectacle in Taunton of Viv Richards scoring 181 not

---

4   The Triumph 2.5 PI (Petrol Injection) was Britain's first fuel-injected family car. Oh, the excitement!

out for Somerset against the tourists. I didn't speak to anyone other than a barman for the entire game. No matter; the summer stretched before me and life was looking pretty good(-ish).

The 1982 Test series was billed as a contest between Imran Khan, Pakistan's fearsome new captain, and England's Ian Botham, fresh from his breathtaking Ashes exploits of the previous year. Imran, with his leaping fast bowling style, didn't disappoint in the first Test at Edgbaston, where he took 7-52 in England's first innings but the home side went on to win the match by 113 runs thanks to Derek Randall's superb 105 in the second innings. It was the first time I had seen Pakistan in the flesh in a Test match and what an initiation it was. Imran had really set his intentions for the summer and he was glorious to watch.

The second Test at Lord's was a different story for England, as is so often the case at the home of cricket, and Pakistan walloped them by ten wickets. Mohsin Khan scored a double hundred in Pakistan's 428/8 declared first innings and England could only make 227 all out in reply. With Pakistan enforcing the follow-on, England were bowled out for 276, with Mudassar Nazar taking six wickets for 32 and, in just 13 overs, Mohsin Khan and Javed Miandad rattling off 77 runs to steer their team to a resounding win.

The series was tantalisingly poised at 1-1 for the final Test ten days later at Headingley and, after a stuttering drive – the Dolomite was really struggling by then and I had spent much of the journey leaning well forward over the steering wheel in an attempt to give it momentum – I arrived at a low-rent bed and breakfast on the outskirts of Leeds. The terraced house where I would be spending the next few nights smelled of chip fat even by the front gate and the landlady was in a suitably greasy floral housecoat when she opened the door to welcome me. It was far from salubrious and I wondered whether the 'B&B' on her swaying sign, which unsurprisingly advertised 'Vacancies' even during a sold-out Test match, stood for Bed & Bugs.

By then, I was as discontented as my poor car appeared to be. It was the end of the summer, I still hadn't got a job and there were none on the horizon. The next morning, though, I woke up to the delicious anticipation that the first day of a Test match provides (and somewhat more appetising than Mrs Grease's fried breakfast), so I put my dejection to one side. Cricket can do that for you. So many questions run through your mind at the dawn of a new Test: who will win the toss? Bat or bowl first? What am I going to eat? Will I see someone I know? What's your score prediction for the first day? It feels like sitting in the dark, hugging yourself in excitement, before the lights go up and the curtains open at the theatre. Ta dah!

I spent most of the match in the Pakistan section of the ground, where the atmosphere was electric, making new friends who delighted in teaching me pro-Pakistan chants. How we all would have laughed if we had known then that Imran would become Prime Minister of his country or, indeed, that I would go on to work for him.[5] One of those events, though, would be rather more important in his life.

The game was a thriller: low-scoring, full of drama and sub-plots, including the inevitable dodgy umpiring decision when Sikander Bakht was given out, caught by Mike Gatting off Vic Marks, by umpire David Constant. The Pakistan fans were convinced Constant had got the decision wrong and were furious. That was the only time I felt less than welcome among my new friends.

Imran, to put it mildly, was not a fan of dubious decisions from the men in white coats and later became a prime mover in the campaign for neutral umpires. Indeed, I often thought he used his editorial column in *Cricket Life*, the magazine on which we would later both work, as a sort of party political manifesto as he wrote about the subject in virtually every issue. He did have a good point, though, and eventually the game's administrators thought so too. Imran played beautifully at Headingley (67 not out in the first innings, 46 in the

---

5 Nor did I know then that my future husband had been awarded a scholarship to Oxford University and was there at the same time as Imran. It is rumoured that one of the two men uttered the famous proclamation, 'I am the best f*** in Oxford'. I will leave you to decide which.

second and a total of eight wickets in the match) and the Test was in the balance up until the fifth day when England won by three wickets and the three-match series 2-1. Imran, the player of this match and of the series, was right that this was a watershed for Pakistan cricket: England would not win another Test series against them for 18 years.

My fond memories of that match are mainly due to the fact that my own fortunes took a definite turn for the better through a convoluted link. One of my father's friends, Ian Davison, who had played for Nottinghamshire in the 1960s, knew the *Test Match Special* scorer Bill Frindall, the late and much-lamented Bearded Wonder (a nickname shortened to Bearders). Frindall managed a touring team called the Malta Maniacs with whom my father, standing as a very amateur umpire, had toured Singapore earlier that year. I had met Bearders at a Malta Maniacs dinner and had mentioned that I was looking for a job in cricket journalism. (Bearders later sent me a postcard asking if I would like to accompany him as a handmaiden on England's tour to Australia that winter. I didn't know what a handmaiden was or did – although even in my naivety I suspected it might involve something more than sharpening pencils – so I declined as politely as I could without burning any bridges.) I timidly made my way up the long flight of steps to the *TMS* box at Headingley to say hello to Bill, who casually mentioned that Christopher Martin-Jenkins, the editor of *The Cricketer*, now very sadly no longer with us, was looking for a secretary. Was I interested in him putting in a word for me?

Was I interested? Now, on one level, this was extremely annoying. I had graduated with plans of earning a starting salary of at least £10,000 a year and saving up to buy a Maserati to replace my Dolomite by the time I was 25. Looking again at *Careers for Girls*, I see that I had put a pencilled X against the section for secretarial and clerical work. The only other mark on that page, forcefully made in fountain pen (and, defiantly, without italic dots above the 'i's), reads 'Gil and Michéle woz here 10.9.74'.

But I put those dreams to one side and arranged to meet CMJ in the Headingley car park after close of play on the fourth day. Characteristically, he was late for our 'interview' and could only just see me over the tower of books he was carrying. I put on my best voice (in other words downplayed my Nottinghamshire accent) and when he asked whether I could type, replied, 'Yes, of course.' I couldn't, but knew I would teach myself. On the strength of that chat, CMJ asked when I could start. I was so excited I forgot where I had parked my car and spent the next two hours wandering the streets around Headingley.

The next morning saw England, after quite a few stutters, complete their win by three wickets, which only added to my celebratory mood. The six-hour drive home passed in a flash – well, as close to a flash as my car could manage – in my eagerness to tell my parents that I actually had a job. And on *The Cricketer*, no less, which, apart from my Haynes book, had been my instruction manual for much of my life. There was no time to rest, though, as I taught myself to type in three weeks, bought a couple of suits from Next with my mother's help and prepared for my new life in the bright lights of Redhill, Surrey.

I should confess here that I had never been sartorially confident. At the age of 21, I had still not grown into my body; my legs were too long, I was too thin, despite eating like a horse, and never seemed to know how to 'carry' myself like so many other young women I saw. On the other hand, my mother, in those days, was always immaculately dressed head to toe in the latest size 6 Jaeger outfit with matching lipstick, so perhaps I thought I just couldn't compete with her. Ever since she was a teenager she had made a performance of 'putting her face on', which involved a very heavy application of foundation and a precisely-placed black beauty spot slightly above and to the right of her red-lipsticked mouth. I used to find it infuriating because it meant I would have to wait for what seemed like hours for the face-painting to be complete.

I would now give you my face to be able to wait for her to do that. Yet another life lesson right there.

But thank God I had swallowed my preconceptions about being a secretary. There was a lot more to the job on *The Cricketer* than making tea and filing, although there was a fair amount of that. Naturally, there were a few green ink letters from some saddo readers pointing out statistical errors in the previous issue but I quickly felt I was at the veritable epicentre of the cricket world. Every day, there would be a letter or phone call from one or more of the game's worthies and it was all I could do not to faint with reverence every few minutes. I mean EW ('Jim') Swanton regularly rang up. And there were all those letters from Harold ('Dickie') Bird. And then there were all the books! I had landed in cricket nirvana.

CMJ, with his commitments as a broadcaster, after-dinner speaker and author as well as a journalist, was not in the office a great deal but I was able to receive first-class editorial training from another legend: Andrew Longmore, again late and very, very much lamented (I am sorry this has become a theme for this chapter), was the magazine's assistant editor. As he was so over-stretched (these days we might call it stressed), he increasingly asked me to do proper editorial work (cutting and pasting, in other words), which I managed alongside handling CMJ's correspondence. Our editor, when he was in the country, was notoriously disorganised and I would often have to fire up the Dolomite to meet him with his mail in a lay-by off the A24 when he ran out of time to get to the office. The job was not at all glamorous but that didn't dampen my enthusiasm for it, even if the £3,000-a-year salary was some distance from what I had planned on earning.

My accommodation wasn't that ritzy either. After a few false starts in other digs, in one of which the landlady prepared half-a-grapefruit with a cherry in the middle for my breakfast every day, I rented a couple of rooms in a ramshackle ancient cottage in Reigate from a Mrs Pye, who was as old as her house and farted every time she took a step. There was no heating and every winter's day I woke up to a frosty wardrobe mirror, hence I had no proper idea of what I looked like when I went to work. I shared a bathroom and a kitchen, which *always* smelled of fish paste, with the landlady, who was a kind woman and had actually led a very interesting life, if I had ever bothered to really listen to her. The folly of youth, though, meant I was always rushing and, in any case, I drove home to Somerset every weekend.

After about a year at *The Cricketer*, and still very much in love with my job, I boldly asked if I could be called an editorial assistant instead of secretary. Miraculously, this was agreed. There was no more money but at last it felt as though I might begin to be a proper journalist. By this time, too, I had worked on eliminating my Nottingham accent, answering the phone with 'Good afternoon, *The Cricketer*' with a long 'a' on afternoon as I thought befitted a young lady in Surrey. It wasn't that I was ashamed of my accent, more that I wanted to sound the part and to fit in.

I wrote book reviews, compiled the Young Cricketer section of the magazine and organised the 'Find a Fast Bowler' competition held at Alf Gover's famous cricket school in Wandsworth. Alf, born in 1908, had played for Surrey and England and was a lovely man. After he retired from first-class cricket he devoted his life to his coaching school, which he founded in 1938. Among many others, Viv Richards had benefited from his expertise.

The contest we held at Alf's school was designed to help rectify England's shortage of quicks and attracted many young tearaway bowlers, mostly from London, drawing plenty of press coverage. Sadly, though, the winner, Junior Clifford, didn't go on to trouble England's selectors. I wish I had known what happened to him and also to Delroy Hercules, who was like lightning and had been my favourite to win. Just as well I am not a selector.

I also arranged non-cricketer interviews for the Young Cricketer but am sad to say that letters to my father's hero, Brian Clough, while answered by the great man, didn't result in a meeting. But Mick Robertson, one of the presenters on ITV's *Magpie*, did feature and he later wrote a letter to thank me, saying, 'It is my proudest possession – shown to all my friends and now framed and hung on the wall. Never has your writing been so venerated.' Well, that was nice.

I absolutely loved my job, every minute of it, but the paltry salary was becoming hard to deal with and I started to receive cheques marked 'Return to Drawer'.

'What does that mean?' I asked my father when I got the first such cheque from Mrs Pye, who hadn't known what it meant either.

'It means you're spending too much and not earning enough,' he replied, which was probably as close to a lesson in financial management as I ever got from my father.

I asked *The Cricketer* for a raise but they said they couldn't afford it and after a few more months of bouncing cheques, running out of petrol in the middle of nowhere and living on mashed swede, I had to face up to the soul-destroying prospect of finding another place to work. I felt distraught at the thought of having to give up my dream job but there was no other way round it: I couldn't afford my rent, let alone anything else.

Yet again, positions open to female sports journalists were not exactly troubling the Sits Vac columns. The only one I could find with sport in the title was as assistant editor on a trade magazine called *Sports Industry*. I went for it and got it. Even now, the thought of it makes me want to curl up in a ball, put my head under a pillow and bash it with a baseball bat. The job mainly involved writing about new sunbed launches and the latest gym equipment, much of which seemed to originate from Germany, where I was able to enjoy a few beery business trips. The sparse high points on the magazine were features about groundsmanship, in which I could at least ask the experts in their field about the preparation of cricket pitches. I had to get my fix where I could.

For the sake of keeping my head financially above water (*Sports Industry* paid me double the amount I earned on *The Cricketer* and a car allowance, which meant I sold my Dolomite with a heavy heart), I sucked it all up and continued to work in trade publishing for the next few years. This included time on a magazine called *Body Business* which, while it was as deathly dull as *Sports Industry,* was not actually for undertakers but for fitness managers. Through it all, I was still determined that it was not going to leech my passion for cricket and I would frequently call in sick during Test matches. That was until my cover was blown at Lord's, where I had gone for the first day of a Test against India.

In those days of free-to-air television, the nation enjoyed ball-by-ball coverage plus edited highlights shown in the evenings. Imagine that. That's seven hours of action to be edited down to about 30 minutes. Unfortunately for me, the BBC kept the footage of me, sitting and laughing next to my friend James (then a student, now an eminent QC), in the edited highlights.

And I didn't look very ill at all. In fact, I even made a miraculous recovery to return to work the next day to be greeted with cries of 'Bueller' after the film *Ferris Bueller's Day Off* since so many colleagues had seen me on TV the previous evening. The nickname stuck for the rest of my tenure, which luckily wasn't for much longer.

Leisure Scene, where the publisher greeted me every morning with a shout of "Ello babe!', was another notch on my CV, which was, by then, taking a definite and unwelcome turn from fair to middling and not the course I had been plotting at all at the start of my career. Virtually the only highlight of my time on *Leisure Scene* was a business trip to Finland but even that weekend didn't get off to a good start with a naked, mixed session in a sauna. I was still quite reserved and a little reticent, understandably, about removing my clothes in front of complete strangers. Perhaps the Finns are, too, but by the time you have consumed your own body mass in vodka, it hardly seemed to matter. My article 'A Weekend Never to Remember if Ever There Was One', subtitled 'Having a Sauna with People You Barely Know', recalled the managing director of the sauna company talking to me in German after drinking so much vodka that he had forgotten my nationality. By that stage, I may even have understood him.

But later that same evening, it seemed that I had not only forgotten my nationality but also my dignity by borrowing a luge from someone's front garden to go sledging through the streets at 4am. I mean, I like middle-of-the-night shenanigans as much as the next person but I'm sorry to say it was not the life even for me. I would have given anything to be back on the boundary.

I was still writing freelance cricket articles, including for the much-loved and much-missed *Sticky Wicket* magazine, and I continued to scour the papers for other jobs, although I knew the position I dreamed of was, frankly, a bit niche. I had almost stopped looking. And we all know what happens when we stop looking.

'Deputy editor for a new cricket magazine' read the advert. It was made for me, surely? By now, I knew I had much more senior editorial experience and, if it was at all possible, an even deeper passion for and knowledge about cricket. I *had* to get this job.

I was invited for an interview at the publishers' offices near Piccadilly Circus, an alarmingly flashy address for a new cricket magazine. A smidgeon of research revealed that Imran Khan (him again) was to be the editor-in-chief with a respected journalist, Shahed Sadullah, the editor. I already felt intimidated but bought the smartest two-piece suit I could afford, a dazzling white shirt and new high-heeled shoes to give me, I hoped, height advantage if nothing else. My heart was in those shoes as I walked in to face the three or four men sitting behind a field-sized desk in the offices of *Cricket Life International* ready to lob what would undoubtedly be tough questions.

I was not feeling at all confident.

The one thing I was quite sure about was that the mere fact of my gender was going to count against me and I was definitely going to have to be in the best form of my life.

Quite often, for situations such as those, I prepared mentally as though I was going to play a tough match. I might swing my arms above my head, *á la* Viv Richards, then I would take my guard, prod the ground a few times to check for any dimples in the pitch, play a couple of practice strokes, squint a bit as though I was thinking very carefully about how to play that one, note where the fielders were and then somehow get myself into position to flamboyantly reverse sweep a bad ball through the gap for four.

'Michéle,' began one of the terrifying grey suits from somewhere miles away behind the desk, 'I see from your CV that you recently got married.'

That's so nice! Perhaps he was going to congratulate me?

But no.

'So will you be planning to have children soon?'

Glory be. I squared my child-bearing shoulders, saw that ball as big as a Super Full Moon and gave it a mighty swipe straight back over the bowler's head.

I shuffled a bit in my seat, sat up as tall as I could and replied, 'Are you asking the male candidates the same question?'

The men on the other side of the desk shifted a little in their chairs, which seemed to squeak in unison, but they didn't reply. That'll be a six then.

With the ground rules laid down, the interview went better than I could have dreamed and they offered me the job. I walked out on to Lower Regent Street and looked up at the dull sky. Pah and double pah to that grey day. I clicked my high heels together, managing not to fall over, winked at those clouds and smiled. My love affair with cricket was back on track and the Earth could revolve more smoothly on its axis again. With everything in my world looking up once more, I began to consider again the people who didn't feel the same about the loveliest of ball games. What on earth was wrong with *them*?

For Non-Cricket Speakers

Test Cricket

FOR THE majority of cricket fans, Test (always with a capital T) cricket is the purest form of the game. A Test match is a contest between two international teams featuring each country's top players and is, quite literally, a test of competence, strength and nerve.

The first day of a Test begins with exquisite anticipation and while some might compare Test cricket to chess, to me a chess game doesn't have quite the same frisson. I am more inclined to equate Test cricket to a long marriage in that a certain amount of stamina is involved after the first few overs of titillation have worn off. And, inevitably in the middle of the game, there will be some frustration when someone isn't performing quite as you want them to.

A Test match is allocated five days of continuous play (although until the 1980s it would be played over six days, with a rest day) but can be completed in fewer days depending on whether a team has scored more runs or taken more wickets than the opposition. A match can be drawn due to bad weather and/or light.

A Test series comprises matches – any number between one and seven matches historically but more recently between two and four, largely for commercial opportunities – between two international teams played over a couple or more months.

A day of a Test match will consist of three sessions with a 40-minute break for lunch and 20 minutes for tea. Drinks breaks are also taken. In England, the day's play begins at 11am, lunch is taken at 1pm and tea at 3.40pm. Lunch or tea can be taken early if the weather (rain or bad light) is troublesome. There is also a ten-minute interval at the change of innings, unless the innings is completed within ten minutes of a scheduled interval or close of play. In that case, the interval will include the ten minutes between innings.

With me so far?

There are four potential innings in a Test match. Each innings will see one team bat and the other bowl and field. There is no limit to the length of an innings. The aim of the batting team is to score as many runs as possible while losing as few wickets as possible. The bowling team tries to stop the batting team from scoring while trying to take as many wickets as possible.

A Test team will pick its best players from their nation. (Note that the West Indies side includes all their member countries and islands as each country doesn't have a large enough population to field a competitive Test side; England includes England and Wales; Ireland includes the Republic and Northern Ireland.) Nations gain Test status by applying to the International Cricket Council and there are currently 12 with status: England, Australia, South Africa, West Indies, New Zealand, India, Pakistan, Sri Lanka, Zimbabwe, Bangladesh, Ireland and Afghanistan.

This may sound quite dry, but spectating at a Test match is anything but. It is a chance to meet up with old friends and make new ones, eat your bodyweight in pork pies (or a vegan alternative) before midday, drink warm beer and dodgy white wine. And, between overs, you will talk and hear more crap than anyone should ever have to. There can be hours when nothing much seems to be happening then in the space of a few overs, a lapse in concentration (of the players, if not your own) can turn a game on its head. Add to that the excitement of watching the highest standard of cricket ebb and flow and you have a potent combination for some of the most memorable and glorious days of your life.

Chapter Two

Is He Asleep?
The World Cup Final 1983

It appeared that even spotting the ball at Michael's inaugural cricket match was going to be the greatest obstacle to his enjoyment of the day. The second problem was that he didn't understand the rules of cricket. At all. The third was that he enjoyed very early consumption of pork products so the combination of him and my father meant I spent most of the first hour worrying that we were going to run out of food. But yet again, cricket came to the rescue. Who really cares about the paucity of a pork pie when you've got a World Cup Final to watch?

IN MARCH 1983, one month before the start of the cricket season and when I was still living my best life in my job on *The Cricketer*, it was fair to say that I had had enough of men. Well, of boys pretending to be men. So if you're only 22, could there be anything better to do than go on a very cheap and cheerful package holiday to Ibiza with a friend? Determined never to speak to a man again (unless at work), let alone have a relationship with one, I planned to drink as much sangria and smoke as many Marlboro Lights as I could while trying to make sure that my Nottingham-grey legs became slightly less pale.

Oh well. I met Michael in a queue to a casino in San Antonio on the first night. He was with his friend, Tony, a cricket-lover who was a sensational impersonator of, among others, John Arlott, the great cricket commentator. I should have been alarmed at that very moment as Michael seemed not to know that Arlott was better known for his cricket writing and commentating than for football.

Many years later, in fact, I found a reply from Arlott to a query from Michael written in January 1973 in which the great man said:

> Dear Mr Johnson,
> Thank you very much for your letter. Not all of us read play in the same way, but my point is that no player, however gifted, can be a major midfield player and a major goal scorer at the same time.
> Best wishes,
> Yours sincerely,
> John Arlott

This was a typically beautiful and tactful response from Arlott to an early example, and a predictor of many thousands of future similar incidents, of Michael helping someone with their thinking.

Michael's misapprehension of Arlott should, of course, have been a warning sign on that first evening in Ibiza. But you ignore chemical attraction at your peril (or at least the fear of being 57 and surrounded only by cats) and I spent much of that week watching Michael sleep soundly on an Ibizan beach. In fact, I have spent much of my life since watching Michael sleep in many locations: school plays; a West End performance of *The Lion King*; face down in his plate in an Indian restaurant; driving. He is perhaps the only man who, according to his friend Jon, could fall asleep waterskiing. Despite his obvious foibles and eccentricities, however, I decided he was The One for me, even though he clearly didn't realise it.

There was also another hurdle that had never appeared on my list of prerequisites for a boyfriend: a few years older than me, Michael was going through a complicated divorce (is there any other kind?). My gut instinct told me, though, that my pursuit would eventually end in triumph.

Incidentally, I lent Michael a pair of tight, red satin sports shorts to wear on the beach in Ibiza. Worth noting because it seems extraordinary that he could ever fit into a pair of my shorts (he is now literally twice the man I married) and, he won't have realised until reading this, that those shorts used to belong to Gord.

The holiday romance unexpectedly continued after we returned to England, although I had the small matter of the World Cup to attend to for *The Cricketer*. As the tournament reached its climax, I secured four tickets to the final at Lord's on 25 June; one for me, one for my father and another for my Uncle Dennis. There were a number of contenders putting themselves forward for the remaining ticket but, rashly, I decided that there could be no better occasion to introduce Michael to my dad. I obviously wasn't thinking straight; in fact, I was completely over-excited by the fact it was the West Indies' third consecutive final and they were widely expected to trounce India, playing in their first. India had been made 66-1 by the bookies at the start of the tournament and no one seriously thought they could beat the reigning champions.

I packed plenty of high-fat products with ample potential for post-match salmonella infection into a picnic bag and Michael and I headed off to the Compton Stand at Lord's, where my father and Dennis were waiting. Lord's was extraordinary that day; a cacophony of horns, whistles, bells and flags. Lord's was usually my least favourite ground; it was too restrained, too many old buffers moaning that 'It's just not cricket'. But that day, it was the best place to be.

Taking our seats, I realised, not for the first time and certainly not the last, that Michael couldn't see very well. He was in the habit of wearing just one contact lens and, when questioned, explained that his eyesight was so poor in his 'bad' eye that it was pointless wearing a lens in it. It seemed to make perfect sense to him. I had even got used to waiting at green traffic lights with him in the driving seat apparently not having seen that the lights had changed.

It appeared, then, that even spotting the ball at his inaugural cricket match was going to be the greatest obstacle to his enjoyment of the day. The second problem was that he didn't understand the rules of cricket. At all. The third was that he enjoyed very early consumption of pork products so the combination of him and my father meant I spent most of the first hour worrying that we were going to run out of food. But yet again, cricket came to my rescue. Who cares about the paucity of a pork pie when you've got a World Cup Final to watch?

West Indies captain Clive Lloyd won the toss, put India in and by lunch they were 100-4. As the players walked off for the interval, I stood up and rubbed my palms together with glee. It was going much better than I had hoped and we all thoroughly enjoyed our lunchtime warm white wine. So far, so good. But, soon after lunch, to my father's absolute horror and disbelief, Michael had to close his eyes.

'It's the World Cup Final and he's *asleep*!' my father remarked, although what he actually meant was, 'What on earth are you doing with *him*?' I'm surprised he ever approved of our marriage. Well, he did in time.

That day, the Windies pace quartet was at its magnificent best: Andy Roberts (taking three wickets for 32 runs), Joel Garner (1-24), Malcolm Marshall (2-24) and Michael Holding (2-26) were supported by Larry Gomes (2-49) and India were bowled out for 183 in 54.4 overs. By the change of innings, I was feeling pretty sure that the Windies had this one in the bag.

At that time, Gordon Greenidge and Desmond Haynes were by far the best opening partnership in the world and the majority of the crowd thought the duo would knock off the target of 184 with ease. But when Greenidge faced his 12th ball, it was my confidence that took a knock. He completely, unbelievably, misjudged a ball from Sandhu, shouldered arms and was bowled on his off stump. Windies 5-1. Okay, that wasn't exactly part of the plan but my man, the best number three batsman in the world ever, will just be in a bit earlier than we thought, so it will all be fine.

Viv came down the pavilion steps, prowled on to the field like a tiger and wheeled his right arm, then his left, above his head. It's just his thing.

Viv was electrifying, imperiously clattering the ball to all corners of the ground, and my nerves settled. I could just relax now and enjoy the ride. Surely? Soon it was 50-1 and surely Viv would wrap this up in no time. But then Haynes drove at a ball from Madan Lal and was caught by Binny. 50-2.

There was still no need to panic because as soon as one West Indies legend was out, another entered the arena, so the Windies – and I – could still feel confident as Lloyd, 'the Big C', 'Super Cat', came in. He was walking a bit gingerly, though, and taking his first single he seemed to pull a groin muscle and called for a runner. Not ideal, but you would still back the reigning champions, wouldn't you?

It is no exaggeration to say that what happened next, in the space of nine seconds, might have changed international cricket – not just Indian cricket – forever.

Viv took his guard and looked round the ground, rolled his mighty shoulders and prepared to face the next ball from Madan Lal. We all heard the thwack of his bat on the ball as he went for the hook. But he had mistimed it. Kapil Dev was running towards the boundary, shouting what sounded very much like, 'It's mine, it's mine, it's mine' and looking over his left shoulder as the ball started to come down from high up in the heavens. It looked as though the ball might go for four but Kapil ran some 20 yards to take a brilliant catch. It had taken nine seconds from Madan Lal releasing the ball to Kapil snatching it out of the air, but it had felt like an eternity.

The noise having woken him up, Michael shouted, 'It's a six!' and punched my arm, the most animated I had seen him all day.

Oh, for God's sake. He couldn't understand why I was rooted to my seat with my head in my hands, oblivious to the excitement of the nearby India fans and to those who had run on to the outfield in an attempt to mob Kapil Dev.

'No, Michael,' I explained. 'Viv's been caught. He's out.'

I had a dreadful feeling in the pit of my stomach and it didn't seem to take long for the unimaginable to transpire. The West Indies were bowled out for 140 in 52 overs in one of the biggest upsets in cricket history. And so you might be able to trace a direct line from Sandhu bowling Greenidge to Kapil Dev catching Viv to the birth of the Indian Premier League and India becoming the game's powerhouse.

But I am getting ahead of myself. I was stunned and upset by the result. My mood hadn't been helped at all by the Yorkshireman sitting behind us who, when Viv strolled out to bat, said, 'I 'ate him, I really 'ate him. 'E's got more talent than any mortal should have.' As if that was a good enough reason to despise someone. Later, however, with Richards safely back in the pavilion, the Yorkshireman proclaimed that he would have liked to have seen more of him. 'It were exciting when 'e were in.'

I'm not even sure that this spectator had watched much of the match. By the tea interval, he had drunk two bottles of wine – French, bought for 38 francs a bottle (38 francs?!) on his recent holiday, as he informed all of us unlucky enough to be in earshot – as well as several cans of bitter. And in any case he hadn't really needed to watch the game because, whaddyaknow, he had forecast the very result the night before in the pub.

I wrote an article about him headlined 'O – for a breathless hush' for *The Cricketer* (kept by my mother in a mouldy bookcase), which got more letters of support than anything I had written before or since. Funny that. But it were good when 'e went home.

Joel Garner later said that losing that final was the biggest disappointment of his career and that the Windies had been over-confident. Perhaps they were but it seems to me now that India made the best of their luck and allied that with moments of sublime skill. Sometimes it is really just that simple.

The 1983 World Cup Final was one of only two cricket matches Michael has attended (the other was the first day, and only the first day, of the 1994 final Test between West Indies and England at the Recreation Ground in Antigua) and it is fair to say that he is no more familiar with the rules of the game now than he was at his first match. He is, however, deeply passionate about Tottenham Hotspur – who play with a bigger ball and have less complicated rules – and I am sorry I have not been able to convert him to the loveliest of ball games. But am I really? Isn't it blissful to have your own little world to escape to, a *Wisden* to remain untouched by no human hand other than yours and experiences in your cricket memory bank that belong to you alone?

So I was able to keep my *Wisden* and the rest of my cricket book collection to myself and in the early days of our relationship at least, I could continue to indulge my favourite pursuit as a solo spectator at cricket games. Other times, I would accompany Michael to White Hart Lane, enjoy the match, followed by a film, then dinner, two bottles of wine and a tumbler of Tia Maria frappé. That combination would probably finish me off now, so I wouldn't attempt it (I would just leave out the trip to Spurs). It's amazing what you can do (drink) when you're deliriously in love, isn't it?

I pretty much gave up trying to make Michael fall in love with cricket and I soon learned that, in fact, I couldn't make him do anything at all that he didn't want to – and that included marrying me. After we had been living together in a suburban semi in Worcester Park for a few months, and still hopelessly in love, I thought we might officially seal what I thought was a perfect relationship so I, as casually as possible, suggested getting married.

I didn't get the rapturous response I had anticipated: Michael rejected my suggestion out of hand, leaving me feeling upset, unwanted and stupid. Had I been a bit more mature, I might have considered that Michael had been badly wounded by his divorce. He is an exceptionally fair man and, even though he had wanted to be with me, the fact that he had caused someone else pain was agony for him and he was not prepared to go through all that again.

Prior to my suggestion to Michael, I might have been better advised to adopt the playing style of Chris Tavaré, the Kent, Somerset and England batsman who once took six and a half hours to score 35 runs (okay, maybe I wouldn't have wanted to be *that* slow). Instead, my callowness saw me take on more the hurly-burly approach of Windies' cavalier batsman Chris Gayle, who was the first-ever batsman to hit 1,000 sixes in T20 cricket and once reached a century in 30 balls.

Feeling utterly rejected I reacted in my customary fashion, going out until all hours and returning home in the dead of night to sleep in the spare room. That situation couldn't continue and, within a few months, I left Michael and began a relationship with a New One.

However, I couldn't stop thinking about Michael and he bombarded me with letters, mix tapes of the saddest songs as well as tearful phone calls. Sod that.

I went sailing on a small boat in the Ionian with New One, playing loud music on deserted, flat seas with the soundtrack of U2's 'I Still Haven't Found What I'm Looking For' accompanying every nautical mile. I returned home to find yet another mix tape from Michael on the doormat.

The tape included an Elvis Presley song, 'You Were Always On My Mind' which Michael patently hoped would help his campaign.

'Yeah, well, you blew your chance,' I thought, and turned it off. Bloody men. I'll stick to cricket, thanks. At least that won't let me down (much).

* * *

My misstep in communication with Michael had perhaps been driven by the example of England's chairman of selectors, Peter May, in 1986. That summer, the England cricket team were a total shambles. They had been thumped 5-0 in the Test series in the West Indies in the spring and then Ian Botham was banned from playing cricket for 63 days for admitting, in a newspaper article, that he had smoked cannabis and was made unavailable for the home Test series against India. The tourists arrived having not won an away Test since February 1981; surely, then, there was a chance for England to recover some pride at least? The home team, however, persisted with eight of the 11 players who had lost the fifth Test in Antigua only two months before and as John Woodcock, eminent cricket writer in *The Times*, put it, 'It may be no easy matter getting into the England side, but just try getting out of it.'

England captain David Gower had been put under huge pressure by the chairman of selectors, who made it apparent that the captain would be on trial for the one-day internationals and the first Test at Lord's against India. It was hardly an ideal – some might say cruel – way to start a series. The tourists beat England by five wickets in the first Test, which resulted in Gower getting the sack. But he wasn't the first person to know that he had lost his job.

Mike Gatting had seemingly been offered the captaincy by Peter May before telling Gower that he was being relieved of it. Gatting survived the rest of the summer, including a three-Test series against New Zealand, which the tourists won 1-0 before preparing for the small matter of a winter tour to Australia for the Ashes. Little was expected of England, with Martin Johnson famously writing that there were only three things wrong with the team – 'they couldn't bat, they couldn't bowl and they couldn't field'. It was a great and memorable line but he was wrong and, remarkably, England retained the Ashes with a 2-1 series win.

It was a false dawn, though, and as I prepared for the Ionian sailing trip with New One, Pakistan arrived in England intent on winning their first Test series against the hosts. Even though Imran was a positively geriatric 34 years old, you wouldn't have guessed as much from watching him bound in to the wicket. In the third Test at Headingley, he took ten wickets in the match, which Pakistan won by an innings and 18 runs.

The series was badly rain-affected, not that it bothered me much while I was in a record-breaking Greek heatwave. I did get back for the final Test at The Oval, where England were frankly lucky to get a draw and, thanks to the Headingley win, Pakistan took the series 1-0.

Just like the England team, though, I was engaged in my own falling-apart phase. Perhaps I would have been better off with Peter May as my personal chairman of selectors and he could have made up my mind for me in what was now turning out to be a close contest between Michael and New One. Michael had made it very clear that he was not going to abandon his attempts to woo me back and had even been to Somerset to take my mother out for lunch, which showed just how desperate he felt as they never had an easy relationship. As the winter of 1987 progressed, I was feeling pretty desperate myself. There was some deep recess in my brain that was signalling I was behaving like a complete prat, but I refused to listen to it. Self-awareness wasn't my watchword then.

Each Friday evening I would drive up to Derbyshire, where New One lived, bomb back to London on a Sunday night, find another letter or mix tape from Michael and then spend the rest of that evening lying on my bed listening to it and crying. All I had to do was listen to my gut and decide who I wanted to be with: slow and steady Mr Angry Michael or untrustworthy

Jack the Lad New One? I wasn't then quite as prone to the volatile hormonal mood swings of my younger days but I wasn't far off and couldn't make a decision because I was still Out of Control.

The England cricket team were also doing their best in that regard. Who knows whether his own hormonal swing made skipper Mike Gatting lose it that winter? England travelled to Pakistan to play three Tests and it became a very ill-tempered series, which reached its nadir in the second Test in Faisalabad. Pakistan had won the first Test by an innings and 87 runs, leg-spinner Abdul Qadir taking 13 wickets, including claiming Gatting lbw in both innings. Umpire Shakoor Rana had claimed that Gatting moved a fielder behind the batsman's back when bowler Eddie Hemmings ran in to deliver the ball and apparently the umpire uttered something along the lines of 'You are a f***king cheat.' Gatting had already been riled by Rana earlier in the series when the umpire donned a Pakistan sweater and on that day of the Test, the England captain had had enough. Pictures of Gatting pointing his finger at Rana's chest as the two of them yelled obscenities at each other went round the world. Rana demanded an apology; Gatting refused. The following day, the umpires and the batsmen didn't take to the field and a day's play was lost. Even the Foreign Office and the British Ambassador got involved in an attempt to calm the situation and to keep the tour on the road.

The next morning, Gatting was forced into writing an apology:

> Dear Shakoor Rana, I apologise for the bad language I used during the 2nd day of the Test match at Fisalabad [sic]. Mike Gatting 11th Dec 1987

It didn't come across as particularly heartfelt, or even well written, but the Test did resume and the match played out to a draw. The next match in Karachi was also drawn, leaving Pakistan 1-0 winners of the series, but the ill feeling from the Rana–Gatting incident lingered and was only heightened by the England and Wales Cricket Board paying a £1,000 'hardship' bonus to each England player at the end of the tour. The incident undoubtedly contributed to the introduction of neutral umpires in 1994, when one neutral umpire stood in a Test for the first time. From 2002, both have been independent.

Turmoil on the field; turmoil off.

As the year turned, I resolved that I had to make a decision once and for all. While New One was away skiing, I decided that Michael was definitely still The One for me and we resumed our relationship. On 3 March 1988, we got engaged and after a spectacular summer for the West Indies, beating England 4-0, we were married that September. It had not been a straightforward romance but somehow we made it to the altar and my father was delighted to tell everyone in his speech at the reception that Michael had fallen asleep during the World Cup Final. Apart from that obvious shortcoming, how lucky was I to have two of the very best of men in my life? So perhaps that made it even more disappointing to meet so many who didn't remotely come up to the mark.

For Non-Cricket Speakers

One-Day Cricket

IF TEST cricket might be compared to a long marriage, perhaps one-day cricket could be viewed as 'the hurly-burly of the chaise longue'.[6] And, indeed, whichever format of one-day cricket you might favour, none gives much opportunity for foreplay. It is perhaps the Tinder of the sporting world.

As it says on the tin, one-day cricket, or limited-overs cricket, is a match played in one day. However, not all one-day cricket is equal as different competitions will have varying numbers of overs: 40; 50; 60; 65. Then you have the T20: two teams playing 20 overs each. And then we have The Hundred, the 100-ball domestic competition so loathed by the purist, so adored by the marketeer, the launch of which was delayed by the coronavirus pandemic.

---

6   Mrs Patrick Campbell, English stage actress, born 1865, died 1940.

The first knockout competition, the Gillette Cup, was played in England in 1963, and was the governing body MCC's response to dwindling audiences for the county game. (Until 1988, county games were played over three days; from 1988 to 1992, some matches were played over four days; since 1993, all county matches have been scheduled for four days.)

The Gillette Cup, sponsored by the Gillette company for £6,500, wasn't even known as that until the following season, so low-key was their patronage. Nowadays, we might expect an ad campaign featuring before and after shots of players, male and female, in various states of hirsuteness and the subsequent transformation into smoother-skinned versions of themselves. Different times. The Gillette Cup saw each team play 65 overs. Those really were the days of increased attention span. The cup was a resounding success, not least in fielding standards, which were dramatically improved as players flung themselves about in efforts to stop batsmen scoring. Christopher Martin-Jenkins, as editor of *The Cricketer* magazine, wrote, 'Hitherto only a few enthusiasts like Tony Lock had considered it worth the dry-cleaning bill to dive for the ball. Now everyone in the team had to be an athlete and a gymnast.'

After the Gillette Cup came the John Player Sunday League, played over 40 overs in an innings, and the Benson and Hedges Cup, which began over 55 overs but was reduced to 50. One of cricket's longest-ever sponsorship deals, the Benson and Hedges competition ran from 1972 to 2002. Since then, domestic one-day competitions in England have included the Refuge Assurance Cup, AXA Equity & Law Cup, the National League, the NatWest Pro40, the Clydesdale Bank 50, the Yorkshire Bank 40 and the Royal London One-day Cup.

A one-day international (ODI) is played by two international teams, usually over 50 overs, and this format was adopted by the World Cup, the first of which was held in June 1975. International T20 matches, first played in 2005, are now hugely popular and the standard extremely high. There is little doubt that T20 cricket has improved fielding exponentially while also giving *carte blanche* to powerful batters.

The most notorious one-day series was organised by Australian media tycoon Kerry Packer and held between 1977 and 1979 and, it is fair to say, transformed cricket forever in terms of players' fitness, the wearing of helmets and marketing. Packer secretly signed contracts with top players from England, Australia, West Indies, Pakistan and South Africa. England captain Tony Greig (of whom there is more in Chapter Five) tempted many fellow players to join the 'Packer Circus' and was pilloried by all sides for his role. He was stripped of the England captaincy and cold-shouldered by the powers that be. Many never forgave him.

If you like to live on your nerves and thrive on heart palpitations, one-day cricket is the format for you.

Chapter Three

#Who? Me? #Me Too

The former Test cricketer put his foot down and accelerated hard as if to remind me that he was still an alpha male who had a penis in full working order despite my rejection. Or maybe he was just angry?

Either way, my plan to jump out of his car wasn't looking very practical. I wanted to cry, or at the very least ring my dad.

'YOU DO know I'm going to fuck you later, don't you?' the former England Test cricketer said as I got into the passenger seat of his Rolls-Royce (no kidding).

He had collected me at some backwater train station north of London to drive me to a new business enterprise he was setting up and I got the impression that his question wasn't a polite enquiry. It was more a statement of fact.

I had not slid provocatively on to the passenger seat ('when the leather runs smooth' as Morrissey's lyric that year in The Smiths' 'This Charming Man' had put it), nor had I looked coquettishly into the man's deep blue eyes. I had simply arrived, professionally dressed, and got awkwardly – I was quite nervous about the assignment – into his car but I was greeted without even so much as a 'Hello' before the question came out of his leery, sneery mouth.

My hand hovered over the seatbelt. I felt completely ill-prepared for such a terrifying situation and how I managed to find the pluck to formulate my reply I do not know.

'Actually you aren't,' I said, now staring at him and still a long way from seductively. 'So if you want to put that out of your mind, we can move on. If not, I will get out.'

Inside, I was shaking but there was no way I was going to let him see how scared I was.

'Oh!' he replied, a slight smirk on his face. 'Okay then. Well, that is disappointing.'

I said nothing while he started the engine and I did up my seatbelt praying that he wouldn't drive down some lane and attempt to have his wicked way with me. I made sure my knees were locked together, my thighs burning from the intense muscle-clenching, looked out the front window and tried to concentrate on the questions I needed to ask for my article.

He drove on and was silent for a while but I didn't have a clue whether he was embarrassed by what he had asked or whether he was trying to think of a way to rephrase his question. I was still feeling frightened and very small. He was a great big hulk of a man, with the powerful shoulders characteristic of an elite sportsman, and I wouldn't have stood a chance if he had tried something on. It wasn't just the size of him that scared me, either. He seemed to have some innate confidence that made me think that whatever he, in his power, decided, ultimately he would make it happen. I checked that my door wasn't locked and worked out how I could unbuckle my seat belt and jump out, even at speed, if necessary. The thought of being splattered on the tarmac seemed far more appealing than the alternative.

He put his foot down and accelerated hard as if to remind me that he was still an alpha male who had a penis in full working order despite my rejection. Or maybe he was just angry? Either way, my plan to jump out wasn't looking very practical. I wanted to cry, or at the very least ring my dad.

I knew I had to get some control, however ineffective it might seem, so took out my notebook and started to ask questions, desperate to change whatever subject (although I think we know, don't we?) was in his head. I tried to concentrate on being professional and polite all the while yet dreading the prospect of having lunch with him. He made a few comments about my blouse (which was, I can assure you, the definition of demure and even if it hadn't been, what was that to do with him?), asked me if I had a boyfriend and said he was looking forward to lunch with me.

I managed to project an air of cool indifference when we reached the site of his new venture. I made sure I didn't stand too close to him, and I didn't smile at him at all, merely focused on not giving him anything he might perceive as encouragement. That was extremely difficult because he apparently viewed the mere fact that I was female and breathing encouragement enough. I really didn't know what to do with myself. Should I have crossed my arms to cover my chest (I am not particularly well-endowed but that probably wouldn't have bothered him). Should I have answered back?

Normally, I am what is termed 'a good eater' but I barely ate anything for lunch and somehow managed to get through the uncomfortable day unscathed and unsullied. I even did a follow-up interview with him a few months later once his enterprise had been officially launched. He introduced me to his wife too. Poor woman. But I have never forgotten what he said, how he behaved and how it could all have turned out horribly differently. Nor have I forgotten how dirty and second-rate he made me feel.

Many times since, I have asked myself if I had unwittingly been provocative or whether I handled the situation as well as I might have done. From what I know now, it is clear that the perpetrators try to make their victims feel that they are the ones to blame and it is only recently, with the plethora of #MeToo publicity, that I realised that I was not at fault in any way. And I was 23 years old, for heaven's sake. I had thought the world had moved on so much that my daughters would never be in a situation like that, although #MeToo plainly gives the lie to that. Should I have called him out? Should I have written about it at the time? I did neither and believe that I dealt with it as well as I could at the time and it no doubt toughened me up for all the many other encounters I faced in the future. So perhaps it gave me some inner strength, even though I shouldn't have needed it.

Those were different days in so many ways. Perhaps we (women) were more resilient and more inclined to sort things out, or not, by ourselves rather than resorting to a public appraisal on social media, even if that had been possible? In any case, this chap has faced investigations over the years, although all for nefarious business activities. In my mind, he has had his comeuppance many times over and I don't feel the need to add to it, so you won't learn his name from me.

However, the incident, and others like it, had another effect on me and perhaps not one you might expect: disappointment.

It is fair to say that I had placed my father on a pedestal, which was no less a position than he deserved, from when I was very small. As well as being the kindest man in the world (fact), for a man born in 1928 he was extraordinarily evolved in terms of how he viewed his daughter (or any woman, in fact) as equal to any boy. He never once waved me aside when I said I wanted to be a cricket journalist and made massive personal and financial sacrifices to send me to a boys' school, which had just started admitting girls, for my sixth form education. 'You'll be working in a man's world, so it'll be good experience,' he told me. He also took me as his companion (my mother had an unfortunate habit of fainting before or at social occasions) to cricket dinners and charity functions, so I became used to talking to men of all ages and backgrounds. And virtually every man, apart from one, my father introduced me to at all sorts of events treated me as an equal too. It didn't occur to me until much later that perhaps Dad had been a human shield and no man would have dared to 'try anything on' in his presence. So I hadn't met anyone before who behaved like the chap who picked me up in his Roller.

Really? What a disappointment! Some men behave like *that*? I found it extraordinary. If that had been an isolated incident, perhaps more men might have got away with me not being disappointed in them. And note I say 'disappointed' not 'hate'. I don't want to be any part of a man-hating culture; I don't have the bandwidth for that. But you may not be surprised to learn that it was not an isolated incident.

In the spirit of *Bueller*, I'll release some edited highlights rather than broadcast the full version.

I'm in a car – again. The man had picked me up to take me to a restaurant, where we would discuss his latest cricket book. Nothing to be alarmed about, you would have thought, especially as the man was known to my father. I felt perfectly safe and was looking forward to an evening in good company, talking endlessly about cricket, with a nice dinner that I could claim on expenses. What's not to like? The only potential drawback I could envisage was that the man was instantly recognisable, which might mean he would be bothered by people coming to talk to him at our table. But that could surely be easily managed by him with a few smiles and a courteous autograph. After all, he was very courteous.

The problem began when he pulled up in the car park. I unclicked my seatbelt at the same time as he did and I reached for the door handle. At that precise moment, and without warning, he quickly lunged at me with his right arm, pulling me towards him. He swivelled to move his left arm, a tricky manoeuvre but he was equal to it, to try to grab my breasts. (Again, I have to point out that I was not remotely provocatively dressed, although even if I had been would his behaviour have been acceptable in any way?)

His slobbery, stubbly chin loomed towards my face and I moved backwards, as if I could escape through the closed car door. But he thrust himself forward and there was no way I could dodge those prodigious bristles. I could feel them on my face as he tried to kiss my pursed lips and force his tongue into my mouth. You would be right in thinking that my firmly-closed mouth might have been a clear sign of rejection, but no. I tried to push him off; by now his breath and whiskers, which seemed to be sprouting like triffids by the second in the horror movie in which I found myself, were threatening to suffocate me. His hand was trying to find a way down my high-necked top but somehow I managed to grab his wrist and force his hand away. The intensity of my push seemed to shock him. He licked his salivating, glistening lips.

'No?' he said, dribbling like a bloodhound.

'Er, no,' I replied, wiping my mouth with the back of my hand, my chin stinging from his unshaven one. I had never felt more like throwing up in my life.

I opened the door, got out, praying my legs would stop shaking, and, thank you God, spotted a current cricketer I knew who had just parked his car. Asking the man to join us – the Bristled One also knew him – I acted as though nothing untoward whatsoever had happened and pretended to spend the evening in good company with a nice dinner attached. I delivered an Oscar-winning performance, even though I shouldn't have had to, and ordered a cab home to avoid any further close contact with the man who was making my skin crawl.

Could I have handled this any differently? I certainly didn't tell my father. I think he might have gone to see Whiskered Willy and thumped him. I didn't tell anyone else either and, again, I am not going to name him because what is the point? Anyway, he is dead now (my condolences).

It had become pretty clear, just as my parents had warned me and as yours probably warned you too, that I shouldn't get into a car with strange men. Or was it with men who are strange? One of the two and I never got in a car with any other interviewee again. My Dolomite, which I was still keeping on life support with daily help from the Haynes manual, was going to provide me with a safe haven for future encounters. Not a chance I was going to let a strange man sully those Bri-Nylon seats.

But even if they didn't darken the Dolomite's doors, there seemed to be more disappointing men around every corner. It is generally believed that you shouldn't meet your heroes and while another dodgy encounter wasn't with one of my heroes exactly, he was an international legend for whom I had the utmost respect. I couldn't wait to meet this cricketing icon and ask him a ton of questions about, well, all his tons. I had been at many Test matches when this genius had virtually single-handedly taken the game away from the opposition. I also really wanted to ask him how he had felt when he ran out one of my real heroes in a Test match. It had vexed me from the day I had seen it. I shook his hand, said I was honoured to meet him and sat down, him on my right-hand side. With seemingly no time for any pleasantries, he reached (or, perhaps more accurately, slid) his arm over my waist, grabbed my left hand and jabbed at my ring finger.

'Oh! You're not married then?' he asked.

I stared at him, the familiar disappointment and revulsion coursing through my veins. I was so disappointed, in fact, that I never asked him how he felt about that run-out. I couldn't even be bothered to hear his explanation, if he had one, and instead asked him a series of bland questions that I wasn't even sure would make any kind of article. He, on the other hand, didn't look remotely concerned, having lost interest when I refused to play his game.

I thought about the encounter when I got home that evening with a growing sense of astonishment and indignation. Was the fact I wasn't wearing a wedding ring a green light for him to make a move? In his mind, was that all it took? Don't get me wrong, I like a man as much as any other robustly heterosexual woman but it was beginning to dawn on me – in my pathetic naivety – that there were an awful lot of men around who didn't compute that a woman might just want to concentrate on doing her job to the best of her ability. In their minds, we simply had to be available for sex with them at any moment of their choosing.

This attitude was further typified by an Olympic gold medallist who began pawing at me and making lecherous comments from the moment we were introduced at an exhibition. By then, I had worked on perfecting a steely glare that I hoped would say, 'What on earth do you think you are doing, you scumbag?' His response to that look was breathtaking. 'Come on, you know you want to!' From the depths of my boots, I somehow uttered, 'Actually, I really, really don't.' He looked very confused for a moment, then laughed in my face as if to say his was the best offer I was ever going to get in my life, so it was my loss. I turned on my heels, feeling utterly humiliated.

Oh, I hear you cry, but you chose to go into a man's profession, so what did you expect? And it was the 1980s, different times! But, remember, I had been brought up by a father who had taught me that I was an equal (if not, indeed, superior) to any man. And I didn't go around shoving my hand on a man's crotch or grabbing his hand to see whether he was wearing a wedding ring, did I? Actually, maybe I should give it a go. Brace yourselves.

As well as all the unwanted physical approaches, there was also the latent sexism to deal with. And there was a hell of a lot of that. Every single day.

When I was with the *Evening Standard*, for example, we hosted a lunch for the 1991 West Indies touring party. After a suitably cheerful conversation with Viv Richards, I sat at an elaborately decorated table next to a Lt Col (ret'd) and former secretary of the MCC.

'Hello,' I smiled, delighted to be in the same room as my favourite players.

'Are you something to do with the catering?' the Lt Col (ret'd) asked, obviously the first question he could think of to ask a 'girl'. Oh, I know, perhaps I should have been more charitable and accepted that he was just trying to make polite conversation, but I wasn't buying that. I now had ten years of experience in cricket journalism to embolden me. Poor chap.

I arranged my not inconsiderable nose into as haughty a sneer as I could muster and, with a sweet smile, replied, 'Actually I'm with the *Evening Standard*. On the *sports desk*.'

I emphasised the words 'sports desk' with a metaphorical comedy arrow over my head pointing at the words to give him a really big clue, but then it became clear that he thought I must be something to do with the clerical side. To give him some credit, how was he to know I had put a pencilled cross against that entry in *Careers for Girls*? Actually, I could have told him that, even then, we were so evolved on the *Standard* sports desk that, in fact, we had a male secretary. Heaven forfend.

'Do you know John Thicknesse [the *Standard*'s long-serving cricket correspondent] then?' he asked.

I resisted the urge to tip some of the (very good as I remember it) catering on to his lap.

'Of course. I'm a sports sub-editor and, as my speciality is cricket, I rewrite his copy.'

'Do you *really*?' the astonished Lt Col (ret'd) queried. He looked completely baffled and, for a moment, I thought he might choke and wondered if I would have to perform the Heimlich manoeuvre on him, thus preserving a venerable cricket dignitary. That would have been a turn-up for the books. I would go on to ghostwrite the columns of England spinner John Emburey for the *Standard* and can only imagine what the Lt Col might have said on hearing that snippet.

Incidentally, the Lt Col (ret'd) was a real poppet (how he would have loved to have been described as that) and really the exchange was pretty inoffensive compared to others.

Indeed, a veteran newspaper cricket correspondent, an otherwise charming man (or so I had thought), attempted to goose me at one cricket function. Did he think I wouldn't notice?

There was an even older (really, really old; hardly able to stand unaided, in fact) former England cricketer who, after five minutes of innocuous chatting at a congenial function, asked me to go on holiday with him. I might have even considered that (I could have done with a break) had it not occurred to me that I might have to function as his carer, or even his handmaiden (eurgh).

Oh, come on, these are sportsmen; just think of all that testosterone racing through their athletic bodies. Well, excuse me, I probably had more testosterone than that really old, barely-able-to-stand former cricketer and, anyway, is that an excuse?

And was it testosterone rampaging through his veins that made a former England captain explain (mansplain?) to me during an interview in the late 1980s that I, as a female, didn't know enough about cricket nor had played the game to any level to write intelligently about it. I asked him whether he thought that by applying the same 'logic' a man couldn't be a gynaecologist or an obstetrician. Reply came there none.

By contrast, I cannot recollect a single West Indies player who ever gave me the slightest suspicion that I was only there for some sexual activity. I was treated as an equal who had as much right as any man to interview them and to write about cricket. The only uncomfortable moment came when I was interviewing Michael Holding in Antigua and an England player walked past, then turned round and said to me, 'We're good too, you know' as if I had just found myself in a primary school playground.

Thankfully, there are more female cricket journalists than ever before now and I really hope that none of them would ever encounter similar incidents to the ones I found myself exposed to. Nowadays, it seems positively antediluvian that I wasn't even allowed into the pavilion at Lord's to have a meeting with my then boss, Christopher Martin-Jenkins.

As long ago – or as recently as, depending on your attitude – 1996, I wrote (thanks for saving it, Mum), 'It is not too far-fetched to imagine that a female cricket correspondent, should a male sports editor ever be brave enough to take one on, could soon sit happily in the press box.'

Whatever will they think of next? Women in cricket administration?

Of course, not all men I had to deal with were disappointing or lascivious. After all, at *The Cricketer*, Christopher Martin-Jenkins and Andrew Longmore were two of the finest fellows you could ever meet. Even at *Cricket Life*, there were occasional glimpses of appreciation for a job well done rather than surprise at the gender of the person doing it, although I won't go into any details about being sexually harassed by a lesbian colleague there.

And I truly walked through the sunlit uplands on the sports desk of the *Evening Standard*. As *Cricket Life* came to its sad, inevitable end due to financial problems in early 1990, I had the audacity to apply to the *Standard*'s then sports editor, Michael Herd, for the vacancy as a sports sub-editor on the paper. They hadn't employed a woman on the desk before but, cricket caps off to them, they offered me the job and I leapt at it.

One of my first assignments on the *Standard* was covering the funeral of Sir Len Hutton, one of the game's finest ever batsmen, England captain and a national hero. It was the first funeral I had attended in a professional capacity and I think I was sent as I would have been able to recognise all the old players who would be there to pay their respects. Much as I was an admirer of Sir Len's peerless prowess as a cricketer, I was also mindful of his attitude towards female players. He had been quoted as saying, 'Ladies playing cricket? Absurd. Just like a man trying to knit.' Olympic diver Tom Daley, famously photographed knitting during the Tokyo Olympics, might have an interesting take on that, too.

My job on the *Standard* sports desk was easily the best I had ever had – and will ever have – with a whole team of men who (bar one who called me 'poppet' until the rest of the chaps put him straight) and the attempted goose by another treated me absolutely and always as their equal. Those were the days when the *Standard* was a paid-for paper, had a circulation of 500,000-plus (and a whopping 821,000 on the day Margaret Thatcher resigned in November 1990) and printed at least four editions a day. It was non-stop, high-energy and joyous to be part of a team that produced cracking sports pages several times a day.

Every morning I walked into the paper's Kensington offices feeling like a giant and excited for the day ahead. It was all going so well.

But, as life reminds us, it is a big mistake to think, even for one second, that you are sailing on calm, sun-reflecting seas with a safe harbour in reach which, that very day, has a rum punch happy hour that also includes a soothing foot massage while you are drinking them.

After being at the *Standard* for less than a year, and shortly before my 30th birthday, I discovered I was pregnant. My husband and I hadn't planned that. Life was about to get in the way of cricket again.

Despite feeling more tired than the most tired person in the history of tired people, I kept the news of my pregnancy from the team. Hard enough that they had got used to a woman on the desk without them having to get used to a pregnant woman on the desk. Anyway, I had not put any weight on at all nor did I feel very well. In fact, I was losing blood every day and I was hardly going to share that unsavoury titbit with them, was I? So I decided not to tell anyone until I was four months pregnant. Just in case.

The day I hit my self-imposed 16-week deadline, I met the sports editor and told him my news then relayed it to the desk. Predictably, they were all thrilled and I pointed out to them it would be business as usual and I didn't want or expect any special treatment.

The next day, I had my first scan and learnt that the baby wasn't developing properly. In fact, the ultrasound technician wasn't even sure the baby was in my womb and said it looked as though I had an ectopic pregnancy (where the baby develops in a fallopian tube). A consultant was called but he gave me no further information and with no hint of a gentle bedside manner, he simply told me to phone my husband to ask him to come down to the hospital.

The afternoon passed in a blur of scans and hushed voices as it became clear that the pregnancy 'wasn't viable'. In fact, the consultant said the developing foetus was so badly damaged by the absence of amniotic fluid that he was surprised I had carried the pregnancy for so long. He added that it was extremely unlikely I would carry it to full term. If I did, it would be highly unlikely that I would give birth to a live baby. And if by some quirk of fate I did, there was absolutely zero chance I would take that baby home. So just 24 hours after announcing my happy news to the office, my husband telephoned them to say I would need an operation the following day. Predictably again, they were the epitome of empathy, told me not to rush back and were the first to send flowers.

I spent a week at home, battling with my feelings of pain, loss and inadequacy (what kind of a woman was I if I couldn't even carry a baby?) as well as big dipper hormonal swings before heading back to work with the imminent start of the new cricket season to look forward to. I immersed myself in statistics and predictions as cricket gloriously came to my rescue again, with a team of men at the *Standard* who were light years away from the disappointing bunch I had met earlier in my career. It is not an exaggeration to say that, to a man, the

Standard sports desk was populated by giants and I was lucky to get to stand on their shoulders.

Yet it could all have been so different only a year earlier. I could have missed my chance of working with them after meeting a man who I might have run away with. Had he asked me, of course, which, very sadly, he didn't.

Bowling

JOHN ARLOTT wrote 'perhaps, indeed, a bowler's action can be the most poetic motion in cricket' and I am certainly drawn more to the beauty of a bowler's movements than his statistics, which is hardly surprising given my issues with numeracy.

To a cricket novice (I would still class my husband as one), one bowler might look the same as another, apart from the fact that even he can tell the difference – just – between a fast bowler and a slow one. Cricket being cricket, though, there are many types of bowling as well as varieties of balls bowled.

Types of bowling include fast/pace/quick; spin, including finger-spin, leg spin, off spin, wrist spin; slow and medium pace. In terms of the variety of balls bowled, terms you will hear include: googly, bouncer, Chinaman, full toss, yorker, half-volley, inswinger, off-cutter, long-hop and many more.

A bowler will be referred to as 'economical' if the batsmen do not score freely off his bowling. He will achieve a maiden over if no runs are scored off his over and a hat-trick if he takes three wickets in three consecutive balls (even if that doesn't happen in consecutive overs).

Extras are included in the batting side's total. Extras are any runs that do not result from a scoring stroke made by the batsman on strike: byes, leg-byes, no-balls and wides. A no-ball is a delivery from the bowler that an umpire deems to be unfair. No-balls and wides are included in the bowler's return, but byes or leg-byes are not.

The umpire will hold his arm horizontally to signal such a no-ball. The position of part of the bowler's front foot must be behind the popping crease (a line 1.22 metres in front of the stumps) and the back foot must land inside the line of the return crease to be a legitimate delivery. A no-ball can also be called if a bowler bowls too many bouncers.

One of the greatest fast bowlers, Michael Holding of the West Indies, was scornful of fast bowlers who repeatedly transgressed the no-ball law. 'They just don't work hard enough on their run-ups and that's unprofessional. Once you're bowling no-balls, it must enter your mind at some stage of your run-up that this is going to be another. Once that happens, it means you're not concentrating fully on putting the ball where you want it.'

Holding had the benefit of one of the forerunners of cricket trainers, the physiotherapist Dennis Waight. He used an extraordinary method of educating the West Indies fast bowlers in the art of running.

'They have to learn to run into the wicket,' said Waight, 'with their eyes *closed*, floating, feeling comfortable.' Of the West Indies' Malcolm Marshall, perhaps the greatest fast bowler of all time, Waight said, 'If he closed his eyes, Malcolm could do it [run to the wicket] a million times, on and off, on and off, and there would be the same footmarks every time.'

Watch any footage of Marshall or Holding and I dare you to say they aren't poetry in motion.

Chapter Four

The Man I Would
Have Run Away With

Peter O'Toole was an older man when I met him but his eyes still shone with multiple twinkles and a weaker woman might have drowned in them. Noel Coward said that if O'Toole had 'been any prettier, the film [*Lawrence of Arabia*] would have been called *Florence of Arabia*'. O'Toole wore a hat throughout our interview, only removing it for the moments (dozens) when he performed impressions of cricketers. And we were shrouded in thick cigarette smoke from his French fags for hours. I tell you, the delectable smell of those can take me right back and make my stomach flip.

ONE OF the advantages of working for *Cricket Life*, probably the only one if I'm totally honest, was that having Imran Khan as the editor-in-chief opened doors, even if some of them should really have stayed shut. Imran was then at Peak Playboy In London and I witnessed many a female fling themselves on the floor of our office as soon as they so much as caught the faintest whiff of his rather delicious aftershave. There was no mistake: Imran was blessed with bags of charisma. My loins, though, remained unstirred. My heart belonged to Viv. (Oh, and to my husband. Nearly forgot.)

Incidentally, my boss at the *Evening Standard*, Michael Herd, once asked me, 'You would definitely sleep with Viv, wouldn't you?' I replied, 'You've got it all wrong, Michael. Do nuns want to sleep with God?' I clearly remember him rolling his eyes at my response.

Perhaps it was the mention of Imran's name (well, it certainly wasn't mine) that paved the way to setting up an interview with the actor Peter O'Toole, famously passionate about cricket and, by some distance, easily the starriest name outside the sport I had ever interviewed. O'Toole had made his name in the Oscar-nominated title role in the 1962 film *Lawrence of Arabia*, regarded by many as the best British film of all time. Subsequently, O'Toole had established a reputation as the poster boy for hell-raisers along with actors Richard Burton, Oliver Reed and Richard Harris. But what I, along with many others, remembered him for was his heart-stopping first appearance in *Lawrence*. Oh. My. God. Those eyes.

O'Toole was obviously a much older man when I met him but his eyes still shone with multiple twinkles and a weaker woman might have drowned in them. Noel Coward famously said of O'Toole that if he had 'been any prettier, the film would have been called *Florence of Arabia*. He wasn't wrong.

In spring 1990, O'Toole was playing the lead in *Jeffrey Bernard Is Unwell* at the Apollo Theatre in London, a role that required him to be on stage for some two hours and to successfully perform a trick every night plus afternoon matinees. The trick involved a pint glass filled with water, a biscuit tin lid, a matchbox and a raw egg. ('I forgot to add, you've got to be at least 50 years old and pissed out of your brain,' advised Keith Waterhouse, journalist and the author of the play, explaining the trick.) O'Toole's performance won an Olivier Award and was an unbridled riot, receiving delirious reviews from critics as well as from audiences who gave him standing ovations every night.

In the midst of this mayhem, when he was being lauded as King of the West End, he agreed to an interview with exceedingly average me in his dressing room at the Apollo Theatre.

I was exceptionally nervous but it turned out to be one of my most extraordinary afternoons and I still have the tape recording (no, not one of *those* tapes). For starters, O'Toole wore a hat throughout the interview, only removing it for the moments when he did an impression of a cricketer (of which there were dozens). And we were shrouded in thick cigarette smoke from his French fags for hours. I tell you, the delectable smell of those can take me right back and make my stomach do a little flip. I am sure you know that feeling.

Before the match started, when it was time for the coin to be thrown up in the air, it would have been a toss-up between me fainting with nerves or throwing myself at his feet. His reputation for outrageous behaviour mattered not a jot to me; I was fully prepared for that. After all, by then, I'd had some experience of fending off uninvited guests. But O'Toole was completely charming and not in a leery sense.

What I wasn't ready for at all was just how hugely knowledgeable he was about cricket nor for the glorious fact that we shared a deep passion for the West Indies. I could also tell him of another coincidence. When I mentioned to my father that I was interviewing Peter O'Toole, he told me that the young actor had been to several boisterous parties Dad had hosted in his flat in Bristol in the late 1950s. At that time, my father had recently left the Royal Air Force and was working in Bristol as a photocopier salesman. O'Toole was performing in the local Old Vic theatre. I never did find out quite how my father in his distinctly unglamorous job had attracted such a guest, although it was some time before O'Toole became a star so, for all I know, perhaps the young actor regularly caroused with office equipment suppliers. O'Toole, in fact, played his first Hamlet at Bristol Old Vic and I am certain that my father wouldn't have seen him in that as he had no time for Shakespeare, preferring his entertainment to come from a jazz band (big band, not that awful trad kind).

On top of everything I thought I knew about him, O'Toole was effortlessly hilarious with, in the manner of a glossy fast bowler, a superb delivery of stories and I had to focus on not being sick with laughter. After a few minutes, I had no choice but to ignore every one of my prepared questions and just let him roll.

O'Toole's achievements in cricket, as in life, are the stuff of legend: he once caught the mighty West Indian Learie Constantine on the boundary, for God's sake. It was towards the end of the war, O'Toole explained, when 'cricket began again' and Arthur Wood and Constantine were the two driving forces of 'larky' Sunday cricket played at Roundhay Park, Leeds. Occasionally, boys were invited to join in and were put on the boundary. 'And I was one of them,' said O'Toole. 'I can see the ball now right here in this dressing room – it was still, it wasn't spinning and it was brick red. I remember catching it and Constantine, with a huge grin, waving his bat. I felt like *God*.'

O'Toole stood up to his full height of 6ft 2in and stretched even more to show just how very God-like he was.

He saw Donald Bradman bat, too, at Bramall Lane, Sheffield in 1948 on the Don's last tour of England, playing for Australia against Yorkshire. Bradman made 54 in the first innings, 86 in the second. O'Toole remembered, 'It was beautiful. I remember the ball never leaving the ground and Bradman scored 86 or 87 before being out. He didn't get a ton. But it was rather wonderful to see a great god *not* make a hundred. I remember him walking back to the pavilion, almost as slowly as he had walked out, and he walked very, very slowly.' O'Toole got up from his chair and walked across the tiny dressing room to show exactly how Bradman walked. 'There was obvious, huge disappointment in the crowd manifest through an absolute silence when suddenly, as Bradman walked back, a man stood up just in front of me and began that clapping which isn't applause – emotional, heavy thuds [O'Toole put his hands together in a slow, thumping clap] – and there were tears from these strong, old, tough Yorkshiremen. It was beautiful.'

To get an idea of how O'Toole spoke, and not just about cricket, the best example I can provide is from the man himself. In the first volume of his (bonkers) memoirs, *Loitering With Intent: The Apprentice*, O'Toole attempted to rewrite the Konstantin Stanislavski technique of training actors by comparing it to playing a long cricket innings. Then O'Toole remembers a match he played in:

'Watch for the one that comes in, or gets big. Face. Feet, feet, feet. Ball, ball, ball. "Good night, Charlie!" Saw it all the way, pitched well up, came down late on her, she slipped under the bat, castled, there's timber all over the shop. Out. Do you see, unless one is a naturally gifted cricketer, with a good, constantly honed technique, Mr Stanislavski, confident and on song, the objectives of putting bat to ball or pitching the ball on the spot turn into a raffle, Mr S., a bugger's muddle, nor can any systematic approach to the job, not only yours, my old segocious, however sound in principle, prove to be anything other than a washout. Saw it all the way, you know, swung in later, just too rusty to get wood on it. Fuck. A duck. It would make you weep.'[7]

I know it is not Neville Cardus, but it makes me laugh more than the Lancastrian cricket writer ever did.

One of the highlights of O'Toole's cricket experiences was playing six games for Halifax in Jamaica in the late 1980s. 'I'd agreed to skipper a side against a young Northants XI,' he recalled. 'I was down having a net when the ball hit me on the foot – as happens – and I did all the ice and things.' O'Toole kept talking while hopping on one leg around the dressing room and described the pre-match meeting with fellow player Stephen Thorpe, who was to be the star of the side.

'I walked into the room and saw Stephen lying on the sofa; his knee had gone. Neither of us could walk. Stephen asked what we should do and I said there was only one thing for it. Both of us would have to open the innings with runners. So we each had a runner

---

7   Peter O'Toole, *Loitering With Intent*, 1992.

and it was only overthrows which kept us alive. It was bizarre. Occasionally, one of us would forget and start hopping down the wicket only to have to hop back. But to our amazement, because neither of us had any pretensions with the bat, we put on 50. That was a major highlight for me.'

Even while O'Toole was wowing the West End in 1990, he made time to have nets at the Lord's Indoor School, 'Just for fun and obviously lunatics like heaving balls as I polish my skills as an opening batsman,' he joked. 'I'm a village green cricketer, you understand. I've never had any pretensions; I just love the bloody game and I love to be part of it, if I can. I shall probably die on a cricket field, standing at slip because I can't zoom around any more.'

At Lord's, he had also witnessed some of England's players preparing for the visit of the West Indies that summer in 1990. 'I watched them practising the other day: [Keith] Medlycott, all cricket that young bloke, a good spirit and a bloody good bowler, and [Graham] Goochie, looking relaxed and funny even after facing that bowling machine flinging it down at 90 miles an hour. I faced that damn thing at 60 and 70 and it was enough to scare the Jesus out of me. I said, "put it in at 90" and, luckily, they put a tennis ball in – I saw a yellow flash somewhere out of the corner of my eye. [Geoff] Boycott summed it up for me the other day in an interview. He said that if you want to know what it's like facing really fast bowling – be it Whispering Death Michael Holding, Malcolm Marshall, Dennis Lillee or Jeff Thomson or any of those tearaways – you get your friend to drive at you in a car at 90 miles an hour and, when the car is 12 feet from you, decide which way to jump.'

On his next visit to Lord's, O'Toole was due to pick up his Christmas present to himself: a new bat. 'It weights 2lb 2oz, has a thin, long handle and is quite heavy enough for me, thank you. I picked up Ian Botham's bat once. I could, probably, if very drunk, toss it in a caber competition but I couldn't lift the bloody thing.'

O'Toole became serious for a moment as he acknowledged the agonies that Botham must have suffered at the hands of the press. His fellow hell-raiser and actor Richard Burton once wrote of O'Toole that he had been the victim of 'press envy'. 'Undoubtedly, Botham experienced that,' said O'Toole, looking rather forlorn, for the first time in our interview, 'and it's very wearing. It affects everything; it affects not only the way you look at yourself but the way that people look at you. And you'll find people saying, "there's no smoke without fire" and "there must be some truth in it" and it's all bollocks.'

At that moment, O'Toole left his chair again and started on another impression, bending his legs, shaking his feet and twitching his shoulders. He looked inquisitively at me and raised an eyebrow.

'Derek Randall?' I suggested.

He smiled and nodded. 'Why he was dropped I shall never know,' said O'Toole, still twitching. 'I had an operation in the '70s, and was confined to bed, so I listened to that 1979 Test from Australia at four in the morning. I can still hear John Arlott now – everyone sounded as pissed as parrots – and he was poetry, wonderful stuff describing Randall's innings.'

O'Toole starts to deliver the commentary in Arlott's voice and the commentator might as well have been in the dressing room as the actor describes Randall's century.

'Randall scored 150-odd that game – and he saved 25 or 30 runs in every match. I'll never know why he wasn't an adornment to the English side to this present day.'

Listening to my tape of that afternoon, I noticed O'Toole's voice turn wistful. He proffered that the English game then, in 1990, might be lacking in pride.

He said, 'It seems, at its simplest, that we've lost our love and great respect for our game. It's a hard game, a man's game, a beautiful game. It's all the old-fashioned virtues, the old-fashioned qualities, plus devil, plus flair, plus guts. And the wish, the need, is to somehow instil in young players, the need to say, "I'm going to give 100 per cent commitment to the loveliest of ball games."'

I know what O'Toole would have made of England being bowled out for 67 by Australia at Headingley in the 2019 Ashes series. But I didn't agree with him even then – or now – about players not giving 100 per cent, although as he did make his point so eloquently I was never going to argue with him. I just wish he had been alive to see the 2019 World Cup and Ben Stokes's Ashes innings at Headingley. I know damned well what he would have made of that.

After three or more hours of me staring at him doe-eyed, it was time to wrap things up so that he could prepare for another peerless performance as Jeffrey Bernard. As I turned off my tape recorder and put my notebook in my bag, O'Toole exclaimed, 'Oh, I nearly forgot. Now this is my absolutely treasured possession.'

He produced a photograph showing him smiling beneath a cricket cap and surrounded by his team-mates in Halifax, Jamaica in his beloved West Indies.

He agreed that we could reproduce it in *Cricket Life* providing I promised to look after it with my life. In addition to that, he gave me two tickets for a performance of *Jeffrey Bernard is Unwell*, a perk of the job that I repaid literally by going to see it twice more. Each time, I joined the rest of the audience to cheer loudly during the standing ovation, which seemed to go on for hours.

But, even more than the memory of his performance in that play, I treasure the afternoon in his dressing room, as a privileged audience member of one, seeing his theatricality shine through in his good-humoured impressions of the game's great players. I wished I had filmed his version of Gary Sobers' walk but you will just have to take it from me that it was without price.

You might think that Peter O'Toole couldn't do anything else to elevate himself to the very top of the pantheon of men who weren't disappointing to me, but you would be wrong. Shortly after the interview appeared in *Cricket Life*, I received a letter from him that he had clearly (judging by the erratic layout) typed himself and signed 'Love Peter'. It was a beautiful letter in which he wrote how perfectly I had represented our little chat. He might just as well have told me that I had won the Nobel Prize for Literature.

Peter O'Toole died in December 2013, only a few weeks after my father. The fact that the world had to carry on turning without those two men bestride it made me howl, as O'Toole himself might have said, heavy, thudding tears.

Such is life that shortly after meeting O'Toole, I interviewed the less glamorous John Major, then the Chancellor of the Exchequer and, although Major was famously cricket-mad, he could not have been more different from O'Toole. Oh yes (as Major's *Spitting Image* puppet might have said). He was, however, friendly and engaging with a firm handshake from which I could just about discern, at a push, what former Cabinet Minister Edwina Currie might have seen in him. He was very charming in an old-fashioned way and the interview was splendid, as Major himself might have said, but almost as soon as I had finished writing it – and probably not just because of that but who really knows? – *Cricket Life's* publishers pulled the plug on the magazine. The money had finally dried up. I was upset that the magazine had crashed just as I felt I was getting into my stride, as well as ashamed that I had talked Adrian Murrell, one of the best cricket photographers in the world, into jumping ship from his long-standing tenure at *The Cricketer* a few months previously.

The John Major interview looked as though it would be consigned to the journalistic spike of history but a few months later, in November 1990, when it seemed that Major would take over from Margaret Thatcher as Prime Minister, the *Evening Standard*, for which I was then working, ran the piece. Two days after it appeared under the headline *Running For Office*, Major was improbably installed at No.10 as the Prime Minister and the *Standard* had had a fortuitous but hardly earth-shattering scoop.

Major admitted that, no matter how heavy or important his workload, he would never neglect cricket. I had a lot to learn from both O'Toole and the Prime Minister because they never once seemed to let life get in the way of their passion for the game. Major, in fact, used cricket terminology in letters to the Prime Minister of Pakistan in the 1990s, Nawaz Sharif, writing on 14 June 1994, 'All in all, I feel as if I have been batting on a fairly sticky wicket, with the ball swinging about and sometimes bouncing unevenly. But we have scored a lot of runs over the last four years, and we are not out and going for more!'

Major's message resonated with me: stick with it, no matter how dodgy the wicket, he seemed to be saying. And even though my life continued to get in the way of my passion for cricket, I was still sticking like glue to my devotion to Viv Richards, even when, like all heroes, he sometimes tested my fidelity.

Batting

IF JOHN Arlott provided an appreciation of bowling as poetry, then cricket writer Neville Cardus imparted an insight about the psychology of batting when he wrote, 'A true batsman should in most of his strokes tell the truth about himself.'

We could consider, then, England's Chris Tavaré batting for six and a half hours to score 35 at Madras in 1981/82, West Indies' Viv Richards hitting his 20th Test century in just 56 balls in Antigua in 1986 or England's Ben Stokes scoring 135 not out at Headingley against Australia in 2019 to see what each of those innings might tell us about the men involved. And we might also learn a lot about the character of W.G. Grace, one of the most important figures in the development of the game who, when bowled first ball, simply put the bails back on the stumps and said, 'They came to see me bat, not you bowl.' Whenever I read anything about W.G.

Grace and the quotes like diamonds that fell from his mouth, I feel a huge pang of regret that he isn't alive today. He was made for Twitter. In an idle moment or two, I like to imagine a quick-fire round of tweets between him and Donald Trump. Verily tremendous Twitter nirvana. Fact.

But I digress. Put simply, the job of a batsman is to score as many runs as possible without getting out. The opening batsmen should, ideally, put on a stand (partnership) of some substance to anchor the team's performance and allow the other batsmen a chance to flourish. The number three batsman can play more freely as a stroke-maker and build on a strong start (à la Viv Richards). Batting order is thus divided into openers, top order, middle order and the late order 'tailenders', also known as 'rabbits', with little or no batting skills. One of the greatest examples of the difference a 'rabbit' can make came at Headingley in 2019, when England's last man in, the bespectacled Jack Leach, scored just one run in the 76-run partnership with Ben Stokes, which won the Test to keep England's hopes alive in the Ashes.

Batting terminology you will hear includes a single (one run); a four, scored when the ball travels to the boundary rope without being stopped; a six, when the ball passes the boundary rope without bouncing; an on-drive, when the batsman hits a ball pitching on or just outside leg stump; an off-drive, the opposite of an on-drive; a cut, an attacking shot made by the batsman hitting the ball towards the off side in an arc between slip and cover; a sweep, a shot played usually to a slower ball into the area between square leg and long leg; a mow, a shot resembling the motion of a scythe.

The contest between bat and ball, especially when it is practised by the game's greatest exponents, is the essence of cricket. And poetry isn't just saved for the best of bowlers. To witness a batsman on form is to feel blessed to be alive.

The West Indian author Ian McDonald, writing about Viv Richards in his poem *Massa Day Done*, perfectly summed up the Antiguan's prowess, explaining how the batsman couldn't be stopped when he was in the mood to hit a big score, hitting the ball like a 'cannon ball'.

Chapter Five

Heroes Don't Have to Wear Capes. Sometimes They Wear Batting Gloves

Viv was ten years older than me so he had shrugged off any immature or uncool elements of his character, had he even previously possessed them, which was highly unlikely. Living life as Viv played cricket and being as cool as him was perhaps going to be too tall an order for me. He played cricket with power, nonchalance, flamboyance, effortless footwork, grace and unselfishness. I had none of Viv's qualities except, and only on a rare day when everything might be going in my direction, effortless footwork.

A FEW months before I first saw Viv Richards announce his magnificence to an unassuming cricket crowd in Somerset, I sat down on a bland grey velvet sofa at home in Derbyshire on a Thursday night to watch *Top of the Pops*. Being a regular reader of *Jackie* magazine, along with 100 per cent of the female teenaged population at the time, I was well acquainted with most pop stars of the day. I frequently imagined myself as a member of Pan's People even though I had only ever seen them in photographs, and not been allowed by my parents to see them actually moving on screen. And the performance of '20th Century Boy' by Marc Bolan and T. Rex on that night's episode made me want to be something else entirely.

Grown up.

Bolan had already established himself as a pioneer of glam rock two years earlier when he sang 'Hot Love' with two glitter teardrops beneath each eye. I hadn't seen that episode of *Top of the Pops* at the time as I was deemed too young and it was, in those dreaded words of our collective youth, 'past your bedtime'. You would have flounced too. However, two years later, my parents had obviously thought I was ready to witness what I can only describe as raw sex and whatever hormones had been lying dormant certainly started to fizz that evening.

'So that's what all the fuss is about,' I thought. I obviously concentrated more on his appearance than his lyrics but the fact that Bolan sang something about Robin Hood clearly meant he was singing to me and all the other girls in Nottingham.

You may or may not have to make the leap to see the connection between Marc Bolan, a diminutive glam rocker originally from east London, and Viv Richards, a sublime cricketer from a tiny Caribbean island. Yet if we look at the way Bolan moved during his performances, we will see it is not dissimilar to our West Indian hero. The nonchalance, the casual choreography was there; the apparent effortlessness of movement in both men allied to supreme mastery of their bodies.

Viv, in my eyes, may just as well have had glitter teardrops.

And perhaps Bolan absolutely had Viv in mind when he sang about moving like a cat because while Bolan indeed did move like a cat, it was more in the manner of a sensual domestic pet than the big cat evoked by Viv. However, my brief flirtation with Bolan did not last long and, as is the preserve of an impetuous teenage girl, I moved on pretty quickly. I have since revisited the relationship many times, and certainly enjoyed it more, but at that time he was much too dangerous for me (I can only imagine the rows with my parents if I had stuck *him* on my walls) and he couldn't replace the (then) much more wholesome and pretty David Cassidy, who had been beautifying my bedroom since 1971.

It was also the musicality and physicality of Viv's batting that floated my boat rather than his stats (again, bearing in mind my lack of appreciation of numbers). It is no coincidence, either, that I, an emotionally unbalanced (hormonal) and anxious young girl, was attracted to the seeming casualness of both Viv and Bolan.

Or perhaps it was my father's decree that 'I think we should keep an eye on that young man, don't you, sweetheart?' when he first discovered Richards' name, which bore deep into my soul – reluctant as I ever was to disobey him. My father would be right, he usually was. From that summer's day in an unremarkable Somerset village, I started to devour all things Viv. In the beginning, there wasn't much (if anything) to be found and I had to content myself with very meagre pickings. From 1974, though, when he joined Somerset, making his debut for the county in a one-day match against Glamorgan on 27 April that year – and scoring 81 not out – it became easier to gather paraphernalia, all of which had been (not carefully) stored in my mother's hoardings. There were a few snippets in the daily papers where I could check on Viv's progress and in the winter of 1974/75, with barely a season of English county cricket under his belt, he won his first cap, at the age of 22, for the West Indies on their tour of India. He didn't get off to a good start in the first Test in Bengaluru: out for four runs in the first innings, out for three in the second as captain Clive Lloyd scored 163 in the second innings to lead the Windies to victory by a whopping 267 runs.

It was in the second Test match in Delhi that Viv launched himself mightily on to the international stage and had everyone talking about him. He scored 192 not out in the first innings as Windies triumphed by an innings and 17 runs. Reading the match report a day later in my father's *Daily Telegraph,* I felt flushed with possessiveness and resentment that so many other cricket fans were now jumping on my bandwagon of Viv adulation. 'I saw him first!' I wanted to shout. Watching the grainy black and white footage now, it seemed there were at least a million people at the Arun Jaitley ground in Delhi, all of them spellbound by the young Antiguan man's performance. Time and again, he would step away as the ball came towards him and whack it to all corners of the ground.

In fact, Viv's physicality would quickly lead to comparisons with the boxer Smokin' Joe Frazier – indeed, one of Viv's nicknames was Smokey – who was renowned for applying relentless pressure to wear down his opponents. That seemed to be true of the majority of Viv's innings but there was already a lot more to him than that.

There weren't just the comparisons to Frazier, though. Norman Mailer's description of Muhammad Ali in *The Fight* comes to mind. 'Women draw an *audible* breath. Men look *down*. They are reminded again of their lack of worth.'[8] Whether he strikes you more as Ali or Frazier doesn't matter much. What I am reminded of when I study that film of him in Delhi flaying the ball all over the park is the vivid memory of not just desperately wanting to be a cricket journalist but also the crystal-clear recollection that I wanted to live my life in exactly the way Viv played cricket: I wanted to Be Cool. Just like him.

---

8   Norman Mailer, *The Fight*, Little Brown and Company, 1975.

Now Viv was ten years older than me so had undoubtedly shrugged off any immature or uncool elements of his character, had he even previously possessed them, which was, of course, highly unlikely. Living life as Viv played cricket and being as cool as him was perhaps going to be too tall an order for me. After all, he played cricket with power, nonchalance, flamboyance, effortless footwork, grace and unselfishness. (I have asked myself many times how many more runs he would have scored if he had been selfish?)

I had none of Viv's qualities except, and only perhaps on a rare day when everything might be going in my direction, effortless footwork. For instance, I am reminded of once falling over on an icy pavement with a matchbox in the back pocket of my jeans. I landed on my bottom and as the box ignited I set fire to myself, so I am fully aware that effortless footwork might not come easily to me. I mean I cannot imagine Viv *ever* being involved in a similar mishap, can you?

So while I may have planned on becoming as cool as him, as a teenager (and beyond) I struggled every day with how I looked and how I felt. *Jackie* magazine, with its weekly Cathy & Claire advice page, was actually supposed to help but finding an issue from February 1975 – obviously kept by Mum – I now read in their guide to 'being at the centre of things' that 'you'll be amazed at how effective a radiant smile can be, how it can light up your face and make you look ten times more attractive. Some girls smile on one side, or smile as if they're trying to hide their teeth [me] or give a twisted sort of grin [also me]. So get in front of a mirror and get yourself a good smile. Then practise it – on friends, on the family. Practise doing it when you don't feel particularly happy and when you're bored, or at a disadvantage [me, all the time]. Then suddenly you'll find it'll come quite naturally and there's nothing more encouraging to a boy than a beautiful smile across a crowded room.'

To my mind, there was no 'suddenly' about it.

But don't panic just yet. Cathy & Claire had even more helpful and profound advice up their sleeves. 'Another useful expression, though, is the pathetic, appealing look, which brings out a boy's protective instinct and has him desperate to get you another drink/ help you on with your coat/give you a lift home. It's best done by opening your eyes wide and drooping the mouth a little, looking (hanging your head slightly) directly into the eyes of the boy you're talking to. Practise this.'

I did indeed decide recently to practise this on Michael's return home from work one day to see if it would bring out his hitherto latent protective instinct. As instructed, I opened my eyes wide, accentuated my drooping mouth and hung my head slightly. But, as I had earlier that day very confidently predicted to myself, Michael thought I was having a stroke.

* * *

In the early days of his career, Viv said that he didn't want hero worship from youngsters (sorry, Viv, a bit late for that now), more that he wanted to be an inspiration. Some youngsters, he wrote in his autobiography *Hitting Across the Line* in 1991, 'might grasp the true meaning of this phrase "hitting across the line", which is not merely a cricketing term or even a concept for this book. It is about self-belief, about finding that inner strength, that sense of determination to develop your talents naturally, in the face of all manner of adversity and negative influence. That's what I mean by "hitting across the line". It's the only way I know.'

Of course, it helps if you have talents that you can develop and if I had had any, they were yet to make their presence felt. It is surely no coincidence that latent is an anagram of talent.

While Viv's inner strength was tested on his first international tour to India, little did he know that in the spring of 1975, my adulation of him would also be fiercely challenged.

It is fair to say that Malcolm 'Supermac' Macdonald was not really an Adonis in anyone's book and, at this distance, I have absolutely no idea why I became temporarily obsessed with the Newcastle United number nine. It may have been because my best friend, Gillian, an otherwise highly intelligent girl, was a big fan of Emlyn 'Emmo' Hughes, the captain of Liverpool and

England. To my father's absolute horror, I also switched my allegiance from his (and my) Nottingham Forest – where we used to spend every other Saturday afternoon listening to Brian Clough shouting – to Newcastle United. It was a short-lived affair, though, lasting only from 1974 until 1976, when Supermac left the club to join Arsenal. I mean. *Arsenal.* There was no way I was going to follow him there; my father would have disowned me.

My mother had, of course, saved my Newcastle/Supermac scrapbook, in which I found my hand-written minute-by-minute report of England's 5-0 win against Cyprus at Wembley on 16 April 1975. My headline read, 'Mac has burst ya nets and will do so for ever more. Supermac rules Wembley O.K.' Well, I was only 14. Macdonald scored all five goals. Emlyn Hughes was a substitute for that game, I can't remember why, but I am sure I must have been an unbearable friend for Gillian as I blathered on about Supermac's supremacy.

It was around this time that I also began to frequent the youth club on Tuesday and Thursday evenings in the Derbyshire village we had moved to, forging a variety of highly unsavoury friendships for my mother to worry and complain about. One in particular, let's call him Jez, was the acme of unwholesome youths and, needless to say, he was the one upon whom I concentrated my affections. He was the (im)perfect antidote to my days at a repressed all-girls' school, a place where even the arrival of window cleaners could cause contagious swooning. But Jez was a living, breathing boy who, I could kid myself, cared deeply for me. He did not. Of course. He had pretty much only one thing on his mind.

All the free counselling from Cathy & Claire in *Jackie* had mattered not a jot. I am quite sure they had promised me that a boy, *any* boy, would increase my self-esteem and immediately give my life some meaning and purpose. Jez did none of this and it seems fair to say that I chose him simply because I knew he would offend my mother on very many levels. Oh, the rows we had. She was gracious enough to invite him in for coffee on several occasions but, the minute he left, she would get out a full carpet cleaning kit and scrub the floor where his brothel-creepers had been. It was during this brief dalliance, too, that my father, for possibly the only time in his life, shouted at me. He would drive around the village in whichever model of Triumph car he then owned until he found me. 'Get in the car, *now*,' he would yell, leaning over to open the passenger door as he screeched to a halt like a driver out of *Starsky & Hutch*.[9] The shame of it. For me, I mean. It is only since becoming a parent that I have realised how anxious my own must have been, for Jez had not a single redeeming quality apart from the fact that, to me, he seemed different and dangerous and my simple little life craved

---

9   *Starsky & Hutch* was an American TV series shown in the UK in the late 1970s starring Paul Michael Glaser and David Soul as two Californian detectives, one of whom (Starsky) wore a big cardigan. Yes, a cardigan.

some of that frisson. An aside is that we often hear how children are embarrassed by their parents. In my experience, it works just as well the other way round.

Jez was a thoroughly boorish boy who wore brothel creepers, a bootlace tie and a variety of leather jackets. He owned a Yamaha FSIE50 (more commonly called a fizz pot in those days and, for all I know, may still be now) and had no intelligent conversation whatsoever. He would have filled my mild-mannered, courteous parents with absolute dread. Riding on the back of the fizz pot caused other problems too, as the legs of my fashionably voluminous baggy trousers constantly got caught in the wheels and ripped. We didn't have a lot of money, certainly not enough to buy new trousers, so I had the added humiliation of having to wear Mum-repaired trousers that featured any material she could get her hands on to disguise the tears.

The other characters at the youth club weren't much better than Jez and a lot of them were Derby County supporters. Which is how I found myself one Saturday morning on the 'Ramaway' Derby fans' away train to see my fleetingly beloved Newcastle at St James' Park. As usual, I was one of the 0.00007 per cent recurring (I looked this up and, apparently, for those who are more numerically proficient than me, it should obviously be 0.000077) of females on a football train and, as I was supporting the other side, I hid my Newcastle scarf under my coat and travelled up with a Derby fan who we will call Bob. He made an attempted foray into my coat – not to touch my scarf, mind – which I swiftly rebuffed (at the age of 14, I couldn't understand what he was doing but did know I didn't want him to do whatever it was) and we settled down for the journey. I say 'settled down' advisedly as these were the days of unbridled football hooliganism and the 'Ramaway' was pelted by bricks thrown by 'fans' as it travelled through Leeds station.

Our arrival at Newcastle wasn't much better. While I don't remember any more bricks, we ran for our lives from the station to the ground accompanied by a posse of police horses. Once there, I was so overcome by the whole experience and half a pint of lager-and-black that I fainted and missed all of the first half. It was my last trip to St James' Park.

Alongside my athletics commitments, and at the risk of sounding like a tomboy (which I certainly wasn't), I was also playing a lot of football and, somewhere in the bottomless pit of my mother's collection of papers, I found a programme from May 1976 of a five-a-side knockout competition in which I played for Derby County Ladies. My notes on the yellowing paper report read, 'Got to S-F [semi-final] where we lost 6-0.' The matches have faded from my mind like the print on the mildewed programme, but I do vividly remember making the first joke that people actually laughed at. We were driven to the competition by the mother of my friend Jackie and, passing a Colman's mustard sign, she said, 'I used to go out with a boy whose surname was Mustard.' Quick as a flash from the back seat, I said, 'I bet he was hot stuff!' Maybe you had to be there.

Spectating was more my thing than playing, though, and for several seasons I went to Nottingham Forest or to Derby County every Saturday with my father and brother. Given the animosity between the two clubs, it may seem surprising today but my father had no problem with that; he was a devotee of Brian Clough (apart from their very different political views) and wanted to watch any side he was in charge of. But while my father's heart belonged to Forest, he went to more Derby games when Clough became manager of the then Second Division side in 1967; two years later they were promoted as champions and in the 1971/72 season won the league. Dad had also become friendly with two Derby players – John O'Hare and Alan Hinton – who lived in the same village, which added a personal element to the games too. We all had a soft spot for Hinton, a thoroughly nice man, whose curly blond hair and white boots had earned him the nickname 'Gladys', although we also called him 'Noddy' because of his running style. He was a legend at Derby and in our family. Hinton retired from the game and left Derbyshire for North America in 1976 with his wife, Joy, after the death from cancer of their nine-year-old son, Matthew, a dreadful event that consumed our whole village in sadness for weeks.

Our attendances at the Baseball Ground dropped off when Clough left Derby in 1973 but when he took over at Forest in January 1975 – after eight months managing Brighton & Hove Albion and then his infamous 44-day stint at Leeds United – our Saturday journeys along the A52, now known as Brian Clough Way, only went in one direction. And what a glorious route to travel. Forest were narrowly promoted from the Second Division at the end of the 1976/77 season, then the following term lost only three of their first 16 league games and only one more game all season, in the FA Cup sixth round. They conceded just 24 goals in 42 league games and won the First Division title in 1977/78, seven points ahead of second-placed Liverpool. That same team had ended Forest's 42-match unbeaten league run, which dated back to November 1977.

All this excitement took my eyes even further off the ball regarding my O levels. Worse still, just as Forest were bring promoted from the Second Division, I contracted pneumonia, as diagnosed by no less an expert than my mum – although I think it was more likely to have been glandular fever – in the middle of the exams. Mum thought that some bracing sea air during the May half-term would prove an instant cure, so we travelled to Dorset to stay in the coldest, dampest motel (a motel in England in the late 1970s would have had a whiff of glamour) in the world. A bizarre excursion when I was so ill, I'm sure you will agree. A photograph taken at the time outside the birthplace of Thomas Hardy in Higher Bockhampton shows me even more emaciated than usual, barely able to stand on painfully matchstick-thin legs. On my return to school for a maths exam (yay!), I was supported by a chair on either side to make sure that, if I fainted, I wouldn't fall on the floor and be knocked out. To be honest, being knocked out would have been much kinder to the poor examiner than the crap I handed in.

Luckily, Nottingham Forest were destined for far greater heights than me and, unbelievably, they went on to win back-to-back European Cups in 1979 and 1980. For an unglamorous club with unglamorous players and fans – my father among them – they were extraordinarily happy times. And at least it took Dad's mind off my stockpiling of poor exam results.

But the glory days of Forest were a sideshow compared to my increasing fanaticism for Viv and the West Indies. In the midst of all the local excitement around Nottingham in 1976, I was concentrating on the Windies tour of England and confronting an issue I had never thought about before, such was the innocent backwater of my upbringing. I say innocent but I was brought up not to notice skin colour, just to see people as, well, people.

But that all changed when, on the eve of the Test series, the South African-born England captain Tony Greig gave an interview on BBC television that caused an immediate outcry.

'I'm not really sure they're as good as everyone thinks they are. If they're down they grovel, and I intend with the help of Closey [the 45-year-old Yorkshireman and former England captain Brian Close] and a few others to make them grovel,' Greig said in the interview.

My father, an egalitarian who had taught me by example to be the same, was outraged by the comments of the privileged white South African. Greig's remarks only cemented my support of the West Indies team and I remain offended on their behalf to this day. In Greig's defence, he carried on apologising for the remarks some 35 years after making them until he died too young at the age of 66 in December 2012.

But in the summer of 1976, I was furious and burned with the desire to see the Windies humiliate England's cricketers and to shove Greig's words down his throat. The Windies players themselves were far more dignified than me; they just let their cricket do the talking.

As Viv later said, 'It was as if he [Greig] had unintentionally handed us the ammunition we needed to win the series.'[10]

The incident opened my pathetically innocent eyes to the racism endured by my heroes and I was on high alert for any offensive comments from that summer onwards. I have been accused many times of being anti-English and unpatriotic for supporting the West Indies

---

10 Viv Richards, *Hitting Across the Line*, 1991.

cricket team (England *are* my second team, though) and for hero-worshipping Viv Richards. Well, tough. Tony Greig did that for me. The brilliant Professor Sir Hilary Beckles (now vice-chancellor of the University of the West Indies) in his seminal work *The Development of West Indies Cricket* wrote, 'It is rare indeed that great men locate their genius within the social circumstances of their humble origins. It is also rare for great men to humble themselves before movements that surround them and which they could ignore to much profit. We felt, then, that Richards was doing something for us. Each century, each double century, peeled away the optic scales accumulated over 400 years of inhuman subjection. The English were thrown into panic, not because of the aggregates – they had seen them before – but because they sensed with Richards it was more than sport; it was the business of history and politics – the struggle against injustice and inequality.'[11]

Just as I had failed to understand sexual discrimination – why couldn't I pursue the career I wanted to? – I had failed too to understand racial discrimination. Until that word: *Grovel*.

* * *

As my luck would have it, the first Test of the 1976 series was to be played at my home ground, Trent Bridge. It

---

11 Hilary McD. Beckles, *The Development of West Indies Cricket, Vol 1, The Age of Nationalism*, 1998.

was a place of pilgrimage for me and, as Neville Cardus so lovingly wrote, it was 'a lotus-land for batsmen, a place where it was always afternoon and 360 for two wickets'.

It would be my first sighting of Viv Richards in a Test match and I felt like the mother of a child about to play Joseph in the school nativity play. 'Please, God, don't let him be bowled first ball,' I thought. 'Please, God, let him score a century.'

And lo, it came to pass: there was no dropping of the baby Jesus, no fluffed lines and no gravy-stained tea towel on a small child's head.

West Indies captain Clive Lloyd won the toss and elected to bat but the openers, Roy Fredericks and Gordon Greenidge, were soon out for 42 and 22 respectively, leaving Viv and Alvin Kallicharran at the wicket just after lunch. I knew Viv would have been galvanised by Greig's 'grovel' remarks and, sure enough, he was at his imperious best, smashing his way to a century from 144 balls. By the close of the first day, he was on 143. On the second day, he raced to his first Test double hundred to an ecstatic reception from the West Indies fans. The match ended in a draw but, to me, it was the sweetest victory.

By the final Test at The Oval in August, the West Indies were two up in the series and I had barely missed a ball. When Richards hit 291, I felt as if I was in paradise and I revelled in the ball-by-ball TV coverage as well as basking in the press reports of Viv's prowess. There was a bonus in seeing Michael 'Whispering Death' Holding [a nickname conferred upon the bowler by umpire Dickie Bird, who said that Holding ran without making any sound on his long run-up] return match figures of 14 wickets for 149 runs. And that was on a featherbed pitch (definition: a surface very favourable to batsmen). The sweetest sight was seeing Holding bowl Tony Greig off his pads in the first innings, which prompted a pitch invasion by West Indies supporters delighted that their heroes had, in fact, made the England captain well and truly grovel. The umpires held up play for some ten minutes, giving me ample time to perform a dance of gratitude around my living room. Captain Clive Lloyd said the Oval Test that year was just like playing a home game, thanks to the volume of the West Indian crowd.

Before that Test, I hadn't paid much attention to many bowlers, apart from Joel Garner, such had been my fixation on every move that Viv made. But that match changed it all. Along with many others during that blistering summer, I had never before seen a sight like Michael Holding on a cricket field. And it was a formative experience. Watching his long, gliding run-up culminating in a balletic leap as he delivered ball after ball of utmost ferocity was poetry in pure physical form.

England's fast bowler, Bob Willis, who played in that Oval Test, said, 'Michael Holding gave the finest display of fast bowling I have ever seen. Having bowled on that pitch, I know what I am speaking about when I say there was nothing there to help the pace bowlers. But Michael managed to make it seem perfect for speed.'

Holding was just 22. Some years later, he remarked that had he been older he might not have bowled at full pelt on such a featherbed pitch and it was his youthful enthusiasm that got the better of him. Actually, it got the better of all of us who saw it, whether you were an England or West Indies fan. Of Holding's 14 wickets, 12 were either bowled or lbw, such was his unerring accuracy. Yet while he was super fast and so beautiful to watch, he doesn't even get a mention in some top 20 fastest bowlers of all time. It isn't all about mph, though, and most of us would surely choose Holding in our own lists.

The man himself remains modest and unassuming, which is remarkable when you consider that one over he bowled in 1981 even has its own website. On 14 March that year at the Kensington Oval in Barbados, Holding bowled six balls to England's opener Geoff Boycott, which have become the stuff of legend. Words such as 'scalded', 'peppered' and 'battered' are used to describe possibly the fastest and fiercest over in cricket history. Ball after ball found Boycott's glove, then thigh guard, then chest and then throat, being torpedoed as the crowd of West Indies slip fielders leapt into the air after each delivery. Then the sixth ball saw the England opener's off stump ripped out of the ground before cartwheeling backwards. Boycott said that last ball 'went like a rocket' and he seems unable to even remember the first five balls of the over (or he has erased them from his memory, more likely) at all.

Back in 1976, Holding's 14 wickets at The Oval earned him a place in cricket lore forever. How thankful I am to have been alive to see it, even if just on television. But Holding's and the team's performances meant much more to many others than to me.

The summer of 1976 was parched by drought and water rationing. It was a real scorcher, and not just on the cricket field. While I remember it mainly for Viv scoring 829 runs in the series against England – even though he missed the second Test at Lord's through illness – that summer became notable too for the Notting Hill riots that occurred some two weeks after the end of the series. Some commentators placed the riots alongside the West Indies' humiliation of England, a special triumph in the wake of Tony Greig's 'grovel' remarks. Professor Sir Hilary Beckles said of Richards in that sweltering summer, 'Richards was reaping that which those who went before him had sown. That is how the struggle for justice evolves everywhere. I understood the meaning of many things that summer. I believed he understood the seriousness of our condition and was prepared to act with all means necessary. We, the wretched of England's inner cities, had never seen the likes of it. I examined his method, his concepts and his sense of purpose. I concluded that the survival struggle for West Indians with respect to post-colonial Englishness was placed at a higher level.'[12]

Viv Richards, without him realising it, opened my eyes to it all: 'the seriousness of our condition'. Of the 1976 Test series, he has said, 'Who wouldn't want to maybe have one-up on your colonial masters at some point? I just wanted to send that message we are all equal. It's pretty simple.'

I was a fairly innocent white teenage girl from the East Midlands, which isn't to say that I would have lived my life in total ignorance of colonialism and the slave trade, but I couldn't have had a better teacher than Viv to initiate me. I started to read widely on Caribbean history and slavery and from then on called out racist remarks when anyone uttered them in my presence. Later on, when I wrote *Real Quick: A Celebration of the West Indies Pace Quartets* with Alastair McLellan, we finally had the chance to highlight some English and Australian writers who were still peddling racist slurs disguised as complaints about the Windies pace attack in the 1990s. For instance, in June 1991, soon after the West Indies arrived for a Test series in England, David Frith, then editor of *Wisden Cricket Monthly*, wrote, 'Another invasion is upon us by a West Indian team which is the most fearsome, the most successful and the

---

12 Hilary McD Beckles, *The Development of West Indies Cricket, Vol 1, The Age of Nationalism*, 1998.

most unpopular in the world. Their game is founded on vengeance and violence and is fringed by arrogance.'

Frith's remarks made in 1991 seem little different to Tony Greig's 'grovel' comment in 1976. In the next issue of the magazine, Frith followed up his editorial with one entitled 'Just to clarify' as he believed his comments had been misinterpreted. Er, okay, then.

And, in his review of *Real Quick*, Frith wrote in *Wisden Cricket Monthly* that the West Indies' famous four-prong attack was 'morally indefensible'. He went on, 'Holding was usually magnificent – as was Wes Hall before him – and Garner and Ambrose were fortunate to be endowed with such long limbs. That will suffice.'

Frith was forced out by the magazine in February 1996, apparently after another race row.

Stay alert, even now, for remarks by other commentators in the same vein.

Even in January 2021, Simon Briggs in the *Daily Telegraph*, wrote, '*There was a period when the West Indies outpaced them [Australia] – in every sense of the word. That spell from 1972 to 1992 was the heyday of the NASTY FASTIE* [my capitals].' And even the avuncular Henry Blofeld, in his 2001 book *Cricket and All That*, wrote, '*In 1976 in England, the West Indies fast bowlers reached a peak of nastiness.*'

Could someone explain to me why West Indies bowlers, and *only* West Indies bowlers, are *still* written about in the type of language that implies violence, intimidation and bullying?

But how much deeper does the wickedness go? In autumn 2021, the cricket world was rocked by the revelations of racism, brought into the light by Azeem Rafiq, at Yorkshire County Cricket Club. And it won't just have happened there.

For me, some three years after my first sighting of Viv Richards, he had become crowned as a role model, not just for his pride in representing the West Indies but as my guiding light as a teacher about racism. And the great man was also blessed with bags of natural talent allied to a strong work ethic, so there was certainly a lot for me to learn there. My bag was, on both counts, pretty empty and a role model can only do so much.

* * *

In amongst the many thousands of damp and nicotined newspapers I started sorting through after my mother's death, I found three pages written by me in the same year as Viv's supreme summer. My adolescent self had a lot of maturing to do.

I wrote: 'I was the first child, so naturally I am freedom-seeking and independent [that is a blatant lie].

'I am fifteen years old. Most of my fifteen years have been enjoyable – but the worst, I believe, is yet to come.'

I then proceed to contradict myself.

'Since I was ten, I have been an extremely moody person with a very quick temper – you just ask my mother and father. Now, I think I am over the top of the hill and I will soon become a nice person once more.'

Ah, the innocence and optimism of youth.

'I quite enjoy my life; even if things go wrong and turn against me it all adds up to experience! I will sum up with a marvellous line: I met a funny thing on the way to the grave. They call it Life.'

Michéle Savidge 12-10-76

Finding these pages so soon after my mother's death moved me on many levels. First, shame that I had been so moody and had undoubtedly given my parents a lot of trouble; second, disbelief at the optimism I seemed to possess but had subsequently forgotten all about; third, sadness that I couldn't run down the stairs at that very moment and show it to my parents and have a misty-eyed laugh about it. Does the missing them ever, *ever* go away? I stood in my old bedroom, surrounded by mountains of rubbish, and cried more tears.

Then I found an envelope addressed to me, annotated 'Received 20-10-76', which made me wonder whether my mother was more ordered in her hoarding than I had ever thought, given that date is only a week after the pages I had written. In the A4 brown envelope were a dozen letters all signed the same way: 'All my love from Tony' with 14 kisses shaped into a triangle.

'Who the hell was Tony?' I asked myself.

In one of his letters he writes, 'Hope you are well after your accident (what a stupid thing to do!)'

'What accident?' I asked myself again.

I read carefully through the mostly very boring letters as the memory of the 'relationship', if not the accident, slowly returned. I had met Tony on a family holiday in the Lake District that summer and exchanged many letters with him. In one, I saw that I had arranged to visit him at his parents' home in Essex and he had drawn a very intricate map showing a lay-by off the A405, where my father would hand me over to Tony's father. I remember very little about my stay with him, other than having a prolonged snog to Real Thing singing 'Can't Get By Without You' and listening in the middle of the night to James Hunt win the Formula One World Championship in Japan. I also remember feeling ill with stomach ache for most of the time. That must have put him off as I never saw him again after the fathers did the reverse transfer in the same lay-by a week later. I'm sorry about that, Tony, but at least you were spared any more of my mood swings – or stomach ache for that matter. (It took many more years for that to be diagnosed and treated as a bipartite gall bladder, which was certainly a new one on me.)

There were more letters, photos and drawings from forgotten boys – a United Nations of inamoratos – which I unearthed in my mother's belongings. And while my memories are that I had had no success in the boyfriend department, many letters profess undying love: perhaps I had simply been a bad picker, choosing to remember the unobtainable 'bad' boys rather than the ones who seemed to care about me. Self-sabotage has perhaps been a recurring theme.

There was a collection of gushy letters from a boy from Karachi whom I had met in Dorset in 1980. While there had been an overlap with Gord, I had actually given the potential paramour from Pakistan zero encouragement, but you would never have guessed that from the perfectly preserved thin blue airmail letters I found.

'My one and only. What do I have to do to make you think of me in a nice way. I have asked you to marry me and I don't think I can do more than that. I have completely devoted myself to you and what have I got in return? Nothing, except a few curses and ill thoughts. I am sure one day you will remember me and say, "God, I wish I could have been nicer, he is such a great guy. Now I realise how much I really do love him."'

He also complained that I was selfish for having gone to a cricket match without him and in his next letter wrote:

'I know how you feel towards me. Some day you will realise that you should have been more than a friend to me. But I won't be around and you will be sitting behind a dustbin in a dark alley with a bottle in your hand. (This is not supposed to make you laugh, but to take a serious look at our lovely relationship.) P.S. Viv

[Richards] was beaten by Zaheer [Abbas, a Pakistan cricketer] in a single wicket challenge.'

I suspect the P.S. was added to make me query my allegiance to Viv and make me switch to Pakistan in the form of my suitor. It didn't work and re-reading those letters just makes me think I had a lucky escape all round.

My mother's 'filing' system meant that letters from four years earlier were mixed up with those from Pakistan and one written in red pen, with an English stamp on the envelope, fell out of the box, urging me to read it.

'You never know, perhaps you were meant for me all the time. I am reading your poem, yet another ingenious masterpiece. [I briefly wonder if his mother had been a hoarder too and had kept my poem.] I like the bits towards the end. I never knew you felt like that but if you want to give it a try I will go along with you. I want to have a really good time because if you do want me, I want it to last as long as possible. But I have got to watch myself because I have got my exams coming up and you said get all of them and all of them I will get. [I imagine I would have found that a very unattractive ambition.] You have made me feel so happy. I love you and always will. Love Rick.'

Perhaps he was a good one that got away? Unlike the next admirer, Marco from Sicily, whose letters read like the ramblings of a madman. In one, he had drawn a smudged sketch in biro of St Peter's Square, captioned with the information that the square was waiting for me and that St Peter would take me to paradise, but his hand has lost the key. No? Me neither.

Another lucky escape. But the ones I really liked didn't seem to reciprocate. I had a fleeting dalliance with a French chap with whom I became temporarily and predictably infatuated but whose letter to me read as if he was firmly trying to keep me at arm's length.

'I will hope to see you again in the future.' To accompany his note, he had also drawn a picture in pencil of a cow called Michele.

Hardly the language of love, I am sure you will agree.

All the letters, apart from the French and Italian ones, mentioned Viv and cricket as if they all thought that was the way to my heart. Well, it was – but not their way. I did put a lot of effort and love into my relationship with Gord, which lasted from 1978 until 1982. That period coincided with many glorious days at Somerset County Cricket Club, which featured Viv, Ian Botham and Joel 'Big Bird' Garner, a supremely quick bowler from Barbados who had made his Test debut for the West Indies in 1977.

Somerset were regarded as an exceptionally unsophisticated county but the potent combination of England's great all-rounder with two shining lights from the West Indies changed all that. On the last two days of the 1979 season, when Somerset won the Gillette Cup and the John Player League, it was the first time for 104 years that the county had won a major trophy. David Foot, the venerated cricket writer from Somerset, wrote, 'During Somerset's golden years, Richards and Garner in tandem, batsman and bowler, both lethal and languid, gave the county a majesty and authority which they had never possessed before – and may never possess again.'[13]

The towering Garner was a joy to behold and often bowled balls that were unplayable. He was a master of the yorker (a straight ball that goes underneath the striker's bat, landing at his feet), a delivery that would cause delight in the home crowd as an opposition batsman stumbled, frequently losing his wicket. The sun always seemed to be shining at the County Ground, Taunton on those days, surrounded as I was by cider and sublime cricket. Those days gave me countless opportunities to study Viv in close-up and to witness how, as David Foot put it, unassuming and accessible he was. I never had the nerve to approach him, though, and thus he still managed to hang on to his mythical status. I sat pathetically agape when he was batting, marvelling at his physicality and the theatre of each innings. I was well aware of his detractors' views that he was arrogant but I never

13 *Sunshine, Sixes and Cider* David Foot 1986

saw that. Like the very best performers or athletes, he was the master of his body as he faced each ball. The power seemed to run upwards from his thighs through his spine and he would then squeeze his shoulder blades together to open the face of the bat and unleash the full force of his shot. I would feel crushed when he was out; I took the loss of his wicket personally, feeling I had placed too much expectation on his mighty shoulders.

It wasn't until the summer of 1984 that I met him for the first time during a West Indies tour match at Grace Road, Leicester, where I had arranged to interview him for *The Cricketer*. I had set off early from Somerset in the Dolomite to allow for any mechanical issues that might arise and felt sick with nerves for the entire journey. It is commonly thought that you shouldn't meet your heroes and a multiple choice quiz was running through my mind. What if he was thoroughly unpleasant/sexist/uncommunicative/arrogant/boring/forgotten all about our assignation?

I was trembling as I got out of the car at 10am and even my voice was shaking with nerves as I approached the receptionist. And then, there he was, not unpleasant/sexist/uncommunicative/arrogant/boring/nor had he forgotten we were meeting. It was quite clear to me that he saved all his swagger for the pitch.

We chatted for about 20 minutes as I sat, doe-eyed and nodding in agreement at everything he uttered.

Thank heavens I recorded the interview because I wasn't capable of writing anything down and didn't really hear anything he said, my head being up in the clouds. When I played back the tape recording, I heard Viv's mellifluous voice accompanied by me saying 'Hmm' a thousand times to show him that I agreed with every word he said. He must have thought I had a tic.

As soon as he left, I went straight to a phone booth and called my mother. Well, you would, wouldn't you? I could tell she was ever so slightly amused by the breathless 'I've met him!' as she gave a gentle, empathetic laugh, the kind our mothers do so well. I watched a couple of hours of cricket to calm down before the long drive back, floating on cloud nine with the knowledge that, sometimes – and certainly this time – meeting your heroes works out just fine. After that meeting, I remained in awe of him.

At that stage in his career, Viv didn't refer to himself in the third person as he went on to do on numerous occasions in the future. But maybe that is how someone copes with intense adulation? Only by standing outside yourself, seeing yourself in the third person, can you manage not to let the whole thing go to your head?

Viv had also become a hero for many people the year before, having twice refused a blank cheque to join a rebel West Indies tour to apartheid South Africa. Years later, Viv said that the former South African president Nelson Mandela thanked him for not going.

West Indies bowler Michael Holding also said that he would not sell his birthright for a 'mess of porridge' in reacting to an offer from South Africa. Ian Botham, too, had refused to tour the country with a rebel England XI in 1981, saying, 'I could never have looked Viv in the eye.' Geoff Boycott, with a characteristic turn of phrase, said Botham's comment was 'puke-making'. Thanks for the feedback, Geoff.

For Viv and his supporters, it was very simple. 'Once I was offered one million Eastern Caribbean dollars, and there have been all kinds of similar proposals. They all carried a political burden and in each case it was a very simple decision. I just could not go. As long as the black majority in South Africa remains suppressed by the apartheid system, I could never come to terms with playing cricket there. I would be letting down my own people back in Antigua and it would destroy my self-esteem.'[14]

It was easy then for me to hang on the coat-tails, and indeed to every word, of this man of high principle and I must confess that my head was turned to the extent that I didn't care much for any less-than-flattering remarks about him.

---

14 *Hitting Across the Line*, Viv Richards, 1991.

Even in 1980, when he was accused by sections of the English press of excessive (some might say intimidatory) appealing to umpire Lloyd Barker for England's Rob Bailey to be given out during the West Indies' fourth Test at the Kensington Oval in Barbados, I merely shrugged it off as over-exuberance and commitment to the cause.

My defence was tested again during the 1990 Antigua Test between the West Indies and England when Viv refused to lead the team on to the field and instead ventured into the press box to finish an argument with an English journalist. The press man had accused Viv of making a V-sign to England's Allan Lamb but Viv believed he could plead provocation for that 'regrettable incident', so I will take his word for it. That's what you do for your heroes, isn't it?

It became something of a joke when I worked at *Cricket Life* that I managed to get at least one photograph of Viv in each issue. I tried that a few times at the *Evening Standard* without any success.

My chagrin on Viv's behalf reached its peak, or perhaps that should be pique, at the end of the 1986 season when, unbelievably, Viv Richards and Joel Garner were not offered new contracts at Somerset in an apparent effort to keep New Zealand's Martin Crowe at the club. Ian Botham resigned in disgust and joined Worcestershire while in an emergency general meeting held for the members at the Shepton Mallet

Showground, the club won the vote to release the West Indies stars. Peter Roebuck, the Somerset captain, wanted to build a Somerset team around Crowe and other young players and, it was said, was 'terrified' by what he regarded as Viv's volcanic temperament. But I believe more Somerset and England bowler Vic Marks's testimony that 'the argument surfaced that the younger players struggled to perform because of Viv's mighty, broody, overwhelming presence. It was an argument that failed to convince me then, it does not convince me now nor did I find it vindicated soon after Viv had been sacked when the output of the players concerned was exactly the same.'

Marks also wrote, 'Most batsmen are vulnerable on nought but Richards, by his delayed, swaggering entrance, could have the palms of bowlers sweating on a cold day before he had faced a ball. He oozed arrogance, a quality that deserted him when he was beyond the boundary, which made him most unusual.'[15]

I have seen nothing to contradict anything that Vic Marks attests to and the fact that Antigua made Viv a national hero in 2006 is a slam dunk.

After Somerset, Viv spent the 1987 season in the Lancashire League with Rishton and, in 1990, joined County Championship side Glamorgan where, true to form, he was an inspiration to the younger

---

15 *Original Spin*, Vic Marks, 2019.

players, helping the side win the AXA Sunday League in 1993.

Meanwhile, his last Test match was played in England at The Oval in 1991 and I was lucky enough to get the last interview for the *Evening Standard*. By August that year, the West Indies had not lost a Test series since Viv had taken over the captaincy from Clive Lloyd in 1985.

Seven years before his last appearance in London, a bare-chested Viv had stared down from Underground advertising hoardings holding a Nike shoe as though it was a hymn book. The slogan announced the shoe was 'Also available to mortals'. By his last summer of Test cricket, though, there were signs of his mortality for all to see. His beard sported flecks of grey and his hair was thinner. But his physique was still like Joe Frazier's and he still walked like a king. In the fourth Test at Edgbaston, where he had hit the winning six to beat England by seven wickets, his West Indies team-mates had formed a makeshift throne to carry him off the field. That victory put the West Indies 2-1 up in the series, so ensuring he would end his reign unbeaten.

His regal manner was still referred to as cockiness and arrogance by his detractors but by that stage he was viewing it as 'God-given confidence ... I just think I'm blessed by the Almighty Father to have the strength of character to deal with certain things,' he told me then, speaking quietly. 'You can still get whatever trouble there is around but inwardly you've said your prayers and no one can mess with you because you've got that inner strength.'

In his final interview with me, he maintained that criticism of the West Indies was generated by racism. The year before, he had been deeply wounded when he was accused of racism himself during England's tour to the West Indies after stating that he was proud to lead a team of African descent, thus offending West Indians of Indian descent. 'It was nice to make that statement,' he said, 'and hope that Indians and West Indians would look at the team as a collective unit. Saying that the team was of African descent – well, it is the majority and I felt there was nothing wrong with saying that.'

Approaching retirement, Richards seemed more ready than ever to air his political views and was scathing then about the recent re-acceptance of South Africa into world cricket. 'I feel the cricket body have done their best but it's up to the government to make it one man, one vote.'

While he was fully aware of his hero status to me – I had written him a personal letter to thank him for the joy his cricket had given me and for opening my eyes to a world beyond the boundary – he found it all, including his unofficial title as 'King of Antigua', a bit embarrassing. 'It's nice, in a way, to have that kind of respect but, deep down, you don't take it seriously,' he said.

From what I saw, it certainly never seemed to have gone to his head. Lesser mortals might have had their heads turned by, for example, a near-riot when the 18-year-old Viv was given out lbw at the Antigua Recreation Ground. 'No Vivi, no play,' the crowd shouted. Or their heads might have become just a little bit swollen by having the street where they were born named after them or a calypso written about them. But not Viv. The Antigua government built him a house on the island but the money he made from cricket didn't affect him, even though it was hardly a fortune by many sports stars' standards. 'I wouldn't say I'm rich in a money sense. But I'm rich in soul and body, my beliefs and my values are intact and, as a black person, I'm proud of that.'

Indeed, he didn't want to be remembered for any particular innings or 'playing this or that pretty shot,' as he put it.

'I'd like people to remember me not for what they saw, not for the way I walked, but for what I've said, for my beliefs and to respect those. Just as a guy who was pretty sound in his beliefs and actually meant what he said.'

Just as Viv was preparing for his final Test match at The Oval, so I had to prepare for it too. And after first seeing him bat 18 years earlier, there was only one companion for me on that final outing. My father travelled up from Somerset the night before the first day of the Test and my fridge overflowed with his favourite components for cricket elevenses, lunch and tea.

This last Test of a wonderful series, which had been played in the very best spirit, had been lazily billed as 'Both v Viv' as Ian Botham, Viv's close friend who hadn't played a Test match for two years, was recalled to the England team. But the hype did add some frisson to the atmosphere. The first day, Thursday, 8 August, belonged to England, who reached 231/4 by close of play in spite of some ferociously fast bowling from Curtly Ambrose, Courtney Walsh, Malcolm Marshall and Patrick Patterson. Fair enough; I'll give England their day. Especially as my father and I had worked our way through a weighty cool bag that was certainly easier to carry home on the Tube than it had been to take it.

The second day saw England continue to have the upper hand, bowled out for 409, with Robin Smith bravely making a superb 109. By close of play on Friday, the West Indies were 90/1. Saturday did not go as I would have wanted. Viv, suffering from a migraine, batted down the order at number eight and was out for two. He did not look best pleased as he left the field. In fact, he looked furious and glared at someone or something in the pavilion. My father and I were none the wiser and ate another flaccid cheese and cucumber sandwich with another bag of salt and vinegar crushed crisps. All was not lost.

But the Windies were all out for 176, England's Phil Tufnell taking six wickets for 25 runs, and England enforced the follow-on: the first time in 22 years that had happened. The Windies reached close of play on Saturday on 152/3, still 91 runs short of making England bat again.

Sunday at The Oval was all set then for Viv's last stand. And there was added pressure. As he had only scored two runs in his first innings, he needed to make 20 in the second to secure a Test career batting average of over 50 and thus join an elite group. It was unthinkable to me that he should not be in that pantheon; indeed, the dread that he wouldn't make it – as well as the sinking feeling that it would be the last time I would see him bat in a Test – had kept me awake for most of Saturday night.

As morning broke the weather was set fair, so there were no worries on that score. But I felt sad that it was the end of an era and I didn't exchange a single word with Dad on our Tube journey to the ground. My mood was plainly out of step with the rest of the crowd, whose high-spirited jostling was apparent even at 10am. England were definitely up for it. But my legs felt like jelly as we walked through the Hobbs Gates. 'Pull yourself together,' I told myself. I took a deep breath, trying to take in what already seemed a momentous day, and looked up at the pavilion.

Way up there in the gods, looking down out of an open window, was Viv. He saw me and waved as though he was the Pope delivering a personal blessing. I smiled a smile of the chosen one, put my thumbs up to wish him good luck and told myself that it was all going to be okay.

Later that morning, Viv walked down the pavilion steps and on to the field to the loudest of cheers and whistles. Unlike the first time I saw him bat, he didn't wheel his arms one way, then the other; this time he held his bat high above his head between both hands as though it was a weighty barbell. His posture proclaimed: 'I am the champion' and then he did a little skippy run towards the wicket, a spotlit prize fighter on his way to the ring. I was on my feet even before Viv had left the dressing room, arms above my head too, clapping for all I was worth and tears already clouding my vision. My father turned his head towards me. 'All right?' he said, the thunderous applause drowning out his words so that I had to lip read. I didn't need to reply: I *was* all right, overcome with emotion but, most of all, by gratitude not just to the man in the middle who had enriched my life through his experiences but also to the man by my side who had held the door open for me.

Viv had never been a player who seemed to focus on statistics but it was obvious that this final innings meant a lot to him and it was a single-minded performance from the get-go. He took no chances and reached the milestone of 20 with a rare all-run four that got me to my feet again. He had hit nine sublime fours, and looked well set for a big score, before he was caught by Hugh Morris off the bowling of David Lawrence for 60. Viv began his trudge back to the pavilion to the cheers of a standing ovation, shaking his head with disappointment at being out, and then taking his cap off to wave to all corners of the ground. His walk slowed even more and he seemed to take an age to get up the steps as he pulled his cap down over his eyes and then disappeared from view.

The clapping subsided and the ground was quiet once more. My father put his arm round me.

'Well, that's that, then.'

My father, laconic as ever, was, as usual, right about 'that's that' but not in the way he thought. The following year, Michael and I had our first wonderful daughter and life certainly got well and truly in the way of cricket then.

The Fantasy Lunch Interval

ONE OF the joys of cricket is lunch (and tea). Everything stops for it and it is why cricket is the most convivial of sports. It was customary to take your own vast packed lunch (and alcohol but restrictions mean you can't do that at many grounds now) to a match but nowadays more people buy food at the ground. They are missing out on the significant pleasure of indulging in homemade warm, squashed sandwiches. This is the moment in *Between Overs* to stop for our own lunch interval, which has an element of fantasy about it as I have invited an XI of guests, some of the greatest characters (not just players and nobody chosen for their statistics) in cricket, to join me. The best thing of all, though, is that I have been able to bring some of them back from the dead. Fantasyland indeed.

* * *

It is a scorching July day, the Saturday of a Lord's Test between England and the West Indies. Midway through the match, it is anyone's game with England's bowlers claiming early bragging rights before the Windies' firepower rips through the home team's top order in the morning session. In the Coronation Garden, behind the magnificent Lord's pavilion, I have spread out a couple of green and blue tartan picnic rugs that boast a few indeterminate stains from previous cricket sorties. I had left my seat a few overs before lunch to grab the space and feel lucky to have got it now that I am surrounded by cigar smoke from men in their egg and bacon MCC ties. I unskilfully, as is my habit, pop open some champagne and begin to fill the first of 12 glasses (naturally, there is one for me).

Unsurprisingly, given his penchant for champagne, my first guest to arrive and bang on time is **W.G. Grace** (1848-1915). He utters a gruff 'Hello' and looks at me quizzically. Perhaps he thought the invitation was from Michael Savidge (he wouldn't be the first to make that mistake) and had only just realised that it was a woman who had requested his company. I won't make anything of that for as far as I know this Victorian Hercules was approving of women's sport and had even supported the all-female Womanhood Bowling (lawn bowls, that is, not cricket bowling) Club at Crystal Palace in the early 1900s. Surely a man ahead of his time in so many respects. I signal to him to sit down and this black-bearded bear of a man struggles with his vast bulk to make it down to the rug. He takes up a lot of space once he does but, for all he has done for us, I will forgive him for that.

The Gloucestershire titan's cricket career spanned 44 seasons; he scored more than 54,000 runs (the exact figure has long been the subject of statistical dispute) and took more than 2,800 wickets. This colossus of the game stood 6ft 2in tall and weighed 15 stones in his early 20s, even more in his older age and is regarded as the creator of modern cricket.

I am not sure whether he will be bemused or possibly not remotely surprised when I tell him that he (or rather a picture of him) played God in *Monty Python and the Holy Grail*. He had a great sense of his own importance and was renowned for his put-downs.

C.L.R. James (1901-1981), the Trinidadian journalist, socialist, historian and author of *Beyond a Boundary*, the greatest book ever written about cricket (but it is about a lot more than that), and who joins us on the rug, said of WG, 'No batsman was more scientific than WG and science was his servant, not his master. He was not one who by unusual endowment did stupendously what many others were doing well. He did what no one else had ever done, developed to a degree unprecedented, and till then undreamt of, potentialities inherent in the game. And it was this more than anything else which make possible WG's greatest achievement. It was by modern scientific method that this pre-Victorian lifted cricket from a more or less casual pastime into the national institution it rapidly became.'

James thus perfectly explained how important WG was to cricket's development. Without him, all cricket-lovers know we simply wouldn't be here and I am sure I would have been visited with wrath from heaven if I hadn't invited him.

WG and James have much to talk about and I am not sure that I will manage to get a word in, but I hope I will be able to eavesdrop on their discussions about the development of the game.

Perhaps I might have more success in conversation with one of my father's heroes – a god, more like – **Keith Miller** (1919-2004), regarded as one of the game's greatest-ever all-rounders. The same height as WG but without any of his bulk, Miller was, according to Dad, astonishingly handsome, 'an Adonis of a man'. Perhaps my father was also in awe of Miller because the cricketer had been in the Royal Australian Air Force during the Second World War and my father had completed his National Service – and stayed on for years afterwards – in the Royal Air Force. My father's favourite Miller quote, oft-cited at various intervals throughout his life, was, 'Pressure? I'll tell you what pressure is. Pressure is a Messerschmitt up your arse. Cricket is not.'

Miller played the game in a spirit of glorious abandon. He had been enormously affected by the war and while he deeply loved cricket, he played it as though it didn't matter much. He didn't get on particularly with the great Donald Bradman, the Australian batsman and captain; they were poles apart in their approach, the one leaning to an anti-establishment view, the other concerned with a more orderly, systematic approach. Post-war, when everyone was craving some *joie de vivre*, it is not difficult to understand why Miller and not Bradman, who was certainly much revered, was one of the best-loved Australians in England. Miller scored over 14,000 first-class runs and took nearly 500 wickets, but his statistics don't do justice to the glamour of his personality. My father thought him on a par with film stars of the day. Cricket's Clark Gable perhaps.

There are many legendary tales, including one that saw him hungover the morning after celebrating the birth of one of his four sons, quickly changing out of his tuxedo, running on to the pitch to play a match for New South Wales, his bootlaces flapping around his ankles, and proceeding to take seven South Australia wickets for 12 runs.

I think I will enjoy my chat – and drinks – with this *bon viveur* and will start by telling him how my father walked for nearly three hours from Long Eaton to Trent Bridge in 1948 to see him play for Australia in the first Test against England that year. Miller squats down on to his haunches and then arranges his seemingly endless long legs to settle on the picnic rug just as my next guest bounds up and twitches towards us.

If Keith Miller was a hero for my father, so **Derek Randall** (b.1951) was one of my first, which is hardly surprising since we both have Nottinghamshire in our veins. He played for the county for over 20 years before retiring in 1993. Like Miller, he appeared to play the game for fun but, unlike the Australian, conversely he often seemed to have worry etched on his face and was constantly fidgeting, whether batting or fielding. He was the most phenomenal fielder, famous for electrifying run-outs. No wonder his nickname was 'Arkle', after the racehorse. His greatest Test innings was made at the 1977 centenary Test against Australia at Melbourne, where he scored 174 runs, and it seemed that everyone in England stayed up all night to listen to it on *Test Match Special*. I hope he won't mind if I relive that with him over lunch. Although at this rate, given the tardy arrivals and the subjects we need to discuss, lunch is going to take the whole afternoon and we will miss the rest of the day's play.

If Randall's walk is idiosyncratic, our next guest is equally unmistakable. He purrs up to us, lithe as a cat, his 6ft-tall frame arranged into glorious lissomness. He became a son of Nottinghamshire too, lent to us by the cricketing gods to whom the county would be forever in debt.

Sir Garfield Sobers (b.1936) was the finest all-rounder in cricket history; some say he is the greatest cricketer who ever lived but I think the Old Man W.G. Grace might have something to say about that. Perhaps they can bat statistics to each other. Sobers is in complete control of his body as he sits down. He looks less tired today than when he retired at the age of only 38 after packing more cricket into his 20-year career than most would in a couple more decades than that. He played for Barbados for 21 seasons, Nottinghamshire for seven, South Australia in the Sheffield Shield for three and in English league cricket for eight. He must have been completely knackered by the end. In his 93 Test matches, he scored 8,032 runs, took 235 wickets and 109 catches. He excelled at batting, bowling and fielding and was intolerant of sledging. He probably wouldn't get a look-in these days, particularly when you consider he was never coached.

One of the events I want to talk to Sobers about is his six sixes in an over for Nottinghamshire against Glamorgan in a County Championship match in Swansea in August 1968. My father still talked about it in his early 80s, when he was still lucid, so much so that you would have thought he had been at the ground when, in fact, we had only listened to it on the radio. Sobers is renowned for being exceptionally modest, so perhaps he won't want to talk about that over and I am struck, just by briefly being in his presence, that such a special man doesn't see himself as special at all.

So it seems entirely appropriate that, at that moment, the ground appears to vibrate with the energy of our next guest.

At 6ft 2in tall, **Ian Botham** (b.1955) doesn't just resemble WG in height. And not for nothing was the famous all-rounder nicknamed 'Beefy' and 'Guy' (the gorilla). He is a man who frequently suffered a bad press but for cricket followers of my vintage he is forgiven (almost) any peccadillo you can throw at him. The fact that he is like a brother to Viv Richards and has brought with hims ome of his own label wine means he is a shoo-in for a fantasy lunch.

Mere statistics do not do justice to Beefy. His Test figures alone – 102 matches, 5,200 runs, 383 wickets, 120 catches – mean nothing if you don't take into account the 1981 series against Australia during which he altered the destiny of the Ashes. He was truly the Ben Stokes – and beyond – of a generation. In the third Test in 1981 at Headingley, his innings of 149 not out (and Bob Willis's eight wickets for 43 runs) steered England to the most unlikely of victories and in the fourth Test he hit a century when Australia's fast bowler Dennis Lillee was at his unbridled best.

And, as fortune would have it, here comes **Dennis Lillee** (b.1949). I have no doubt that there will be plenty of ribaldry now that he has arrived, particularly with his old sparring partner. Lillee was the most extraordinary fast bowler who, with his Aussie team-mate Jeff

Thomson, subjected their opposition to rigorous and regular examinations. Colin Croft, the former West Indies quick, said that Lillee got his vote 'for the best of all time. He came back from a grave injury, reinvented himself and transformed into a more cunning and productive bowler.'[16]

Lillee, with Thomson, was in fact ultimately responsible for the West Indies becoming world cricket's dominant force after a torrid series in Australia in 1975/76, when Clive Lloyd and his team lost the six-match series 5-1. Lloyd never wanted to endure another series like that and set about devising a plan to beat the Aussies and the rest of the cricket world with the introduction of the West Indies pace quartets.

Lillee was renowned for his fearsome commitment to the cause of winning and was no stranger to controversy. The most notorious incident occurred during the Perth Test against England in December 1979. Lillee came out on to the pitch with an aluminium bat made for him by a friend's bat-making company and proceeded to hit a ball for three runs. Australia captain Greg Chappell thought he should have hit it for four and told 12th man Rodney Hogg to take out a conventional bat to give to Lillee. While these negotiations were taking place, England captain Mike Brearley complained to the umpires that using an aluminium bat (there were

---

16 *The Cricket Monthly*, March 2015.

actually no rules against it) was against the spirit of the game and was damaging the ball. But Lillee refused to change it, conferring with Brearley and the umpires for another ten minutes before Chappell put his foot down and insisted Lillee use a new bat. Lillee's response was to throw the aluminium bat down in disgust. He was not censured for the incident, merely given a warning by the Australian Cricket Board.

Lillee took 355 Test wickets in 70 Tests and the 'caught Marsh, bowled Lillee' [Rodney Marsh was Australia's wicketkeeper] combination appeared 95 times in Tests, a partnership record that has not yet been matched.

I know that our next guest will have much to debate with him and I am hoping there won't be a punch-up. **Mike Brearley** (b.1942) played for England in 39 Tests and captained the side for 31 of them, winning 18 and losing four. A softly spoken man who at first seems serious but is in fact never far from a wide smile, Brearley was an extraordinary captain. He was so in tune with his men, worked out exactly what made them tick, where their anxieties were founded and did his utmost to mollify them. The Australian Hogg famously commented that Brearley had 'a degree in people' and just watching him interact, as he listens with an activeness that is very unusual in comparison to the other guests at lunch, makes me feel honoured to be in the presence of such a great mind. After he retired, Brearley became a psychoanalyst and psychotherapist, becoming president of the British Psychoanalytical Society, as well as president of the MCC. I wonder if I could talk to him about everything that has bothered me during my life? Maybe not. In 1985, he published *The Art of Captaincy*, one of the greatest books written on cricket, and I suspect that he and C.L.R. James will form their own huddle to discuss their magnificent tomes while the larrikins may indulge in less cerebral conversation. Of course, I could be proved wrong; I often am.

Brearley, writing in *The Guardian* in July 2011, said of our next guest, 'Is he too good to be true? I particularly admired his courage in England four years ago when he was, by his standards, struggling. He had had shoulder and elbow injuries. England's bowlers hit him several times on the body and gloves. He was reduced to being an ordinary mortal, several steps down from the divine. Yet he never flinched from the contest, never went for glory above resolution.' In the same article, he called him 'the most complete batsman I've seen' and few would disagree with Brearley about **Sachin Tendulkar** (b.1973), known the world over as the Little Master. In 1988, the year before his Test debut and aged just 15, Tendulkar and 16-year-old Vinod Kambli, who also went on to play for India, put on an unbroken 644-run partnership for Sharadashram Vidyamandir against St Xavier's High School in the Harris Shield semi-final in Azad Maidan. St Xavier's bowlers were apparently reduced to tears and you could hardly blame them for that.

Tendulkar went on to make his Test debut in November 1989 at the age of 16 and played his final Test, his 200th, in November 2013. The game's most prolific scorer, he returned 15,291 runs at an average of 53.8 in 200 Tests (329 innings) and 18,426 runs at 44.8 in 452 one-day innings.

One of the problems with being in close proximity to Tendulkar is the chaos he attracts. He is worshipped by millions of people, not just in India but around the world. People seem to throw themselves at his feet. Even Australia's Matthew Hayden said, 'I have seen God, he bats at number four for India.' A mass of people are already staring at him and I want to ask Tendulkar many questions about his extraordinary career but, as I spot the tall, gangly figure of my next invitee, **Christopher Martin-Jenkins** (1945–2013), I decide that he would be much better placed to ask the questions. CMJ, my first boss at *The Cricketer* magazine, was much more than a cricket journalist. The game was part of his DNA and he had an encyclopaedic knowledge that enabled him to write or edit at least 25 books on the subject. He was also extraordinarily good company and a brilliant impersonator of cricket characters, some of which he delivered to the delight of listeners of BBC's *Test Match Special*. He joined *TMS* in 1973 and made his last commentary in the England v Pakistan match in Dubai in February 2012. In between those times, he edited *The Cricketer* (1981–82) and was cricket correspondent of both the *Daily Telegraph* (1990–91) and *The Times* (1999–2008). He was a prolific writer with an enviable work ethic and taught me pretty much everything I know. It is a tragedy that he died so early.

I wish he had known that the Christopher Martin-Jenkins Spirit of Cricket Award was established in his memory the year after his death. An entirely fitting tribute to a man who went out of his way to always promote the way the game should be played.

One of CMJ's standout impersonations was of the legendary commentator **John Arlott** (1914–91) and it seems impossible not to have him at the lunch. As well as being a marvellous writer and broadcaster, Arlott was also a poet and wine connoisseur and known to have enjoyed the company of another of our guests, Ian Botham, over a bottle or several. I feel that now Arlott is here, the party can get going.

There is no point in me making any introductions, so I simply offer a few welcoming words which, I hope, spell out my gratitude for their lives on cricket's behalf. We are three bottles of champagne down and have eaten a lot of cheese rolls and vegetable samosas (they flummoxed WG at first) before Botham opens a couple of bottles of his 76 series Chardonnay. There are only 15 minutes of the lunch interval left and there is plenty of laughter as well as in-depth debate.

'Come in, come in,' calls Botham, waving the hand that doesn't hold a bottle. I turn round to see he is beckoning Michael Vaughan (b.1974), the former Yorkshire batsman and England captain. I think about shaking my head to Botham to indicate that Vaughan can't join us as I don't have enough wine glasses, and my panic only increases when I see Ben Stokes (b.1991) running to catch up with Vaughan.

Lunch is spinning out of my control now and I realise we're going to miss at least the first few overs of the afternoon session as I haven't even brought out the cake yet. I had spent two days making and decorating it, knowing that my guests, in common with many cricket followers, are highly sophisticated cake connoisseurs. I carefully unwrap the four-layer Victoria sponge, full of cream and strawberries and topped by small iced figures resembling each of my guests presiding over a green-iced cricket pitch. I feel bad that it is missing Vaughan and Stokes but remind myself that they weren't on my initial list. Then I feel bad that they weren't on my initial list.

There is a moment of silence when I cut the cake and then appreciative murmurs as it is devoured. Keith Miller lies down on the rug and puts his hands behind his head. Then Arlott begins to mesmerise the group with a poetry recital delivered in his rich Hampshire burr. I start to clear up, trying not to make a sound, as Arlott's magnificent voice rises and falls with the words he is reading from a yellowing, crumpled sheet of paper that looks as though it could have come from my parents' house. He wipes a crumb from his chin and begins:

> Aunt Anna mellows as I take
> Another slice of home-made cake
> She rustles in her stiff grey gown
> And takes her endless knitting down[17]

For who knows what reason, hearing the voice for all ages enunciate *endless* brings a tear to my eye and a wine glass slips out of my hand. It lands on the grass without breaking and as I look up I see there is not a soul left in the sunlit garden.

---

17 John Arlott, *Tea With My Aunts.*

Chapter Six

You Burn, I Earn.
A Pilgrimage to Antigua

Vats of rum punch were being carried around St John's Recreation Ground and the music was turned up even louder. The sides of the ground weren't at all in sync so it sounded as though 'Rally Round the West Indies' was being performed as a close canon. I could have fainted with joy and the game hadn't even started.

The music continued until the first ball was bowled, reappearing between overs and at the fall of an English wicket. That was quite a lot of music then.

THERE WAS an hour to go before play began and I could swear that the Double Decker stand at the Antigua Recreation Ground in St John's was moving. And I mean *moving*. At first I thought my raging hangover was playing tricks on me and I did a double take. But it was true. The stand was indeed swaying very gently one way and then the other.

And then Gravy started to perform. Oh my eyes.

A legend beyond Antigua, Gravy – real name Labon Kenneth Blackburn Buckonon Benjamin – had been entertaining the crowd at the Antigua Recreation Ground since 1988 and would continue to until 2000, when he retired wearing a white wedding dress. Of course. A cross-dresser with a penchant for towering and glorious, absurd platform boots, Gravy would gyrate in time to the music and swing upside down from the Double Decker's rafters with special performances every time the water carrier came on to the field. I had never seen anything like it.

Viv Richards once told him, 'Gravy, what you're doing, keep on doing it, because the world is happy when you do it.' I imagine it wouldn't be to the taste of most MCC members in their egg-and-bacon membership ties and stuffed shirts but Gravy certainly made me and plenty of others happy.

On the ground level of the Double Decker stand, a woman had brought her own percussion instruments and her downbeats somehow seemed to keep the stand anchored to the earth. Already the day was better than anything I could have dreamed of. Hangover or not.

Growing up in the East Midlands in the 1970s, my family holidays were the standard fare of the time: days out with my parents to Skeggy (Skegness in Lincolnshire) or days out with my grandparents to Weston-super-Mare. Those of you who have been to Weston (or even brought up there such as my friend Rachel) will know that being by the sea was merely conceptual since the tide was always out. Many postcards featuring donkeys in hats sent by me to my parents and, needless to say, kept by my mother read, 'We went to Weston but the sea wasn't in. Granny and Grampy bought me a new bucket.' I wrote that on every postcard. I must have had dozens of brightly coloured buckets that were never to be joyfully filled with sea water.

But no: my memory plays tricks again. One postcard I found from 9 August 1967 read:

'Dear Mummy and Daddy and Mark, Having a lovely time at Weston I went in the sea I have a new bucket and spade. See you Friday love from Michele xxx'

For a few years, plainly feeling rather more upwardly mobile, my parents took us on exotic trips to the Isle of Wight – oh, the sense of adventure going across the Solent on a ferry – where we alternated dodgy pub meals with scampi in a basket and chicken in a basket. The baskets were a forerunner of the pre-Covid fashion for slates as plates and it's a miracle we didn't get food poisoning.

Nottingham is a long way inland, which is perhaps why even now I love the novelty of being by the sea. As I hit my 20s, moved out of the family home and became fully entrenched in my love of all things West Indian, I began to learn more about the Caribbean. It didn't seem to have much in common with the seaside at Weston. It seemed impossibly glamorous and out of reach for the likes of me, but I made it one of my life's ambitions to one day get to Antigua and swim in those clear turquoise waters.

In April 1990, while working for *Cricket Life*, I somehow managed to organise a trip to cover the fifth Test between the West Indies and England in St John's, Antigua. For a reduced fare, I flew on the now-defunct BWIA, known as Bee-Wee, who were one of *Cricket Life*'s biggest advertisers, and for the first and only time in my life was upgraded to first class for a flight to Trinidad, where I would stay for a night before flying on to my destination. Strangely, the novelty of lying down in a plane while drinking champagne helped to alleviate any threat of homesickness and of missing my husband, but by the time we landed I was feeling a bit wobbly, and not just from the alcohol. It was the first time I had travelled alone overseas and my innate anxiety was rampant. My arrival at the rundown hotel, close to the airport, didn't make me feel any better and after a solitary dinner I went to my room, where I didn't sleep a wink all night.

Excitement no doubt played a part in my insomnia. As a young girl, travelling to Viv Richards' birthplace, let alone interviewing him and reporting on a Test match there, seemed as probable as me becoming a mathematical genius.

The moment I landed in Antigua the next day, I wanted to kneel on the tarmac and kiss the ground. I didn't do that, obviously (I am not the Pope), and merely made my way to a little beach club at Runaway Bay, where James and Ruth, two of my best friends from England, were also staying. As it was my inaugural overseas cricket tour, and theirs too, we did not stint ourselves. The beach club was brimming over with England cricket fans, one of whom we nicknamed Jeff the Pest and who soon gatecrashed our introductory afternoon pina coladas. He droned on for some hours about how much he knew about the game, which was actually not that much. He was infatuated with all things cricket and I would not have been at all surprised to see him walk out on to the ground each morning with the England team.

Every day, I would spot him wearing a natty beige polyester safari-type suit (he had clearly got his continents mixed up) as he made his way to the England team's hotel, where he doubtless hoped to befriend a player's unsuspecting mother and bore her into submission. But another very unfortunate side-effect of my first afternoon in Antigua, apart from being unable to escape Jeff the Pest, was dreadful sunburn. The prevailing wind's coolness as I sat in the sun listening to his monologues had made me believe that my Nottingham-grey skin wouldn't burn.

The next morning, the eve of the first day of the Test, I awoke to a hideous headache, intense dehydration, severe sunburn and volcanic mosquito bites. It was not a good look. Somehow, I managed to keep my breakfast down and made my way to the overly bright beach, where I lay under a palm tree, covered myself in suncream (too late) and tried not to worry about the coconut hanging perilously from the top of the tree, which I predicted would soon fall and knock me out. I closed my eyes and fiercely gripped both sides of the sun lounger, listening to the gentle lapping of the Caribbean waves.

'You burn, I earn! You red, I fed!' boomed a voice that grew louder as its owner closed in on my sunbed. I managed to squint at him through a swollen, sunburnt, mosquito-bitten eyelid. He was holding a few long, prickly leaves in one hand, a bottle of lotion in the other and presenting me with the most gorgeous smile, which was designed to give the impression that I would be the lucky recipient of his assistance that day.

'*This* is what *you* need!' he yelled. 'Aloe vera.'

To be honest, I looked as though I had been in a fire and at that moment I would even have been happy to see my Auntie Vera jetting in from her house in Weston-super-Mare to give me some comfort, never mind Aloe vera. Never heard of her.

'What is it?' I asked him, hoarsely, my voice a shadow of its former self from chain-smoking Marlboro Lights the previous night.

'It will make you better,' he shouted, beginning to squirt the lotion over my scarlet swollen legs. It was as cold as ice and I felt able to breathe for the first time in hours.

'That feels so nice! I'll have it. How much?'

He mentioned a price and, not in a mood to haggle, I bought three bottles.

'Thank you ma'am. You burn, I earn! You red, I fed!'

'Yes, yes,' I smiled weakly to his disappearing back as he went off in search of another mug. I ladled on more of his 'treatment', aware that the next day was the first day of the Test and three days later I was due to interview Viv at his house, a home given to him by the Antiguan government in recognition of his service to the island. So I had a few days for the aloe vera treatment to stop me winning an Elmo lookalike contest. All was not lost. Yet.

That night, though, I managed to power through several more rum punches as James, Ruth and I dodged Jeff the Pest. We could still hear him pontificating to other guests. 'Of course, Mrs [insert any England cricketer's name here] told me that her son had the most dreadful night's sleep, so it's not that surprising that he didn't bat well in Guyana' and 'I had a drink the other night with [name] and you'll never guess what he said.' On and on and on he droned. He is probably still there.

The next morning, we were up early for our bus to the Recreation Ground. I was still dehydrated and had a headache but that couldn't dampen my excitement for my debut at a ground I felt I already knew so well. But it soon became obvious that I was not remotely prepared.

The Recreation Ground in St John's, Antigua, is a long way from Nottingham, about 4,500 miles in fact, but there were many similarities to Trent Bridge: a boisterous passion for cricket for a start, and the friendliest of people for another. But the noise! I hadn't been prepared for the delirium, the chaos, the exuberance. Even the slightest memory of it now can make me quiver.

Most of the spectators milling round the entrance to the ground seemed to be human sound systems, carrying stereos the size of small cars. I wasn't sure that all of the people trying to get in actually had tickets but were simply being awarded entry depending on the size of their equipment. If the speakers were taller than you, I reckoned you could have a whole stand. Then there were the oil drums for cooking in and the steel drums for playing. It was a riot of laughter, good cheer and excitement, with the over-riding anticipation that England were going to be well and truly whupped.

I had paid for a ticket for the five days of the match and also had a pass for the press box, but one look at the dry and dusty inhabitants, none of whom looked like me and were not very welcoming either, made me quite sure that it wasn't the place for me. I was used to that, though. It never mattered which press box I entered, it never felt like home. I don't know whether I was too sensitive, shy or whether the cabal of cricket correspondents really didn't want me in there but, no matter, I knew I would have much more fun in the crowd.

I was covered from neck to toe in swathes of fabric to camouflage the hideous sunburn and mosquito bites, an outfit that made me extremely hot (I don't mean I looked hot). I had drunk four litres of fresh pineapple juice at breakfast on the beach in an effort to rehydrate but all it had done was make me feel very, very sick. Nor could I walk very well because the third-degree burns behind my knees meant I couldn't straighten my legs. It is fair to say my day hadn't got off to the best start and I looked a sight. But still, I was there at a ground where I had always wanted to be and it didn't take long for the cricket to kick in and make me feel a whole lot better. Trust me, cricket can always do that for you.

I watched the Double Decker stand swaying, took in Gravy's inaugural performance of the day and continued my slow walk round the ground, soaking up the atmosphere, before settling in a low-level stand opposite the Double Decker. I noticed a few locals giving me some strange looks, not unwelcoming exactly, but I felt a bit uneasy and realised I was going to have to work hard to win them over. I began with a display of the sort of sashay that I hoped would say, 'I've got rhythm' and a few of them smiled warmly, or maybe it was piteously.

Women began arriving carrying the remains of a small poultry farm, oil drums were lit and the cooking of that day's menu was under way: fried chicken and corn fritters. The cooking station was set up underneath the roof; still, the stand didn't burn. The players were out on the field warming up and the wonderful smell of the food wafted towards them but perhaps, as they had just had their breakfast, they were able to ignore it. The Windies jogged, sprinted and stretched while the England players threw a couple of balls around for some apathetic catching practice. A man standing next to me said, 'If you can't catch 'em now, you's never gonna catch 'em!' and I agreed with him.

Meanwhile, vats of rum punch were being carried around the ground and the music was turned up even louder. The sides of the ground weren't at all in sync, though, so it sounded as though 'Rally Round the West Indies' was being performed as a close canon. I could have fainted with joy and the game hadn't even started.

The music continued until the first ball was bowled, reappearing between overs and at the fall of an English wicket. That was quite a lot of music then.

Before travelling to Antigua, I had learned by heart the words to 'Rally Round the West Indies' but there was a big difference between practising it in my kitchen and hearing it sung *en masse* in St John's. It moved me then, and it moves me still. Released by the Trinidadian calypsonian David Rudder in 1988, it became the officially adopted anthem of the West Indies cricket

team in 1999 but it had become the fans' anthem almost
from the minute it was first played:

> For ten long years
> We ruled the cricket world
> Now the rule seems coming to an end
> But down here
> Just a chink in the armour
> Is enough, enough to lose a friend
> Some of the old generals have retired and gone
> And the runs don't come by as they did before
> But when the Toussaints go the Dessalines come
> We've lost the battle but yet we will win the war
>
> Chorus:
> Rally, rally round the West Indies
> Now and forever
> Rally, rally round the West Indies
> Never say never
> Pretty soon the runs are going to flow like water
> Bringing so much joy to every son and daughter
> Say we're going to rise again like a raging fire
> As the sun shines you know we gonna take it
>   higher
> Rally, rally round the West Indies
> Now and forever
> Rally, rally round the West Indies

There is everything in the full version of Rudder's song: history, lament, pathos, passion and humour. And while the West Indies team now sings it with real spirit, I have never heard it sung as intensely or as melodically as on that first day of the 1990 Test match in St John's. I sang it heartily, too, squinting into the sun with tears in my eyes, trying not to choke on the line 'Little keys can open up mighty doors'. I still thought of the West Indies as the little guys even though they had slain every team put in front of them. To my mind, the Windies team had faced bigger battles than the rest, overcoming paltry development funds for the game in the Caribbean as well as facing downright prejudice wherever they went.

As the midday sun bore down just before the lunch interval, I felt more strange looks directed my way and then I heard the comment, 'Go back to your own stand, man.' Confused, I looked around me and then around the ground, noticing England fans dotted in every stand; there were none that had been set aside for the visitors. I said nothing; after all, I had always, *always*, wanted to be there. It was odd though and the barbed comment was not at all what I had expected. I sat tight and clapped even louder when a Windies cricketer played well. I was, of course, on their side, which would undoubtedly have caused me even more grief if I had been sitting next to England supporters.

But, thanks to my watchful behaviour, I made new friends during the interval. The women gave me chicken and corn and the men gave me beers. No charge. They had finally realised I was on their side and appreciated my good sense. The fact that I was writing in a reporter's notebook maybe helped too. I doubt the men in the press box were being treated so generously and I silently congratulated myself on being in the crowd.

After lunch, the ground reached boiling point and the Windies bowlers seemed to have gained a yard or two in pace. Robin Smith and Allan Lamb looked liked Judy confronted by Punch, their heads moving as if on springs, trying to dodge the supersonic bowling of Curtly Ambrose and Courtney Walsh.

'Scalp him!' shouted the crowd with one voice as Ambrose sprinted in. Within hours, the T-shirts were on sale: *Ambruisin' England.*

By the close of play on the first day, England were 203/6; a woeful return on a good pitch. They were fortunate to have a rest day, unusual after just one day of a Test, and I was lucky too as I had arranged to meet Viv at his house for an interview. I arrived to find him mending his squeaky front gate, which just goes to show that heroes have to do chores on their days off too.

He was in a mellow mood, belying the headlines 'What's wrong with Viv?' and 'Richards on the rampage', which would be in the London papers the next morning after he had apparently made a V-sign to the England batsman Allan Lamb. The English press seemed intent on getting copy for a story based on a headline dreamed up in London: 'Is Viv Mad?' In fact, Viv didn't lead the team out on the second day of the match, perhaps unwisely choosing instead to visit the press box and vent his displeasure at the *Daily Express* cricket writer. As I wrote earlier, there had been a lot of press talk around this Test match about the West Indies' supposed arrogance and authority, which some saw as thinly veiled racism and yet another attack on short-pitched bowling. I think Viv had just had enough of it all. But he had also been criticised more locally after speculation that he had missed two Tests in the series because of illness, which a Trinidad politician had said was a manufactured malady and that his absence was, in fact, 'tactical'. The leader of the opposition in Trinidad had said Richards would not be welcome on the island until he retracted statements he had made in Guyana about his team being of African descent.

Richards seemed unequivocal to me at his sun-filled house that morning. 'I feel pretty strongly about what I believe in and, if certain things were taken out of context by some people who don't have the vision to see what I am saying, I can excuse them and I apologise for those things. But whatever I said, I said with conviction.'

Viv, the king of the island, was secure in the knowledge that his fellow Antiguans forgave him completely. He probably knew I did too and was gallant enough not to mention that I appeared to be wearing a pair of floral curtains in a pathetic effort to camouflage my burns and bites.

After my interview with him, Viv went to a team meeting at a local hotel and was confronted afterwards by the *Daily Express* man James Lawton. Viv apparently told him, 'You write anything bad about me and I'll come and whack you. A lot of crap is written about me and it's time someone was sorted. I'll start with you.'

I didn't want this incident to ruin my trip to Antigua and, being very confrontation-averse, I largely and characteristically ignored it, other than giving it a cursory mention in my *Cricket Life* reports, and concentrated instead on enjoying the remainder of the Test match as well as lying in the shade under palm trees.

England succumbed on the fourth day to a mighty West Indies by an innings and 32 runs, with the finest of England's press focusing on the home side's arrogance, if not insanity. And for arrogance, read 'short-pitched bowling'. Windies openers Gordon Greenidge, run out for 149, and Desmond Haynes, who made 167, were completely commanding in the first innings with their partnership of 298 and crushed what was left of the tourists' morale. It was as fine a display of opening an innings as you are likely to see. Sadly for me, Viv, coming in at No 5, was out for one, caught by Robin Smith off Devon Malcolm's bowling.

The England team in Antigua seemed a far cry from the side at the beginning of the tour that had thrashed the West Indies by nine wickets in the first Test at Sabina Park in Jamaica. There were reports during that game that Viv was 'sulking' and seemed not to know what to do in the face of defeat. Doubtless he had a mighty shock but the series still finished in a 2-1 win for the West Indies.

It was easy then, with cricket restored to its natural order with a Windies win, to stay in a paradisical bubble under a palm tree and to ignore any news from home, although I had tried several times to phone my husband, who had left two messages at the hotel reception. I had thought a bit strange as he is not one of the greatest communicators, even (especially?) to his wife.

And so I didn't know until I landed back at Heathrow, where Michael was collecting me, that his father had died very suddenly and very unexpectedly at the age of just 59 while I had been away. The funeral had been held the day before my return. I had done nothing to support Michael and felt guilty as hell that I hadn't been there as well as shocked and saddened by life bowling such a nasty ball. Needless to say, I wouldn't talk about my trip at all to Michael for many weeks even though I was secretly already planning my next trip to Antigua and resolved that he would be coming with me.

As we have seen, though, life has an annoying habit of getting in the way of cricket and there were many more curveballs to try to fend off. A year after that inaugural visit, I suffered from the aforementioned doomed pregnancy and a little over a year after that I gave birth to our beautiful daughter, Lucy, in August 1992. I worked at the *Standard* until seven weeks before her birth even though I was the size of a Zeppelin airship and had put on four and a half stone. And she wasn't even a big baby.

My father, with his customary ability to find just the right words for any occasion, said my weight gain was 'support services' and, as usual, he was right as I lost four stone within weeks of the birth. But. The birth had not been easy, largely due to the fact, as explained by an obstetrician who had been absent on the day bedside manners were taught, that I had a pelvis shaped 'like a wellington boot'. Who knew that was even a thing?

My mother came to stay for three weeks, hand-feeding sandwiches to me while I stayed in my dressing gown feeding continuously and generally being a great mum. Her, that is, not me. I did not feel a great mum at all and was convinced that Lucy knew it.

Four weeks after the birth, exhausted by 24-hour non-stop feeding of a non-sleeping baby, I suffered a post-partum haemorrhage. I rang Michael at work to explain what was happening and, with a turn of phrase to rival my father and the obstetrician, he said, 'You pick your moments.' Bleeding heavily, I packed Lucy into her carrier and waited for Michael to drive me to St George's Hospital in Tooting, where the necessary procedure was carried out and Michael managed to deal with baby care for as short a time as possible. I believe he changed a nappy.

After the birth, the haemorrhage and my hormonal history, it was perhaps not at all surprising – although it was to me – that I succumbed to post-natal depression. It was a relief to confess my feelings to an angelic and aptly named health visitor, Liz Wombwell, who scooped me up into an imaginary comfort blanket and made me realise that I was not a bad mother, was not going mad and simply needed support, some of which involved her listening to me. I gained the most support from Rachel, one of my oldest friends and a midwife by training, who scooped me up and looked after me as though I was, in fact, the baby. All well and good, in theory, but I was going to return to work in 12 weeks so I didn't have very long to 'pull myself together' which, at that time, was the standard treatment for post-natal depression. Those were the days of very short maternity leave and there was no choice but to get back to the office since we needed my salary to keep us going. By now living in a small and noisy flat with a leaking roof in Battersea, we were, along with millions of others, well into negative equity territory.

Several stone lighter and a good distance from my former self in terms of my state of mind, I resumed work on the *Standard* sports desk in November. I asked for, and expected, no quarter from my workmates and they were faultless to a man. However, I was a long way from feeling well; I was still sanitary-padded up as well as getting through boxes of breastpads a day and squeezing my arms across my chest to try to stop the lactation spurts from soaking my shirts, embarrassing myself as well as the chaps in the office. I felt very much like a changed woman physically but something else had shifted in me too and I certainly hadn't expected it.

I had been looking forward so much to returning to work and to the job I loved. It represented pre-maternal joy, a blithe spirit, great camaraderie and a purposeful life. But those days vanished with the afterbirth. I felt very confused. How come I loved my job before but fell out of love with it so quickly? It just didn't seem as important any more and I couldn't explain why. The headline that needed to be written in 90 seconds, the caption to be done *now*, the copy to be cut from 550 words to 220 in less than a minute no longer fired me up. And I was anxious the whole time about Lucy. Even though we had arranged wonderful childcare in the form of our own Mary Poppins called Jackie, who was *Standard Sport*'s secretary's girlfriend at the time, Lucy's needs had become more significant than sweating the fudge (the term for a few words for the late news box) on the back page. Don't get me wrong: I still cared, very much, about doing a good job and I absolutely cared about not letting my colleagues down. But I couldn't, as much as I tried, ignore the fact that it no longer seemed as important to me as feeding, protecting and being with my baby. And who knew? I had certainly not expected to feel that way.

I had felt an outsider many times in my life – as a gawky teenager, as a woman daring to have a go in a male-dominated profession – and was beginning to feel the same as a mother. I couldn't square having a baby with doing my job. I felt like the uncapped David Steele in 1975 making his debut for England against Australia at the age of 33. Seemingly so unprepared, and coming in to bat at No 3, Steele got lost on his way out to the middle and ended up in the basement of Lord's pavilion. Steele conquered his fears and nerves, however, had a very successful summer and was even voted Sports Personality of the Year in 1975. I thought of the example he had set but I couldn't cut it.

For a few months, I sobbed every morning on my early commutes to the office. That was after I had got up at 5am, breastfed Lucy, changed her then changed her again, had breakfast and changed into my work clothes and sometimes changed again after Lucy had been sick over me. Looking back, I can see I was completely exhausted: by the difficult birth and what came after as well as by my characteristic determination to try to carry on as 'normal' without asking for help. Michael was also in the process of setting up his own business so, even if he hadn't been an unreconstructed Fred Flintstone-type of man, he really wasn't much use.

This process continued for a few months until, finally, I admitted defeat. And that is indeed what it felt like. A timeless Test match, in searing heat and facing unrelenting, sledging fast bowlers from both ends of the pitch while being continuously booed by spectators, had literally brought me to my knees.

I sat down with Michael and a calculator and we worked out that we could, with some struggle and lots of mashed swede (again), just about afford for me to give up full-time work doing the job I loved. The *Standard*, and my boss, were understanding and agreed to me doing a couple of days' shifts a week as and when I could but I would give up my contract and all the benefits of a secure job that entailed.

Many times I have been asked, and asked myself, whether I regret my decision. When the children were young, I would say a wholehearted 'no', believing the early years of care I gave them was vital, if knackering. In later years, though, I have wished I had then had the courage to speak up and ask for what I wanted, which was a bit more time and rest after the birth and a bit more help in the first year. Who knows whether I could have carried on full-time if that had been in place? I am not exactly envious of the benefits of maternity leave that women have now – envy is a pretty pointless and energy-sapping emotion, after all – but I hope they can achieve a better work-life balance and one in which you don't feel ripped apart from all sides. Even now, though, I have yet to meet a woman who can have or who has made a success of having it all. Some constituent has to suffer – and it is often the mother.

If I had been hoping to enjoy a few lie-ins and rest after stopping full-time work, I was disappointed. Lucy continued to be a non-sleeper. In fact, she didn't sleep a full night until she was about six years old.

But while life definitely got in the way of cricket quite a bit during the first year(s) of Lucy's life, it still had the potential to bowl some interesting overs. A colleague, Alastair McLellan, I had worked with during the less-than-halcyon days of *Leisure Scene* magazine – although he had worked on another of the publishers' fascinating emissions (and that is definitely the right word for it), *Glass and Glazing* – was equally obsessed by cricket and we particularly shared a passion for West Indies fast bowling. Over a glass or two of something inspiring, or it might have been Strega, he suggested that we write together about the West Indies quicks and so our book *Real Quick: A Celebration of the West Indies Pace Quartets* was born. One of the many advantages of working with Alastair was that he was an excellent cricket statistician with a phenomenal memory, so I didn't have to worry my silly little head with all those damn numbers.

A big advantage of the *Real Quick* project was that I could plan another trip to Antigua where, fortuitously, England were playing the final Test of their 1993/94 tour. I just had the small matter of bracing myself to leave Lucy with my parents who, if truth were told, jumped at the chance to look after their first grandchild. I also knew that my mother would take copious notes in my absence, so I would have a minute-by-minute account of Lucy's every movement (bowel or otherwise).

Michael was another matter. He wasn't that keen on travelling to the Caribbean to watch cricket (I *know!*) and I initially pretended that we were going on a beach holiday and there would be no cricket. 'No, I'm sure there won't be,' is probably what I said, with my fingers crossed behind my back. The fact that he believed me despite the television at home blaring out the Test cricket coverage from the Caribbean says a lot for my powers of delivery. You think he might have noticed. Once he had twigged, I agreed that his exposure to the game could be limited to the first day of the Test. After some persuasion, he seemed happy enough with that.

I completely 'forgot' to tell him, though, that I had arranged to meet a group of friends in Antigua who would be staying at the same hotel as us. Now Michael, who has many and varied qualities, is not really, shall we say, much of a people person. He is happy with his own company and only very occasionally (usually when the moon is in its waxing gibbous phase) barely tolerant of others. You can see why I didn't tell him. He was completely shocked to see our best friends, James and Ruth, on the beach when we arrived and when we were joined by four more friends his startled face was priceless. I chose to ignore it.

Michael's first (and only) day at the Test match was remarkable for many reasons, and not just because he was there. England were 3-1 down in the five-Test contest so had no chance of winning it. But they were fresh from winning the fourth Test in Barbados, where they became the first side to win there for 59 years. So the England camp was buoyant (some might even say arrogant but I couldn't possibly comment) in a way that some England teams can be even if they are on a losing wicket. They lost the toss on the first morning and West Indies captain Courtney Walsh chose to bat. But England soon had the home side on 12/2, leaving Brian Lara, the young Trinidadian who had made his Test debut in 1990, and the Jamaican Jimmy Adams in the middle.

There was always an air of crackling anticipation whenever Lara, nicknamed the Prince, was batting but this match had a different feel somehow. He was in great form – he had scored 167 in the second Test in Georgetown – but knew he needed to return consistently big scores and by the close of the first day in Antigua he was on 164 not out. Michael had witnessed the beginning of history being made but how was he to know? He was more than happy to spend the next day on the beach but I was enraptured by the Test match and the second day didn't disappoint. As usual in Antigua for the Sunday of a Test, most of the home fans missed the start of play because of church. But as the ground began to fill up, the crowd was already starting to talk about Lara beating the world record Test score of 365, which had been set by West Indies' Gary Sobers against Pakistan in Jamaica in 1958. Sunday saw Lara continuing to bat like a god. He was supremely focused and didn't take any chances while his bat appeared to be the size of a barn door, such was his mastery. And there was a strange atmosphere around the ground; an air of inevitability that he was going to break the record. How did we all know? How did he?

In the last session that day, Lara reached 300 and by the close was 320 not out. Such was the excitement that I, along with most of the rest of the crowd, would have been more than happy to sleep in the Recreation Ground.

I had to get back to the beach, though, where Michael, by now a big fan of the local Wadadli beer as well as the rum punches, was having a marvellous time and seemed, for a while at least, to have become a people person. I had begun to wonder whether someone was spiking his drinks. I was up early the next day, Monday 18 April, my birthday, to race to the ground and get into pole position for what we all unequivocally knew would be history in the making. Everyone was so sure of it; there was no way Lara was not going to make it. Yet it wasn't that England weren't trying to get him out. They were, even though they seemed knackered. It was more that Lara seemed to possess a God-given right to fulfil the destiny that had been written on high.

And by 11am, he had done it. Lara was on 365, equalling Sobers's score, when England's Chris Lewis bowled a long hop that Lara despatched past midwicket to the boundary.

And then it was bedlam. As you now know, the Recreation Ground is not restrained at the best of times with thousands of people jumping and singing, but as the ball left Lara's bat it was pandemonium. Spectators sprinted on to the field and then out walked Sir Garfield Sobers, flanked by security guards (who were not actually concentrating on the great man or the crowds but more on celebrating) and TV camera crews. Sobers approached Lara and congratulated him and you might have thought play would resume pretty sharpish after that. Not a bit of it. Press reports have the break in play as anything from six minutes to 20 minutes but, as I was there, I can tell you it seemed more like an hour. The ground itself seemed to levitate, such was the euphoria and energy of the crowd, and I was having an out-of-body experience, looking down on the most extraordinary scenes. I had never experienced anything like it and wouldn't again.

Needless to say, Lara was exhausted, both mentally and physically, from his exploits and focus on milestones as well as the weight of expectation he had been carrying. He was soon out for 375, caught behind by Jack Russell off Andy Caddick's bowling. No one remembered that.

Someone next to me in the crowd said that West Indies captain Courtney Walsh should have declared when Lara hit the record boundary so that he could have been not out, but who really cared?

The day seemed to sum up for me the best of Antigua and why I had fallen in love with this tiny dot on a map of the world. The joyfulness and exuberance in celebrating the extraordinary achievement of a little master from another island playing for their collective pride and, further, the *commitment* to their celebration was visceral. As a fairly typical buttoned-up Pom, female at that, being given permission to make merry at a cricket match felt pretty good. There would be other occasions in my life when I also felt I had permission to feel blissed out (notably at several Glastonbury festivals even though I seemed to be the only person in a 200,000 throng who didn't rely on chemicals to feel that) but my birthday at the Antigua Recreation Ground in 1994 is the stand-out.

There was excitement of a different sort in the beach club bedroom that night (and whatever you might be imagining, it wasn't that) when I was woken up in the small hours by Michael screaming loudly. It sounded as though he was being attacked and he was sitting up in bed shrieking from the back of his throat.

'What on earth's wrong?' I blearily asked.

He carried on wailing, one of his arms flailing about. By that stage, I was convinced he was having a heart attack. But no. His right arm had fallen on his face in his sleep and he thought he was being assaulted. Which, in fact, he was. By himself.

The next morning, guests at breakfast were animatedly chatting about the disturbance during the night and who had been attacked. The security guards had not been able to find an assailant, so there was much concern that a murderer was on the loose. Michael and I didn't say a word.

Instead, I concentrated on the work I still had to do for *Real Quick*; interviews with Viv, Dennis Waight, the West Indies physio and Michael Holding among others. I interviewed Viv on the beach and recently found in my mother's collection a note from the beach club saying, 'Apologies, Mr Richards is running a little late.' He could have been as late as he liked because the interview was gold and, afterwards, he agreed to write the foreword to the book. His hero status in my eyes remained undiminished.

Dennis Waight was equally delightful. Waight, an Australian, had joined the Windies after the Kerry Packer World Series Cricket in 1977/78 and would stay with the side until 2000. He had the job, first of all, of convincing the players of the benefits of training and then he turned them into a supremely successful machine. He helped to prevent injuries, particularly to the fast bowlers who had, traditionally, broken down due to the strain under which their bodies operated. Waight kept the quicks focused both physically and psychologically. I enjoyed a couple of hours quizzing him on his techniques and mental training; remember, this was years before sports psychology became mainstream. But he not only inspired the West Indies to become greater than the sum of their parts; he inspired every other Test-playing country to change the way they prepared too.

There was no doubt that he got the best out of Michael Holding, whose 'Whispering Death' nickname is at odds with the fact that he is possibly one of the nicest human beings who has ever lived. Further evidence of this was provided in the summer of 2020 when Holding, during the first Test between England and the West Indies at Southampton, delivered an eloquent and passionate four-minute unscripted speech about racism and the Black Lives Matter movement. 'Racism is taught,' said Holding. 'No one is born a racist. The environment in which you grow, the society in which you live, encourages and teaches racism. We need to go back and teach both sides of history and until we do that and educate the entire human race, this thing will not stop.'

His speech went viral and the *Daily Telegraph* called it the 'finest spell' seen on an English cricket ground.

Some 26 years before his impassioned address, Holding was impassioned in the hours of interviews he granted me. Quite rightly, he didn't hold back in answering some of the criticism that had been lobbed at the Windies quicks. Indeed, his view of the intimidation debate was typical of members of the pace quartets.

'It would be naive and misleading of me to claim that I never bowl bouncers without trying to intimidate the batsman,' said Holding. 'On the contrary, I want him to be aware that if he gets on to the front foot against me he might find himself in trouble – in other words, he might get hurt. But that is quite a different thing from actually *wanting* or *intending* to hurt him. I have no desire to hurt anyone. But I do want to get batsmen out as quickly as possible, and if that means pitching a few balls in my half of the wicket in order to keep him on the back foot, I – like any other fast bowler – will do what the law and the umpires allow.'

Critics of the West Indies pace quartet were motivated by a number of reasons: a belief that the game was being devalued, a concern for the safety of batsmen, as well as jealousy and, yes, racism among them. The vast majority of those critics came from beyond the boundary, in various press boxes and broadcasting units, rather than from opposing batsmen. The criticism didn't, by and large, come from the crowds either. Every Test match featuring the West Indies was a sell-out and spectators revelled in seeing athletes at the very peak of their powers.

Alastair McLellan and I had great fun answering the West Indies critics in *Real Quick*, even beginning the book with a Q and A:

Q: Why did two white English cricket writers decide to write a book about West Indian fast bowlers?

A: To set the record straight.

Q: What's the problem?

A: Well, read this: 'Until we can breed 7ft monsters willing to break bones and shatter faces, we cannot compete against these threatening West Indians. Even the umpires seem to be scared that the devilish-looking Richards might put a voodoo sign on them!'

(Letter to *Wisden Cricket Monthly,* June 1990)

Reading that again now, written in the language of street gang culture but actually about a superb professional sports team, still makes me feel sick in the pit of my stomach and I find it unbelievable that David Frith, editor of that magazine, published it. I can take some heart from the fact that such a letter, surely, wouldn't be printed now. Would it?

As Lara's Test in Antigua chugged on to its inevitable draw, I had amassed vast bundles of notes for *Real Quick*, a few more mosquito bites and possibly minor liver damage. But I couldn't ignore the deepening feeling that all of that seemed inconsequential because I was missing my daughter – not merely missing so much but *aching* in that way you do when you are apart from your children – and just wanted to cuddle her for hours.

Needless to say, Lucy had been cared for indulgently by my parents and seemed completely untroubled on our return.

But after finishing *Real Quick* that summer, I vowed not to leave Lucy again, not even for my spiritual home in Antigua. But life would throw even more at me to get in cricket's way.

For Non-Cricket Speakers

Fielding

IN THE panoply of cricket terminology, it is probably fielding positions that leave the non-cricket speaker stumped.

The wicketkeeper is pretty straightforward to spot as he is the one standing behind the stumps. Often an eccentric character (compare goalkeepers in football), it used to be said that you could tell an old wicketkeeper by his hands, although I am not sure that holds true today in this modern era of superlative glove technology.

When you picture a fast bowler at his quickest, imagine the ball travelling past the batsman into a wicketkeeper's gloves. You would have to be mad, then, to stand there. You would also need extreme levels of concentration and physical fitness. One of the greatest keepers of all time, the extravagantly whiskered Godfrey Evans, who played 91 Tests for England between 1946 and 1959, was according to my father a supreme athlete and probably set the bar for the future.

If the wicketkeeper is easy to spot, then the uninitiated can struggle with many of the other field placings.

'What does it all mean?' a friend once asked me. I drew him a very rudimentary diagram from which he was none the wiser, apart from 'silly point' which, as he rightly observed, is 'a bloody silly place to stand' as it is so close to the bat. But I lost him when explaining the difference between silly mid-off and silly mid-on.

My friend also failed to grasp the difference between the leg ('on') side and the off side. Leg means the side of the pitch on which the batsman stands to receive the delivery of the ball and is separated from the off side by an imaginary line going between the two wickets. Simples.

The slip fielders – an attacking field will feature a slip cordon comprising three or even four fielders standing close together – will stand closer or further from the batsman, depending on the pace of the bowling. Fast reflexes and concentration are key in the slips and, like me, you may become irritated when you see a slip fielder resting his hands on his knees as the bowler runs in and, like my father was prone to do, scream, 'Pay attention, for God's sake! Make your hands ready!'

As I said to my befuddled friend after trying unsuccessfully to explain the fielding positions, it is not worth getting bogged down. The more you watch, the more you absorb by osmosis. For now, revel in the athleticism where there is some and groan knowingly when there isn't.

Chapter Seven

Trent Bridge, a Lotus-Land for Batsmen ... and My Father

My father became mute and almost completely paralysed by dementia. He would aim the foulest swear words at my mother, at nurses and lose interest in everything, even his beloved Nottingham Forest. I would tell him the latest cricket news and he would look past me with not a flicker of recognition. Little by little, this spirited and wonderful man disappeared as though a kidnapper was taking him away, cell by cell. We would have sold everything we owned to pay the ransom demand.

'Sausage roll?'

This early (10.45am) and plaintive request came from my father as we huddled together under two umbrellas – his, golf, mine less sturdy – on a typical English summer Sunday at Lord's. Our seats, where we had also spent the previous two days, were high up in the newly-opened Edrich stand, all the better to see the gamut of that morning's billowing downpour throwing itself around St John's Wood.

I delved into our enormous blue-and-white striped cool bag, furtling around for the sausage rolls. My left hand was holding the umbrella trying to keep the rain off the food while the fingers of my right hand closed round a crinkly Cellophane wrapper. Dad, meanwhile, angled his umbrella to better protect me and his elevenses but even so, a rivulet of north London's finest precipitation found its way round and down a spoke and splashed into the bag.

Lunch was going to be soggier even earlier than usual.

'Never mind, sweetheart,' said Dad.

I triumphantly pulled out the packet of sausage rolls, managed to open it with one hand and squeezed one to the top of the Cellophane for Dad to grasp.

He was quiet for a while, enjoying the puffiest of pastry while listening to *Test Match Special* on his headphones. At 11am, I felt a nudge on my right elbow.

'Cup of tea?'

I wedged my umbrella between my left shoulder and chin and pulled out the Thermos.

Handing the cup to Dad, he beamed, sipped heartily and made that 'Aaah' sound that is a speciality of tea drinkers.

He was quiet again then, apart from the slurps of his tea while enjoying CMJ and Johnners on *TMS*.

Not for long, though. At 11.15, there came another nudge.

'KitKat?'

And so we went on. By 12.30, there was still no sign of play so we opened the wine – from memory, I would guess a warm and presumptuous Australian white (that would be the wine, not a nearby spectator) – and started to tuck in to our feast. Cheese and tomato sandwiches were the first to go, followed by squashed salmon and cucumber and then we could get on to the sweet treats: perhaps a slice of Battenberg followed by a smidgeon of chocolate cake. In those days – BC, Before Children – I would have made the chocolate cake myself. I liked to spoil my father whenever I got the chance.

We had missed the first day when Viv was 60 not out by the close and the West Indies 317/3. But on the second day, we saw Viv out lbw to Phil DeFreitas for 63 and the West Indies all out for 419 with Carl Hooper having scored a magnificent 111. On the third day, England made 354 with Robin Smith scoring 148 and the mighty Curtly Ambrose taking four wickets for 87 runs, so we had hardly been short-changed.

Sunday was looking to be a wash-out, but still Dad and I sat there for most of the day under our umbrellas. The unspoken rule was that we wouldn't leave until an official announcement had been made that play was called off for the day and, in any case, there was another directive that we couldn't go until the cool bag was empty.

My father and I shared dozens of such days, rain or shine. They always followed the same pattern: continual grazing, sporadic listening to *TMS* and the occasional plunge into deep and meaningful conversation.

'Are you okay, sweetheart?' Dad asked in the early afternoon on that rainy Lord's Sunday.

'Yes, yes, I'm fine. Honestly. Don't worry.'

This apparently anodyne exchange was actually chock full of unspoken concern from my father and was really about whether I had got over my traumatic and unsuccessful pregnancy four months earlier. But we didn't need to go into great detail any more than we needed to say 'I love you' every minute, or even every decade for that matter.

My father was fairly typical of his generation for getting on with things, not dwelling on heartache and not discussing it at all. His attitude wasn't wrong or right; it just was. Dad would sometimes complain that some young people then didn't have any 'stickability' and I allow myself a smile now when I imagine what he would say to today's youngsters who, 'according to a recent survey', apparently find full stops intimidating and aggressive.

My assurances that I was fine were enough, then, for Dad, who reacted in his customary fashion with a lop-sided smile. But his relief wasn't from the fact that we didn't have to talk about it – I am sure he was quite prepared for an in-depth discussion if that had been what I wanted – but from the reassurance I had given him.

We settled down again, companionably, and put our respective headphones in, although I'm not sure how much Dad would have heard after lunch as he had a little snooze, still holding on to his umbrella while the downpour continued around us.

I might have dropped off myself too but for, some time later, another nudge on my elbow.

'Have we got any cake left?'

I delved into the last full Tupperware that contained our tea provisions. Had I told Dad about that earlier, he would have polished off those too. By this stage, you might be thinking Dad was a bit chubby. But far from it: he weighed virtually the same – ten stone – his whole life. So he was perfectly entitled to another slice of chocolate cake. Oh and 'are there some grapes in there?' he asked. 'I'll have a few of those as well, thank you.'

Inevitably, we finished our tea well before the tea interval and it was equally unsurprising that, with puddles all over the Lord's outfield, play was called off soon after. And thus we were free to leave, the weight of the cool bag having transferred to our bellies and with the knowledge that we had done everything in our earthly power to subjugate the rain gods. Although we had not seen a ball bowled or struck, cricket had still awarded us a priceless day together, a luxury peculiar to the loveliest of ball games.

And Dad had been by my side, as he always was.

* * *

'Hello!' said the smiley giant as he emerged into bright sunshine from a thicket of privet in West Park in Long Eaton.

'And *whose* little girl are you, then?'

Seemingly all alone, I looked up with my big brown eyes at the enormous man, completely unaware of stranger danger, and said, very confidently for one so young (I was four), 'Daddy's!'

The jolly man took a few steps forward but at that moment my father appeared beside me – he wasn't far away, after all – and wrapped my hand in his.

'Come along, sweetheart!' he said with a smile.

You see? He was always there.

Until he wasn't.

* * *

After several years of being systematically dismantled in a savage and one-sided fight against dementia, my Great Protector died on a Tuesday afternoon two days before Hallowe'en, a day I had always disliked anyway and hate even more now.

Later that week, someone had the temerity to ask me whether my father's death had been expected.

'This may sound utterly ridiculous to you,' I replied, 'but I *never* expected him to die, so it wasn't. No.'

How, after all, could I have lived a day of my life with that thought? How could I have imagined a single moment without the silver-backed gorilla, the man I had loved the most and the longest in my life? Even when he was being beaten up by the dementia bully, I didn't (couldn't) think about him not being here. Life without him? Pah! I wasn't going to contemplate that. Well, more fool me. I should have been prepared. And that undoubtedly explains my primal howl when Mum phoned to tell me that he had died.

Only 24 hours before she called me, I had made my weekly drive to Somerset laden with sweet treats for Mum as well as essential groceries. As soon as I arrived, I had played Dad one of our favourite Frank Sinatra songs, 'The Lady Is a Tramp', and he had moved just the middle finger of his left hand in time to the music as I sang about the lady being broke but it was 'oke'.

He sort of smiled at me as I sang while I gazed into his unseeing, watery eyes, and he whispered 'it's oke' – the first words he had uttered in months – in time with the music because, just for that moment and only for that cursory moment, everything was oke.

Dad used to have the darkest brown eyes in the world but now they were the colour of sludgy sand. Whenever people said I was the image of my father, what they really meant was that I had his eyes. Oh, and perhaps his not inconsequential nose.

'Goodness me, you don't have any pupils, do you?' a former boss, staring at me (I was terrified) in a lift, had remarked. That's how dark my eyes are and my father's were. Twins in the eyes department, for sure. And in our dodgy backs.

It is a few years since his death now, yet there is never a day when I don't feel heartache for his absence as well as despair that there is nothing, simply nothing, I can do about it.

You might be thinking that I adored my father and you would be right. I hope you adore yours too and, if he is still around, that you let him know. Some people think that adoration carries too high a tariff, but it's a price I would pay again.

Looking at my father's life, it might seem pretty unremarkable to an outsider. A good one, definitely, and lived well, certainly, but how do you *actually* measure a life? Runs scored? Wickets taken? Stumpings made? Achievements or accolades? Money or masterpieces? Trophies won or lost?

In truth, my father didn't really return big scores by any of those markers, although there are a few RAF football and hockey medals in a box which, as far as Dad was concerned, were at least each equivalent to an FA Cup winner's medal.

But to those who knew and loved him, he paid in far more than he ever took out. When we were planning his funeral, I found a poem called 'Success' written in 1904 by an American writer, Bessie Anderson Stanley, which seemed perfectly to sum up my father and other men like him. (Incidentally, this poem is often incorrectly ascribed to Ralph Waldo Emerson or to Robert Louis Stevenson, which hardly seems fair so I wanted to reproduce Bessie's poem here in full.) My husband read it movingly and beautifully at the service. Or at least so people said; I was too heartbroken to notice.

He has achieved success
who has lived well
laughed often, and loved much
who has enjoyed the trust of
pure women

the respect of intelligent men and
the love of little children

who has filled his niche and accomplished his task

who has left the world better than he found it
whether by an improved poppy
a perfect poem or a rescued soul

who has never lacked appreciation of Earth's beauty
or failed to express it

who has always looked for the best in others and
given them the best he had

whose life was an inspiration
whose memory a benediction.

Perhaps the fact that my father 'left the world better than he found it' might be a good measure of success and contribution; as well as the 'benediction', which was key for me as I did feel, and still do, mightily blessed to have had such a warm and affectionate relationship with my father who, born in 1928, might not have been naturally predisposed to sentiment. It was his tender-heartedness that emerged as a common theme in the letters I received after he died: a wonderful, decent, gentle man; a rare breed of gentleman; a sincere and caring nature; an immensely kind man; a decent and lovely man; a hugely proud father. I delivered these words during my eulogy at his rain-sodden funeral; he would have called it a 'filthy, rotten, lousy, stinking day', words he always used in that order in foul weather. I somehow managed to get through the tribute, with the gentle vicar standing behind me if I fell in my task, until the very end when I crumbled while reading a line from Frank Sinatra's 'From Here to Eternity'.

I managed to look at Dad's coffin as I stumbled from the pulpit steps. He was beside me still, wasn't he?

* * *

Family lore has it that my grandmother, a tiny (4ft 8in tall) and meticulous woman, told the nurses to take my father away when he was born as he weighed in at an eye-watering ten pounds (4.53kg). She must have been in a state of shock because, of course, she did have him back.

He was a clever boy and entered the local secondary Upper School as a beneficiary of a 'special place' even though that place remained in doubt until the week before term started as my grandparents struggled to afford the uniform. He mostly worked hard and excelled in sport. But his departure from the school early at the age of 15 is shrouded in mystery. He maintained that he wasn't actually expelled but was 'asked to leave', although he never confessed to his family exactly what transgression he had committed.

Whatever the wrongdoing, it didn't preclude him from joining the Royal Air Force on 16 July 1946, an enlistment that was 'much to his surprise', he writes in his beautiful Chinagraph-inscribed photo album, which is among my most prized possessions. 'I took the oath and became 35000788 AC2 ACH/GD u/t FME. At that time, I was somewhat green and not a little naive.'

His unworldliness seemed to change once he joined the RAF. While not depicting a Jack the Lad, the black and white images are of a smiling and assured young man clearly enjoying his life and in the prime of it. I detect a hidden subtext from some of the captions in the album. For instance, writing about his posting to Berlin from June 1948 to March 1949 for the Airlift, he says, 'Work hard, play hard was true in this case.'

And that seemed to be his formula for perhaps the happiest time of his service. In June 1951, he boarded the troopship MV *Empire Pride* at Liverpool bound for Singapore, but not before, as he recounts, asking the skipper of the tug for the latest score in the Test match at Trent Bridge. Luckily, he embarked mid-Test as he would have been disappointed by the eventual result: South Africa beat England by 71 runs, despite 137 from local star Reg Simpson and 112 from national hero Denis Compton.

A few weeks later, via a stop in Port Said, Dad's new home in Singapore became H Block West Camp, RAF Seletar, a busy air force base that was heavily involved in the Malayan Emergency. It seems that it was here that Dad found firm friends, all of whom have been preserved for posterity in his album and some of whom became life-long. He also embarked on his love affair with aircraft as testified by the countless pictures of Beaufighters, Spitfires and Mosquitoes.

Those planes held pride of place even over a much more famous visitor to the camp, who merely got squashed in at the bottom of a page in the album with the caption 'Mrs Roosevelt, etc', where Dad has included small black and white photos of America's First Lady. He adds, 'Apart from Mrs Roosevelt, other interesting callers were Douglas Bader [the famous Second World War RAF fighter pilot] and mosquitoes of a particularly belligerent nature.' I inherited my father's vulnerability to mozzy bites too.

And much more important still than photos of some American woman are the images of football teams in which he played, usually with a trophy or shield, including the Flying Wing, which won the inter-unit competition at Seletar, in October 1953.

There was competition of a different sort a few months later with five pictures of aircraft as Dad writes, 'The only time we ever managed to get all five Beaufighters airborne together at one time. The whole camp had a half-day holiday.' And there are plenty of black and white photos of 'various festivities' featuring bright young men, accompanied by pints and fags, in assorted stages of disarray or, on other occasions as Dad remarks, 'whistled'.

He returned to 'Blighty' in January 1954, by now an urbane young man in comparison to the whippersnapper who left on the boat from Liverpool, and there we see in his album, for the first time and with no explanation, a striking-looking woman captioned 'Butch', although she looked far from that. And while Butch is featured at a Christmas dance in 1954, at which the apparently renowned Tony Kinsey Quartet performed, no doubt delighting my jazz-obsessed father, she is replaced a couple of years later by an even more dazzling woman named Joyce. Joyce looked like a film star and in one photograph sports an exceptionally glamorous 1950s swimsuit. She was obviously not enough for Dad, though, as she then finds herself supplanted over the page by an unnamed girlfriend cutting her 21st birthday cake, with Dad by her side, at a table laden with jam tarts, jars of pickled onions and cups of tea, which just goes to show that people knew how to party then.

An action-packed ten years after signing up, Dad left the RAF with a service record proclaiming his conduct 'exemplary', 'very good' leadership and co-operation and a 'very smart bearing'. Particularly noteworthy were his special capabilities with Goblin Engines, which were skills that, as far as I know, he was never called on to use again. Still, at least he had them, which is more than can be said for a lot of us. I mean, when my day of reckoning comes, my tally will not include special skills with Goblin Engines. More likely my record will state: 'Showed exemplary use of a corkscrew in times of dire need, special skills with lighters in gale force winds and formidable prowess at sitting in the same place for hours at a time during cricket matches even when they were being played out for a draw.'

The final comment on his service record states that Dad was 'a keen and enthusiastic worker who has been an asset to the RAF'. Needless to say, he continued to be a keen and enthusiastic worker in everything he did and going through his belongings I did wonder whether I might have been a disappointment to him for not being the same.

His priceless album tails off after his return to Civvy Street. There are no photographs of the beginning of his relationship with Mum, for example. My guess is that he was hit by a whirlwind. She would have kept him so much on his toes that he would have had no time for mounting precision-straight photos with silver corners and neat captions in Chinagraph pencil.

My parents-to-be had met in 1959 across a crowded street in Bristol from the vantage point of respective first-floor office windows, where they had caught sight of each other. Mum, a striking young woman, had had a string of boyfriends, some of whom I only found out about after her death among letters that she had kept. It seems that a few of her suitors were resolved to chase her even after she had become engaged to my father.

My father saw them all off, although whether a swashbuckle was involved I cannot say, and they were married in Somerset in September 1960, the only time in her life that my mother had been on time for anything. Dad had told her that he wouldn't wait, which was undoubtedly the incentive she needed. However, Mum looks clearly terrified, a nervous wreck in fact, in the black and white photographs. Her stage fright seemed at odds with her belief as a teenager that a Hollywood director would appear in sleepy Somerset and sign her up there and then to star in a blockbuster. Such was her anxiety on her wedding day that she forgot all her luggage for their honeymoon in Babbacombe, Devon and had to buy a whole new trousseau. Good move – although I imagine the chances of Mum finding a glamorous outfit in Devon were quite slim.

Mum was very close to her parents and four siblings, of whom she was the eldest, and it was undoubtedly a big shock for her to move up to the East Midlands. But Dad's heart had never left there and moving back with his young bride to take on a new job, they found a flat equidistant from Nottingham Forest's City Ground and Trent Bridge cricket ground. The man had his priorities! These teams, and even the sports they played, had never previously figured majorly in Mum's life. And when I was born some nine months later, Mum's state of shock must have been complete, particularly as she nearly died giving birth to me. As a result, my father, even while working full-time, played a hands-on role in caring for me from my earliest days as well as looking after my birth-battered mother. Characteristically, he would not have complained because, as was the convention in those days, he would just have got on with it.

While not a moaner, he wasn't especially forthcoming either in the proclamation of endearments, although I do remember him bringing Mum flowers many times. There was never any question of his depth of feeling; it just wasn't spoken about much. There may have been occasions, though, when Mum might have appreciated a little more romanticism. Writing home during his Malta Maniacs cricket tour with *Test Match Special* scorer Bill Frindall to Singapore in 1982, he finished a business-like postcard with 'Cannot phone too often. £4 a minute'. Sometimes you've just got to tell it how it is.

But then I found some of his letters, which might be seen as more impassioned.

Monday 12.4.82

Sweetheart,

I really am very sorry about the blasted boiler problem. I never dreamed that you would have all this trouble.

Yesterday, we played cricket at RAAF Butterworth, which is on the mainland. We go over there by ferry, which runs every seven minutes and is very efficient. We beat the Aussies by 70 runs, much to my delight and everyone else's, I might add.

Today I hope to go to Georgetown and spend a little time by the pool. I wanted to play golf but I am still having trouble with my back, blast it.

That's all for now, my love, give my love to the children. I hope they are behaving themselves.

My love to you, my Darling, and do take care.

God Bless,

Bill xxxx

It is his last expression of 'God Bless' that also surprised me as my father was an avowed agnostic and would refer to his religion as Church of Turkey. I did not know then, nor do I know now, what he meant by that. Nor did I know whether that was offensive and if it is now, I can only apologise.

But his last in the series of thin airmail paper letters kept by my mother perhaps more adequately sums up his true feelings.

> Oberoi Hotel
> Tuesday 20.4.82
> My Darling,
> I will probably be home by the time you receive this, but I felt like writing to you.
> Whilst I have enjoyed this trip, make no mistake I have missed you dreadfully and can't wait to get back home. Saturday can't come soon enough for me and I hope you too.
> Take care, my love, and see you soon.
> All my love,
> Bill xxxxxxxxx

Such an unexpected romantic discovery among my mother's possessions gave me a warm glow and the knowledge that, for all their occasional disagreements, they really did love each other. As a young child, I was sometimes terrified, as perhaps all young children are, that my parents would split up. My father would always dismiss my concerns even if I noticed him sometimes admiring another woman. I would always pick him up on it.

'Just because I've had my dinner doesn't mean I can't still look at the menu,' he would say to reassure me.

In fact, he became a minor legend for such pithy remarks as exemplified in Andrew Collins' evocative book *Where Did It All Go Right?: Growing Up Normal in the 1970s*. Writing about the unimaginative diet we all enjoyed in that decade, Collins recounts the story of when my father turned up in Nottingham at my brother's university digs:

'Writing of our adventure-free tastes remind me of the story a music industry friend of mine called Phill [my brother changed his name from Mark after he left school although the family continued to call him Mark] used to tell about his infamous dad – a conservative sort – visiting him at his first flat and refusing a cup of tea because Phill only had Earl Grey. "I haven't got time for experiments," his dad said. That should have been the Collins family motto.'

It could well have been a motto for all of us at the time.

The BBC DJ Stuart Maconie recounted the same story on one of his 6Music radio shows and thus Dad's reputation spread further. My younger daughter Sisi named one of her fashion collections after a piece of advice Dad gave to my brother after a particularly fraught lunch at home when the teenager, ever mindful of his appearance, took an age to get ready for a family shopping trip. Dad had had enough of waiting. He could, of course, have lost his temper. He could have yelled. He could have thrown something on the floor. He could have left in a huff and slammed the door. A lot of people would. Instead Dad said, snappily, 'It's not a fashion parade. We're only going to Yeovil.'

And thus that line became a family aphorism whenever someone dared to make a fuss about anything. Except much, much later on, when Yeovil played a bigger and darker role in my life.

* * *

To some people – well, therapists – the relationship with my father was neither good nor healthy for me. But I had never seen it that way for a second. A few months after having a sort of nervous breakdown (I think of it as 'nervous-breakdown-lite' and I don't mean to be disparaging by saying that) at the end of 2001 and the start of 2002, I embarked on a week of experiential residential therapy in East Sussex. The Hoffman Process is renowned for being intense, both physically and emotionally, as well as transformational.

I had been having therapy on and off since 1996, specifically hypnotherapy, to help me deal with anxiety during my second pregnancy. Throughout Lucy's pregnancy, largely because of my experience the year before, I was sure that something would go wrong and by the time I got to hospital in advanced labour, I had convinced myself that she would be stillborn. After an hour or so of being settled into a labour room in St George's Hospital in Tooting, a nurse bowled in and unceremoniously asked me to move to another room as 'we're having a stillbirth in here'. She had also obviously missed out on the bedside manner training day. From that moment, I was in a state of such terror that I didn't say a single word for the rest of the labour or during the birth. This was hardly surprising since anxiety, whether about exams, boyfriends, work, money, pregnancy, childbirth, cars, cricket or whatever, had been a lifelong companion. Witness my earliest recurring dreams of my father somehow falling out of the car at speed, leaving me to drive it and thus him behind.

My husband told me later that I barely made a sound throughout 16 hours of labour. When it was all over, I lay back with a towel over my face and thought I must have died. So Michael held our tiny baby, already terrified about the prospect of how he would deal with future boyfriends, while I learned how to breathe normally again. I didn't realise it at the time but that was one of the easier parts of motherhood.

A gifted hypnotherapist, Marisa Peer, helped me get through the pregnancy and birth of our second daughter, Sisi, in July 1996, but by then having small children had merely added to my heightened state of fear. Foreboding about what calamity might befall me or my parents was a mere bagatelle compared to the terrors I imagined were lurking round the corner to snatch my children away. And as I know now, if you don't deal with whatever your demon is (in my case, generalised anxiety), it will hide in some dark corner and reach with its long, witch-like hand to grab you at the very moment when you are off guard. Surely, and I know this now, it must be better to behave like any decent batsman and spend as long as you need to check with the umpire that your bat is in the right position in respect of the stumps? You might then be better prepared for any type of bowling you might face. With hindsight and a good deal more knowledge, it is obvious that I was severely affected by perimenopause symptoms. My hormones, once again, had taken control.

11 September, 2001, a day of horror and loss for so many people, unwittingly became a day when my guard was definitely askew. I was not in the habit of watching the lunchtime news on TV but that day, for whatever reason, I sat down with my favourite cheese and tomato sandwiches to see repeated footage of the first plane fly into the North Tower. I rang Michael to tell him what had happened and watched live as the second plane crashed into the South Tower. Like everyone else, I was profoundly shocked. Unlike most other people, the next day I ordered 400 biological warfare suits. That was a mistake. I had actually only ordered four. When the delivery man arrived two days later with a lorry load of boxes, I told him, 'I just want to save my family, not the whole street.'

He looked at me as if I had lost my marbles, and he was right.

We were then living in Clapham, right under the flight path to Heathrow, with planes flying over every 30 seconds or so, every one of which, I thought, was going to plummet nose-first into our roof. Somehow, I held myself together for the next few weeks until 23

December when, after having drunk a glass or two more of wine than I was used to, I woke up in the middle of the night unable to breathe and thought that I was going to die. Michael called an ambulance, thinking I was having a heart attack, and the paramedics swiftly arrived to cart me off to St George's Hospital. It wasn't a heart attack but the first of many panic attacks and fainting episodes. I had several brain scans to try to find out the cause of my constant and severe headaches. Some days, I lay in bed with my hands either side of my head; all I could see was blackness and I was too scared to move. By then, I was sure I had a brain tumour. But I also had numerous episodes of heart palpitations, which obviously presaged the fact that I was going to die of a heart attack if the tumour didn't get me first.

I had a 48-hour electroencephalogram (EEG) to record my brain activity, which came up with a diagnosis of epilepsy. I was devastated and reacted to that news with utter fear. Uncharacteristically, I decided to challenge medical opinion, change my mindset and then have more tests. I had two big incentives not to have epilepsy: we wouldn't be able to move out of London because I wouldn't be able to drive, nor would I be able to visit my parents.

Two old-fashioned books became my constant companions: *You Can Heal Your Life* by Louise Hay and *Self Help for Your Nerves* by Dr Claire Weekes. Neither mentioned the life-saving properties of cricket but Hay's book provided a mantra opposing epilepsy for which I developed an inner rap tune to be repeated on a loop in my throbbing head. The book is still by my bed, just in case, and many pages fall out whenever I pick it up. However, Dr Weekes' book, published in 1962 and still in print today, has been the most important I have ever read in my life. She teaches the sufferer how to heal themselves by facing the fear, accepting it, letting it float over them and gradually letting time pass. It looks simple on paper but when you are in the grip of a nervous illness that process can take all your strength. I was still having severe panic attacks, sometimes several a day, but with the advice of Dr Weekes I learnt to sit in a chair, hold on to the arms (for dear life, most of the time) and breathe my way through them. After a few weeks, I became less frightened.

Three months later, I had another series of brain scans that included a 24-hour EEG. This time, there was no epileptic activity and I remain eternally grateful to Louise Hay and Dr Claire Weekes.

I know now that anyone can have isolated epileptic events that do not become routine but this sorry chain of events taught me something much more profound: I could, with a great deal of application and intent, reprogramme my mind to cope with stress. It was not a magic bullet and I still had frequent panic attacks when I thought I might die, but I got through them. Each one I survived made me feel less afraid.

It was the search for a cause behind my panic attacks and general anxiety that led me to the Hoffman Process. Believing this would hand me the key to inner peace and lead me out of my dark place, I arrived at a large house in East Sussex with 20 other troubled souls to begin a week of intense experiential therapy. Just being away from home for a week caused consternation, not least to my mother when I explained that I wouldn't be able to ring her. At all. We were used to speaking on the phone at least once a day and she thought it unbelievably cruel that I would forego even this paltry commitment. And as for leaving my part-time job and my children, what was I thinking of? They, however, were perfectly capable of surviving without me, even with Michael's legendary non-cooking skills. One of his best endeavours, after I had just come out of hospital after childbirth, had seen him leave the plastic base on a pizza, which melted over the oven floor. That's not even cooking!

To make up in some small way for potential malnourishment, I set a treasure hunt for the children every day I was away. I explained that I was going on a 'meditation camp', a description they seemed happy with even if my mother wasn't. She became concerned that it was a bit more than meditation and that I would be advised that all my problems, real or imagined, would be laid at her feet for blame. She need not have worried. While I certainly struggled with my relationship with her for a while once I returned from 'camp', I focused on the core message. A large part of the 'process' is forgiving our parents and it took me longer to work through forgiving my mother for perceived slights until I finally absorbed the message that parents are just doing their best and no one is to blame.

Unwittingly, however, the process deepened my love for my father and when one of the therapists, or coaches, said that my unconditional love for Dad was at the root of my issues, I snapped at him. I didn't see it as a problem then, nor do I see it as a problem now. I just feel lucky. I'm sorry about that, Mr Therapist.

The price of love is ultimately grief and three months after Dad died, I still felt physically unable to bear the pain of his loss as well as mentally beaten. I developed headaches that were so severe I couldn't move my neck, nor lift my left arm. A trapped nerve in my neck and cervical stenosis were diagnosed (in addition to my existing degenerative lumbar spine) and I set off on a treadmill of hospital procedures involving nerve ablation and steroid injections. Nothing worked for long. My insomnia worsened and the pain became so intense in my left shoulder that on a drive to collect my youngest daughter from university, I contemplated driving into a bridge. I would have done anything to get rid of the pain but I had strong words with myself and kept going.

I tried to find solace in cricket but there was none there either. That winter, the England cricket team lost the Ashes 5-0 in Australia, a 'Pomnishambles' that can still make grown men shudder. I know what my father would have said.

* * *

A few years earlier, and shortly after my return from Hoffman, the England cricket team were again in Australia and lost the Ashes 4-1 in a horror show of a series. Each morning, Dad and I would talk through the previous night's play, which we had listened to on our respective radios. He kept repeating the line trumpeted by journalists that England 'can't bat, can't bowl, can't field' and it was hard to argue with him. But how could any team face down such a buoyant and proficient Australian side?

The first four Tests weren't even close. England lost the first by 384 runs, the second by an innings and 51 runs, the third by an innings and 48 runs and the fourth by five wickets. Only England's 225-run victory – led by Michael Vaughan's second-innings score of 183 in the fifth Test at Sydney – stopped the whitewash.

England were not, then, in the best frame of mind for the visit by South Africa in 2003 and Dad and I only made a brief foray into the series by going to Lord's for the first Test at the end of July. Michael Vaughan had just become England captain after Nasser Hussain handed in his resignation after the drawn first Test at Edgbaston earlier in the week, but it wasn't at all a happy handover. England were bowled out for 173 in their first innings and South Africa went on to score 151/1 by the close, with Graeme Smith unbeaten on 80. It gave Dad plenty to chunter about. I wasn't too chuffed myself as it would be our only Test cricket that season as Michael and I had decided to move our family to Hampshire, which would mean my journey time to my parents would be much shorter. Dad seemed a bit more tired than usual and had a few more naps in his seat in the Grandstand but he was, I reminded myself, 75 so perhaps that wasn't surprising.

He still talked to everyone around us in the stand, as usual making friends wherever he went. Walking along any street in London, he would always say 'Good morning!' to anyone he passed and wasn't at all bothered that he got strange looks in return rather than an amiable reply. He was in his element in a football or cricket crowd. At The Oval in August 1984, as England were being utterly humiliated on their way to a 5-0 series loss against West Indies, Dad was infuriated when England's Allan Lamb was out for one in the second innings, and loudly voiced his displeasure. I seem to remember he actually stood up and sort of waved his fist, which was very out of character. He turned round to look at the West Indies fans leaping up and down and shrugged his shoulders.

A West Indies fan smiled at Dad and said very loudly, 'Sir, I'll tell you why Allan Lamb can't bat. Because he's *tooooooo* fat and he's *tooooooo* small.' Dad laughed, as did the whole of the Vauxhall End, and then he applauded the man. The pair chatted for the rest of the day and I was surprised that Dad didn't invite his new friend to come home with us.

Years later, my father would be rendered mute and almost completely paralysed by dementia. He would aim the foulest of swear words at my mother and at nurses, and lose interest in absolutely everything, even his beloved Nottingham Forest. I would tell him the latest cricket news and he would look past me with not a flicker of recognition. Little by little, this spirited and wonderful man disappeared as though a kidnapper was taking him away, cell by cell. We would have sold everything we owned to pay the ransom demand.

When Leonard Cohen wrote in his poem, 'There Are Some Men' that mountains should bear the names of some men for all time, I am pretty sure he was writing about my Dad.

* * *

Who could tell when Dad's vascular dementia started? When he tripped over the dog's lead, breaking his hip which led to a mini-stroke? When he had a minor op for a bit of prostate trouble? Or was it the time we took my parents out for a pub lunch during which my mild-mannered, polite father proclaimed to all around us that the waitress was 'fat'? Was that the first sign? Or was it when he had a minor car accident and knocked the wing mirror off? We put those incidents down to just one (or two) of those things that can happen. Nothing to worry about, he was obviously just tired. Or maybe he needs new glasses? Or was it Alzheimer's or dementia? And what bloody difference anyway does a label like that make? Either way, it very slowly robs a person of all their faculties and their family of the person they love.

After he broke his hip, walking became more difficult. I suggested that he might like to try Tai Chi, if we could find a class in the depths of Somerset, to help him with his balance and mobility. But he said he didn't feel like it and he continued with his new gait: a shuffle, a bit of a limp and a sideways approach to any object he wanted to close in on. I suggested that driving might not be a good idea, not only for his own safety but for the sake of others too.

'You don't need to worry about that, sweetheart,' he replied. 'I can't walk very well but I can still drive.' His answer didn't reassure me. But it didn't take long for his mobility to decline to the point where he couldn't walk to his car, so we could cross driving off the worry list. I would occasionally take him out in my car but it would take at least 30 minutes to help walk him the 20 yards from his front door to getting him into the passenger seat. Shuffle, stop, sigh. Shuffle, stop, sigh. Shuffle, stop, sigh. After a few weeks, he stopped trying even to do that.

'What have you been up to this week, Daddy?' I asked him once. He was sitting, slumped in his chair, in exactly the same position he had been when I left him the week before.

He smiled up at me. He was always pleased to see me, as I was him. 'Playing a bit of golf,' he replied, lop-sidedly. I swallowed hard and tried to believe that, really, if he thought he had been playing a bit of golf then that was surely some comfort to him.

Dad's armchair became his sanctuary, submerged though he was under the *Telegraph* once he had forgotten how to turn the pages. I would try to put it back in order for him but that would last for only a few minutes before the pages fluttered to the ground again or on to his lap. Sometimes I would read the sport to him and there would be a flicker of amusement in his eyes. By the end, though, he showed no interest even if I read out the Nottingham Forest match report. It was as though he had never heard of them. I kept reading, though, in the hope that it might remind him of good times.

To try to stimulate his brain and rekindle good memories, Mum and I would show him family photographs too.

'Who's that?' Mum asked him, showing him a picture of one of his grand-daughters.

'Oh that's Paul McCartney,' he replied.

Sometimes you just had to laugh.

But Mum wasn't laughing much. She became exhausted looking after him, even with the twice-daily visits of the carers, and she developed leg ulcers that refused to heal. I summoned up the courage to mention the possibility of Dad going into a home for some respite care but, oh no, she wasn't having any of it.

'If he goes in somewhere like that, he will never come out,' she replied. I didn't bring it up again.

She was still managing to cook him nutritious meals and for a couple of years he just about managed to feed himself. We fed him like a baby for the last year. Except you don't know it's the last year, do you? He was having statins, blood pressure medication, blood-thinning tablets and his vitamin D supplements, so he could go on for years and years, couldn't he? But how selfish was I to want him to? I couldn't bear the thought of losing him even though we were all, in fact, losing him every day.

After every visit to my parents' home, I drove for a few minutes, stopped in a small passing place in a deserted country lane and sobbed with the sadness of seeing my father, the anguish at my mother's hoarding and her exhaustion. Then there was the frustration that I couldn't do anything: it would all come out before I began my long drive home. The next week, I would begin it all again but my mother was doing it all day, every day.

For better, for worse,
For richer, for poorer,
In sickness and in health.

I learned a lot about marriage vows from my mother and I had a profound lesson about resilience. Forget your one-day game or a hundred balls bash. This was a timeless Test and Mum played herself in, buckled down and prepared to score a slow double hundred no matter how long it took. For her, though, there was to be no player of the match award or, indeed, any prize other than the knowledge that she used every ounce of her love and energy to look after her husband as well as she could. And after he left us, it was obvious that I owed her that too, no matter how much darker life became.

For Non-Cricket Speakers

How To Be Out. And Umpiring

STANDING AS an umpire can be a thankless task, as Joel Wilson discovered during the 2019 Ashes series. On the last day of the first Test at Edgbaston, some wag altered Wilson's Wikipedia entry to read, 'Joel Wilson is a blind international cricket umpire.' By lunch on that final day, the players had reviewed Wilson's decisions on 12 occasions: eight were overturned. His Wikipedia entry was actually one of the more polite comments. I can only hope he never saw any of the vile tweets that were posted. And to think the Decision Review System (DRS), officially introduced in a Test match between New Zealand and Pakistan in Dunedin in 2009, aimed to improve an umpire's lot. As long ago as 1921, *The Cricketer* magazine wrote, 'Many umpires are too old, and their sight not good enough.'

Cricket being cricket, there are multiple ways of losing your wicket, including some obscure entries in a scorebook such as 'handled the ball' and 'hit the ball twice'. You will also see lbw (leg before wicket), bowled, run out, stumped, obstructing the field, caught, timed out and hit wicket.

The lbw rule is perhaps the most difficult for a newcomer to cricket to understand. The umpire will consider an appeal for lbw (the bowler will shout 'Howzat?') if he thinks the ball would have hit the stumps if it hadn't been obstructed by the batsman's pad or body.

The umpire also has to consider whether the ball pitched outside leg stump. If the ball lands outside the line of the leg stump, the batsman cannot be given out even if the ball would have gone on to hit the stumps. Nor can a batsman be given out if the ball hits the bat before it hits the pad.

An umpire will also reject an appeal for lbw if he believes the ball struck the batsman's pad outside the line of the off stump, even if the ball would have gone on to hit the stumps, *unless* the batsman makes no genuine attempt to play a stroke.

If the ball has pitched on the stumps and hit the batsman on the pads in front of the wicket, the umpire can give the batsman out as the ball has not pitched outside the line of the leg stump and has not hit the batsman outside the line of the off stump.

Before making an lbw decision, the umpire also has to weigh up the height of the ball's bounce, the swing and spin of the ball, where the ball hit the pad and whether the batsman is genuinely attempting to make a stroke.

The umpire has to weigh all this up in just a couple of seconds. TV replays added to the drama of lbw decisions but put umpires under even more pressure. Thankless task, indeed.

Thus DRS was established to aid umpires in that task and to try to rectify errors. The system allows onfield umpires to consult the third umpire to review decisions and their communications are broadcast.

There can be an umpire review or player reviews with each side allowed two unsuccessful reviews in each innings of a Test. In one-day internationals and T20 matches, only one unsuccessful review is allowed. The first time an ICC men's T20 international saw DRS in use was at the T20 World Cup in 2021, with each team allowed two reviews per innings. Due to international travel restrictions during the Covid-19 pandemic, when only home umpires could be used, the number of unsuccessful reviews allowed in each Test innings was increased to three.

But the DRS is not without controversy. The 'umpire's call' in lbw decisions means the umpire's verdict will be given the benefit of the doubt when technology fails to provide conclusive evidence.

The venerable W.G. Grace believed that the laws of cricket were 'good and sufficient' but needed to be made clearer for the umpires, 'who evidently did not always understand them!' Perhaps the greatest cricketer the world has ever known, whose career spanned 44 seasons, was entitled to make such a disparaging remark. I take a more compassionate view, even if the man in the middle is the unfortunate Joel Wilson.

Chapter Eight

This Is Not a Space[18]
... And My Mother

I completed the kitchen assault course and initiative test to emerge victorious with a cup of Typhoo's finest. There were no fanfares or fireworks.

Forget *I'm A Celebrity*'s challenges or *SAS: Who Dares Wins*.

Just ask the contestants to go into a champion hoarder's home and to attempt to successfully finish a simple household task.

IN AN unimaginable and unsolicited chapter of the Circle of Life, it transpired that my mother's eyes were the first I ever saw and mine were the last eyes she looked into.

I owed her that, of course, and much more.

---

18 'This is not a space' were words written by Mum on a yellow post-it note to indicate that a 10cm empty square area on the cluttered worktop was not, in fact, a space to put anything.

A few minutes after she died, a cuddly nurse walked into the room and put an arm round my shoulder as I sobbed as though my heart would break. She gently told me how privileged I was to have been able to spend the last five days with my Mum as she was dying. I didn't understand what she meant as I didn't feel remotely privileged to have watched my mother slowly and not at all peacefully slip away. Covid caused me to rethink that when we heard harrowing stories of people dying alone, unable to have their hands held by the people who loved them most. So, yes, now I do understand I was privileged, even if it was not an honour I would ever have wished for.

A few minutes after that enlightened nurse left me alone to whisper the Lord's Prayer at the foot of Mum's bed, another, perhaps less compassionate (but you be the judge) nurse, walked in and said, 'Well, she wanted to go out with a bang, didn't she?' It was Bonfire Night.

Remember, remember the fifth of November.

A week before, two days before Hallowe'en, it had been the fifth anniversary of my father's death. I hadn't ever liked the time of year when the clocks went back and now that period is doubly difficult, wreathed as it is in the remembrance of both my parents.

On that miserable anniversary, I had been at my mother's for my customary weekly visit. Uncharacteristically, she didn't come to the door when I knocked and said, 'Only me.' I waited for a few minutes because I knew she could only walk very slowly. Giving up and, I'll admit, feeling a bit exasperated, I opened the door with my key and called out as I went in. 'Mummy?'

There was no response as I weaved my way through the rubbish in the hall and into the living room. She was sitting on the sofa, where she had spent every night for the past 15 years.

And, thank the Lord, she opened her eyes.

'What time is it?' she mumbled. My mother was not a great sleeper and certainly never overslept, so it was clear she wasn't well. It was obvious that she could hardly move either. I tried to help her up but, with yelps of pain, she refused so I went into the dark, filthy kitchen to make her a cup of tea. A normal enough task but not in that kitchen.

For a start, there weren't any clean cups or teaspoons. To get to the tap to fill the kettle, I had to dismantle a towering inferno of brown plates out of a sink full of grey, scummy water. Then I had to find a space on the worktop to put the cup, which I had made a feeble attempt at washing. There were a few plates with unidentifiable mould (there were more of those in the hall, too, but when I had complained about them Mum always replied, 'They made penicillin from mould' as though that gave her licence to grow her own). There were also hundreds of scrunched-up tissues and bits of used kitchen roll. Spent matches were all over the worktop and the floor was covered in newspapers, which made for a skating rink under my shoes. After Dad's death, we gave Mum an iPad so we hadn't bought her any newspapers for five years but, anyway, many of the papers were decades old.

On an island unit in the kitchen among curling photographs, empty bottles of Dettol, dried flowers and thousands of handwritten notes was an ashtray featuring the last half of a cigar enjoyed by my Dad. That cigar must have been several years old as Mum wouldn't let him smoke when he had dementia.

She said he was a fire risk.

The mountain of papers and other rubbish was obviously safe, so I wasn't to worry at all about their flammability. For the merest smidgeon of peace of mind, I had installed a smoke alarm but when that started beeping one day my mother, by that stage badly afflicted by macular degeneration and hardly able to see, had climbed on to a white plastic garden chair (the sturdiest she could find) and taken the batteries out.

By now, you can probably imagine her response when I suggested one of those alarm button necklaces.

So that's all good then.

Mum hadn't allowed me to go into the kitchen for the last few years but I had known it was bad even if I hadn't seen it. Thousands of times, I had asked Mum to let me help her and to clean the house. I had said I could clear out the clutter but on one occasion I offered, pleaded more like, she got so angry with me that she threw a filthy glass at my head. I ducked.

Her answer was always, 'I'll do it.'

I completed the kitchen assault course and initiative test to emerge victorious with a cup of Typhoo's finest. There were no fanfares or fireworks. Forget *I'm A Celebrity*'s challenges or *SAS: Who Dares Wins*. Just ask the contestants to go into a champion hoarder's home and to attempt to finish a simple household task.

'Should I call the doctor?' I asked, knowing what the answer would be, even though she looked ashen and was twisted with pain.

'What on earth do you want to ring *him* for?'

'When did you last eat something?' I moved some bits of papers off the arm of the sofa and attempted to rest her teacup there.

'Don't move those notes. I need those!'

'When did you last eat something?' I repeated.

'I had some rice pudding last night. And some cream.'

I bit my lip. At least it was something. Then she tried to stand up. And couldn't. Her leg, which looked twisted to me, couldn't support her. About a month before she had had a 'slight' fall, so she said, and on that occasion the police had gone round as one of the nurses hadn't been able to get her to answer the door. Mum had given the policeman short shrift (he called me after the event) but had obviously spent the last few weeks in

THIS IS NOT A SPACE … AND MY MOTHER

agonising pain. I was very worried that she had broken something but she seemed to think not.

A few years before, she had had a fall and my father spent four days carrying her round the house after Mum refused to let him call a doctor. It transpired then that she had broken her hip.

I could see history repeating itself, so I spent the next hour arguing with her about ringing the doctor before deciding that I would just have to incur her wrath. I made the mistake of telling her when I went back into the house.

'What on earth have you done that for? I don't want him here.'

I had repeatedly, over the years, tried to intervene for the sake of my mother's health and wellbeing and she had determinedly resisted my efforts. She had also refused to give me – or indeed anyone – power of attorney. The fact that I didn't want to see her in any pain or sadness and just wanted to make her life as easy as it could possibly be – and, I'll admit with some shame, also relieve some of my immense stress – seemed to hold no charm for her. So it was quite clear that she was not going to co-operate with the doctor that day.

I had spoken to him on a few occasions and he seemed perfectly nice and competent to me. He had worked out my mother, though, and knew what he was in for.

'Shall we consider getting you into hospital for a while so that your leg ulcers can have a proper chance to heal and you can rest?' he asked, very gently. I noticed him glancing at Denis Compton's biography, one of Dad's cricket books that was on the closed piano lid.

My mother kept her head down and stared at the floor. I half expected her to stick her fingers in her ears and start singing, 'La la la.'

I softly repeated the doctor's words. 'You'll feel so much better when you've had someone looking after you 24 hours a day and made you completely better. And then you'll have much more energy to do all the things you want to do here.'

I looked despairingly round the room at all the detritus and then at the doctor. He didn't know, as I did, that Mum was also incontinent, and I feared she had some kidney problems. It might take a bit more than a few weeks to cure her of all her ailments.

'If my mother hadn't gone into hospital, she would still be here,' Mum replied, continuing to look at the floor and beginning to hum something from *The Sound of Music*.

Now my grandmother Freda, an extraordinarily life-affirming woman, had died four years before, just a few weeks before her 102nd birthday, but I decided not to dispute my mother's narrative. She clearly thought my grandmother would have celebrated her 106th birthday.

The doctor retrieved a sheaf of papers from his old-fashioned bag and started to read out the list of Mum's afflictions, beginning with the leg ulcers, which had begun to plague her when she was under the huge stress of caring for Dad. The year he died, she was diagnosed with age-related macular degeneration but too late for any preventative measures as she had refused to go to the optician when she first complained to me that she couldn't see very well.

At Salisbury Hospital a few months before that, she had an investigation of the circulation to her legs and was recommended to have a stent, a fairly routine and successful procedure. We actually got as far as making an appointment for that but two days later Mum made me ring the hospital to cancel it. The nurse I spoke to, and who we had met at the hospital, said she was so sorry and asked if I was getting any help as I must be finding the situation very stressful. It was kind of her to ask but I told her I was *completely* fine and had barely a note of hysteria in my voice as I said it.

I looked at Mum, who was avoiding looking at the doctor. 'If you could wave a magic wand and I could make things better for you, what would you want?' I asked her.

Quick as a flash, she replied, 'To have Mum and Bill [my Dad] still here.'

It was my turn to look at the floor.

The doctor started to go through some questions with Mum, none of which she answered rationally. When he asked her whether she had a good diet, she sniffed and replied that she had plenty of double cream, thank you, which meant she was getting enough calcium, thank you.

'And Michéle brings me a homemade roast dinner for me to heat up on Mondays.'

That was true, but I had already seen that last week's offering was still in the fridge in the hall. By now, you don't need to ask why the fridge was in the hall. There was also a freezer in the hall, another fridge in the kitchen and two in the garage. Some of them were even plugged in.

At the end of his list, the doctor asked my mother about resuscitation. I flinched but he said it was absolutely routine as well as very important to ask the question. So he ploughed on, asking whether Mum would want to be resuscitated and outlined various scenarios to her. Mum kept staring at the floor and slightly upped the humming volume so that I could recognise 'Climb Every Mountain'. Raising her head and directing her hazy eyes towards me, she smiled but didn't speak.

'I know what you would say, Mummy. You would want to be resuscitated.'

'That's what she would like,' I told him.

He outlined other possible events, each one more alarming than the last. 'So even if you had had a heart attack and might end up severely incapacitated, you would want paramedics to do chest compression, which in itself could be damaging, and still be resuscitated?'

Mum nodded. At that moment, she reminded me of Geoff Boycott after an innings seeing off the world's best bowlers and refusing to give his wicket away.

The doctor muttered something that could have sounded exactly like 'extraordinary' and wrote it down.

My mother had had enough even of humming by now, so the doctor stood up to his full 6ft 8in and narrowly missed skimming the ceiling. It was just like having Joel Garner in the room but not nearly as much fun.

'I'll make sure the nurses come later,' he smiled at Mum.

She smiled at him for the first time but, if she had had the strength, I think she would have preferred to have got up and punched him.

I went outside to walk with him to his car.

'We both know the way this is going to end, don't we?' he asked me, not needing a reply.

I didn't, actually. Not properly, anyway.

'I just don't understand,' I replied. 'Why doesn't she want anyone to help? I mean, mentally she is completely with it.'

'I'm not sure that's true,' he said. 'And you can't help someone who doesn't want to help themselves. She is very stubborn. Forgive me. There are definitely some signs of dementia and anyone of a sound mind would be able to look after themselves a bit better than your mum.'

'That's because she hasn't been physically very well for a while. When she's better, she will be able to,' I said, worrying that I was beginning to sound just as delusional as my mother. She had seen off numerous health issues in the past and my brother and I used to joke that she would live forever, surviving on a diet of Fruit Pastilles and Benson and Hedges (not together, that would be disgusting).

'Ring any time you're worried,' said the doctor as he got into his car.

Well, that wasn't going to happen.

I spent the rest of the afternoon trying to make Mum some food and to get her to eat it. I even notched up a small victory by being allowed to wash some skirts for her. I hung them up around the dining room over chairs and radiators (which hadn't worked for years as a heating engineer I had booked said the house was too dangerous for him to work in) because there was no point taking them upstairs where she wouldn't be able to get them.

'Would you like me to stay?' I asked her, when I had finished as many jobs as I was permitted to do.

'No, thank you. You need to get back. It's dark now.'

I felt torn as well as sick with worry but put the phone on the arm of the sofa and made sure she had some food and drink. The nurse would be in later to change the dressings on Mum's legs, a procedure that always made her yell in agony, so at least there would be someone coming in.

I shut the front door and began my two-hour drive home feeling even more anxious than usual and wracked with frustration. Countless friends, with the best of intentions, had told me to take control and clear out Mum's house for my sake as well as hers. But the psychology of a hoarder is so complex and extreme that, despite my best efforts and all the research I did, I accomplished absolutely nothing. I knew that everything I took into the house would never come out. And that included food.

For a few months, Mum had been telling me that she thought there was a tiny hedgehog in the house. As she could hardly see at all by this point, I thought it was unlikely to be a mini hedgehog but I didn't see any mice either. I put lots of mouse deterrents around but there was never any evidence that a rodent had been anywhere near them. But then, why would they when there was food all over the place?

Driving home, I was aware that I was hardly breathing such was the tightness in my chest and when I arrived, delighted as I was to see my front door, I struggled to put one foot in front of the other to walk through it.

'What's happened to your eye?' asked Michael.

'What do you mean?' It had felt a bit gritty and sore on the way back but nothing to affect my vision.

'It's full of blood!' he exclaimed.

I got a mirror out of my bag and saw that, yes, the entire white of my right eye was bright bloody red. But that's okay, surely? I was just tired and a bit wrung out.

'Are you sure you're all right?' he asked. 'I'll pour you some wine.'

That always did the trick.

Spurs were playing that evening so Michael disappeared to shout at the television while I sat in the kitchen. Within a few seconds, though, and despite a couple of sips of wine, I was not feeling at all okay.

'Michael, can you come here a minute, please? Sorry.' Interrupting a Spurs match was strictly *verboten*.

He walked in to see me, as he said later, grey, shivering with cold but pouring with sweat, which with my eye still bright red was a bit concerning. He tried to take my pulse. There didn't seem to be one.

'Right, I'm ringing 999.'

My head was throbbing by that stage and I was in no fit state to speak, so just let him get on with it.

Within 15 minutes, the paramedics walked in and soon established that I hadn't had a heart attack but that my blood pressure was almost off the scale. Giving me the option of going to hospital or staying at home and seeing my GP the following morning, I chose home,

My father, aged 20, off duty during the Berlin Airlift in 1948, at Fassberg Air Base. He wrote that it was one of the happiest times of his RAF service

Early days: Viv Richards in his first season at Somerset County Cricket Club

Making a point: England's Tony Greig is bowled for one by West Indies' Michael Holding in the fifth Test at The Oval in 1976. Before the series, Greig had said he intended to make the West Indies 'grovel'

Fast, fierce and full of charisma: Pakistan's Imran Khan bowling at Headingley against England in 1982

The day cricket changed: India's Kapil Dev is leapt on by a fan after catching Viv Richards on the boundary in the 1983 World Cup Final

A cricket connoisseur: Peter O'Toole as Jeffrey Bernard

That's entertainment: Antigua cricket fan and crowd pleaser 'Gravy' takes advantage of a rain break to dance upside down on a table

One of the best places to watch cricket: the 'Double Decker' stand at the Recreation Ground, Antigua seemed to sway in time with the spectators' sound systems

Sunburn and mosquito bites: Viv Richards was typically gallant enough not to ask me why I was wearing a pair of curtains to interview him at his house in Antigua in 1990

Catch it like that: the author talks through fielding tactics with the West Indies captain at an Evening Standard *lunch in 1991*

The ground levitated: Brian Lara is enveloped by spectators in Antigua after passing Gary Sobers's world record Test innings score in the fifth Test against England in 1994

King of the Jungle: Ben Stokes roars as England beat Australia by one wicket at Headingley in 2019

A long way from Trent Bridge; beach cricket in Antigua is taken seriously

mainly because I thought Mum could phone me and I might need to drive to Somerset again.

The next morning, my GP changed my blood pressure medication and checked my eye. She knew of the situation with Mum and that I was under immense stress, which had caused the hypertensive 'incident'. Under instructions to remain calm (oh, yes), I went to the health food shop and bought litres of beetroot juice (this became relevant later when, without going into details, I thought I had developed bowel cancer) as I remembered reading that athletes drank it to lower blood pressure.

I rang Mum when I got home. No answer. I tried 20 times. There was nothing for it but to ring my parents' elderly friend, who lived in the village and had a key. I rang him about 20 times too before he eventually answered and I persuaded him to go round. He found Mum still sitting in her chair, unable to move, but she didn't want the doctor. The friend stayed there until late that night but it was clear this situation couldn't go on. However, Mum was refusing to budge on seeing the doctor and wouldn't contemplate going into hospital.

I spent another sleepless night wracked with distress and guilt, but tried to focus on my breathing (futile) and imagining lying on a beach in Antigua (couldn't manage even that).

The next morning, Mum actually answered her phone but said she couldn't speak for long as she couldn't stand up. This didn't make much sense to me as I had left the phone on the arm of the sofa so I thought she would be sitting down to answer it, but I knew better than to interrogate her. Later phone calls were unanswered, so I rang my parents' friend again. No answer. I had no other option but to call the police (they had given me a number to ring after the last incident). When the policeman got there I gave him the code for the key box, he let himself in and rang 999 for an ambulance, which took two hours to get there. The policeman rang me several times to keep me updated and every time I heard Mum shouting in the background. Then the paramedics phoned me, telling me that Mum was refusing to go into hospital but saying that they couldn't leave her as she was. This dialogue continued every half an hour until 2.30am, when after more persuasion and cajoling from me, Mum agreed to go in the ambulance to Yeovil Hospital after I assured her I would be down there first thing in the morning. And, yes of course, I would stop at the house on the way to turn off the immersion heater, unplug the television and make sure the place was locked up.

After a third sleepless night, I rang the hospital to learn that Mum had already had a brain scan and chest X-ray and was 'comfortable'. An overnight bag would be all I needed, I thought, but I packed my copy of Michael Manley's weighty *History of West Indies Cricket* just in case and, bleary-eyed, headed for Somerset, stopping off at the house as promised. The paramedics had created a right old mess to add to the chaos caused by the rubbish. In fact, it looked as though two opposing teams of burglars had been in there.

I turned the immersion off, left the radio on as Mum would have wanted, unplugged the television and collected a few things for her, including some of the freshly laundered skirts, Fruit Pastilles, cigarettes, perfume and bright red lipstick. All the things she would need for when she came out.

Because she was coming out, I was sure of that.

She needed just a few days to repair whatever had happened to her leg, then a short spell of recuperation in a cosseting care home being spoon-fed hearty meals. She would also be cured of her leg ulcers, kidney problems and circulatory issues and that would be just the ticket to restore her to full and vibrant health. Not much to ask, was it?

I found my way to Mum's cheerless ward among the web of bleak corridors in Yeovil District Hospital. She was lying in a bed in the corner and plainly didn't want to be there. Truth be told, neither did I.

I unpacked her bag and put her things in the bedside cabinet.

'Can you give me a cigarette, Michéle? *Please.*' She waved the hand that wasn't connected to a tube at me.

'You can't have one here! That might be one of the reasons you're in here,' I replied.

'They won't see! You can light it for me.'

The woman in the next bed laughed. I smiled at her and raised my eyebrows, which silently said, 'See what I've got to deal with here?' Her expression changed to one full of pity.

Mum was wincing and screaming with pain. I could see from the shape under the bedclothes that her leg was horribly twisted. In fact, it didn't even look like a leg.

'Have you broken it? Are they going to operate?' I asked.

'I don't know,' she replied as a doctor approached her bed.

I introduced myself as the daughter and the doctor asked me to go with him to his office.

On the way, I asked him what tests they had carried out since Mum's arrival and he reeled off a long list of scans and X-rays that seemed very efficient. God bless the NHS.

Sitting at his desk, he rustled through a sheaf of papers. 'Chest X-ray clear, a few tiny things to note on the brain scan and looks like she has broken a bone at the top of her leg.'

Taken aback by the fact that she had a clear chest X-ray, which gave the lie to her 20-plus-a-day habit, I was just as unprepared for the next bit.

'Your Mum is really very sick. She has extreme kidney damage. But the biggest issue is her leg and the chronic damage caused by the ulcers. Have you seen her leg?'

'Not really,' I replied. 'Obviously it is heavily bandaged all the time, so I only get a glimpse of it if I am there when the nurses come in.'

'We are going to assess the tissue viability but I have to be very honest that, with the damage to her kidneys and to her leg, as well as the complete heart block issue, there is not going to be any sort of easy fix. And there might not be any fix at all because she is not in a good way to survive an operation.'

His bleeper buzzed. 'I have to meet a colleague who is looking at your Mum's leg. Will you be okay to stay here?'

I mumbled something and bit my lip as he left the office. He was gone a long time and I remained sitting in his untidy room, making full use of the box of tissues on the desk. I had – admittedly, foolishly, with all the evidence of the past few months/years which I could have paid more attention to – imagined that going into hospital would be the panacea to get Mum on the road to fully restored health.

And perhaps the doctor was wrong, anyway. I mean, he didn't know her, did he? Of course she could survive an operation! Stupid man – as Mum might have said.

He returned after about 45 minutes to my ashen face. The look on his own wasn't much better.

'I am terribly sorry,' he began.

My heart stopped.

261

'Your Mum's leg has started to become gangrenous and we have looked again at her blood tests. Her kidneys are failing. I am afraid she is not going to last long.'

'How long?' I whispered, unable to speak loudly in this version of hell.

'Not much beyond the weekend. I am so sorry.'

Four days?

'What do you mean? That doesn't sound right at all. Couldn't you amputate her leg?'

I couldn't believe I had asked that question. 'And then the rest of her body could start to recover. Surely.'

'I am so sorry. Her body just wouldn't survive any operation like that. So if you need to call people, I would do it right away. Do you have any siblings?'

'A younger brother. And should I call her brothers and sisters?'

'Yes. As soon as you can. I am so very sorry,' he repeated, as I began to sob with great shoulder heaves.

I sat there for a few minutes, not able or willing to compute what he had told me. He remained seated, not looking discomfited at all by my emotional incontinence. I think he kept saying, 'I'm so sorry.'

'Thank you,' I eventually spluttered and stood up.

I couldn't face seeing my mother just then and so I began my calls with Michael because I had to put off ringing my brother. Where do you begin with that?

It is fair to say that Michael has not always been renowned for his empathy nor even for answering his mobile at work but, this time, he impressed me with his compassion and said all the right things. I left it to him to tell our daughters the news of their adored Granny. They would be heartbroken.

I went outside the hospital to ring my brother, said something like, 'She hasn't got long' and we cried together for a long time. I mobilised my eldest uncle, asking him to call the rest of my aunts and uncles, and arranged for them to come to the hospital, apart from my aunt in Australia. Mum's best friend would also come but I told them all that they weren't to say goodbye to Mum as she didn't know the truth and I wanted it to stay that way. Was I right to protect her from that?

I had to get back to Mum's bedside after washing my face in the bleach-bombed ladies' toilets, reapplying lipstick and practising smiling in the mirror.

It was lunchtime and I helped Mum to eat through her screams of pain. I realised as she devoured three courses, as only someone who was ravenous could, how terrible she had become at looking after herself. But why had she always refused to stay with me and let me look after her for a while?

Her stubbornness, which may have served her well at some times in her life, undoubtedly shortened it. I quelled the knot of anger in my stomach and tried to remember what her GP had said earlier in the week. 'You couldn't have done anything differently. You have tried your absolute best.' And a few months before, a friend who used to be a nurse advised, 'We were taught that you can't care about a patient more than they care about themselves.'

None of that helped me as I sat by her bed. I just saw my little mum, without a single grey hair on her head nor a wrinkle on her face. I just saw my little mum dying and there wasn't a damned thing I could do about it.

Among the endless procession of nurses, doctors and specialists who visited Mum that first afternoon in hospital was a tall man who asked if I could have a quiet chat with him off the ward. This was my first experience of a palliative care nurse and I was almost overwhelmed by his compassion and understanding. I soon realised that he would be my guide as he quietly explained what was wrong with Mum and what would happen over the next few days.

He paused every time I started to weep and, when I felt strong enough to ask questions, he answered every one truthfully and at length.

When he mentioned giving Mum morphine to ease her pain, I told him that she thought that morphine had accelerated my grandmother's demise.

'We have to make her more comfortable,' he replied. 'You can see the terrible pain she is in. We have an absolute duty to alleviate her suffering.'

'Yes, of course. But if you have to use it, can you just use the bare minimum?'

'We will.' He looked me squarely in the eyes and I believed him.

Mum had already told the nursing staff she wasn't going to have any morphine 'thank you very much' and I felt utterly treacherous in agreeing to it being used. But how could I or anyone else have watched her screaming in unimaginable pain without doing something?

Even as the morphine started to be administered, Mum said, 'I'm not having morphine, thank you. It killed my mother. That's not morphine, is it?' She looked at me.

'No,' I lied, hating myself for it. 'It is just something, paracetamol I think, to make your leg stop hurting.'

Every time the nurses came to move her or change the dressings on her oozing leg, she screamed and screamed. At least this would take the edge off.

At the risk of becoming as paranoid as my mother, I checked the level of morphine being dripped into her and Googled it. It seemed okay.

Later that evening, I left her, bought a limp, grey sandwich and headed to the hotel. I hadn't slept all week but, strangely, I didn't care. Earlier that day, when I had been feeling a bit irritated at not being able to get anything to eat or drink and feeling exhausted, I had had a stern word with myself and self-chided, 'This isn't about *me*.' Those words became my mantra for the next few days and got me through it all.

The next morning, my brother met me at the hospital. We had a teary hug and I took him into my mother's stifling ward. She was asleep when the hospital chaplain announced himself and asked us if we would like him to say a prayer. My brother seemed uncomfortable but I said, 'Mummy would like that.' We sobbed through the prayer and my mother, still sleeping, didn't notice or hear.

I left my brother alone with Mum then to say whatever he needed to, not knowing until many months afterwards what he said. He also read two letters from his daughters to her, which I hope she heard somehow.

We went to Pizza Express for lunch, which I couldn't eat, although I did gulp down two glasses of wine. I was crying all the time but I don't think my brother was embarrassed even though everyone in the restaurant kept looking at me. He was going straight back to London after lunch as he obviously couldn't handle it. And that was okay. 'This isn't about me,' I told myself again.

My two uncles came back to the hospital, as did my aunt, who had driven from Devon, and I marvelled at their kindness and love for their big sister. When Mum was awake, they talked about their childhood, their parents and they even made her laugh. As she drifted in and out of sleep, she asked me if Mark had visited.

She seemed to be getting further away and I kept holding her hand, determined to hold on to her for as long as possible. When I left the hospital late that night, I asked the nurses to ring me at any time, to which they agreed, but they said she would be fine. How did they know?

On Saturday morning, we were three days in and Mum seemed okay. She was still eating voraciously. Her pain had subsided too, thanks to the morphine, and she was surprisingly lucid.

'She's going to get better,' I told myself and I said the same to the palliative nurse when he visited.

He looked alarmed and began to tell me again how sorry he was, explaining again, just so I understood, that she would only last a couple more days. Well, he wasn't the oracle, was he? He might be well versed in end-of-life situations but he didn't know my mother, did he? Stupid man.

The scene around Mum's bed became more crowded during the day as my uncles came back with my aunt. Mum's best friend came too.

'What are you doing here?' Mum asked her. I explained that she was doing some shopping in Yeovil and had just popped in. She must not know that these were visits to say farewell.

When Michael arrived, I casually explained to her that I had run out of clothes and he was delivering them. She only had three mouthfuls of her dinner that night. I kissed her and said I would see her in the morning and knew that I would.

That evening, Michael took me out for dinner, made sure I ate and held me close so that I slept properly for the first time in days.

The next morning, cold and bright, we walked to the hospital. Mum wasn't in her ward. My heart dropped to my feet.

She had been moved to a single room at the end of a long, cold, dark corridor. How was I to know this was entirely usual as patients approached their end? It soon dawned on me, though. This was a dying room.

Mum didn't seem to be conscious at all.

My uncle came in early and the hotel chaplain arrived soon after. Michael, my uncle and I stood quietly, staring at the floor, as he read the King James version of *The Lord Is My Shepherd*:

He maketh me to lie down in green pastures;
He leadeth me beside the still waters

Before he finished, I left the room to cry on my own.

I returned to find Mum blearily awake but not making much sense and she soon went back to sleep. When Michael and my uncle left, after an important discussion about rugby, I sat alone with her for hours just stroking her hand, which occasionally twitched.

At one point in the afternoon, when it was almost dark through the rain-streaked window, she opened her eyes widely and, in terror, said, 'Bill? Mum?' I stood up and put my face about two inches from hers and stared into her eyes. 'It's alright,' I said, 'I'm here. Everything's fine, don't worry. Please don't worry.'

She closed her eyes again and I sat back down, still holding her hand but upset by her outburst. Were my father and grandmother waiting for her? Is that really happening?

Nurses came in every couple of hours to move her so that she didn't get bedsores and every time they moved her, Mum's breathing became distressed. By the fifth time, I asked if they would just stop.

'She's dying,' I said, although I wanted to shout it. 'What is the point of upsetting her? I know you are on a timetable but it really doesn't matter if she gets bedsores! Does it? Really?'

One of them mumbled something about having to follow the protocol but a glance at my pale and defeated face told her not to finish her sentence and they left. I straightened the blue cellular blanket (just like the ones you swaddle babies in) over my Mum's twisted body and pulled it to cover her swollen hands.

The day before, a nursing assistant had said that hearing was the last sense to go, so I had bought a book to read to Mum; it was about trees, which were her favourite things in the world.

I also had to alleviate, however briefly, the terrible stagnancy in the room and to feel that at least I was doing *something*.

I read aloud from *The Hidden Life of Trees* by Peter Wohlleben and it certainly started well. It was a beautifully written book that I hoped Mum was able to hear. So far, so good. But I hadn't got very far into the first chapter when I began to read about how each tree is valuable to the community 'and worth keeping around for as long as possible. And that is why even sick individuals are supported and nourished until they recover.

Next time, perhaps it will be the other way round and the supporting tree might be the one in need of assistance. When thick, silver-gray beeches behave like this, they remind me of a herd of elephants. Like the herd, they, too, look after their own, and they help their sick and weak back up on to their feet. They are even reluctant to abandon their de...' I choked on the word and stopped reading. I didn't want Mum to hear that.

I sat holding her hand for the next few hours, listening to her breathing, which sometimes rasped and quickened, and at other times quietened and slowed. A very few times, there would be the tiniest, contented sigh.

I decided then to play her some Elvis Presley to see if that might perk her up. After all, according to her, he was the 'most beautiful man who had ever lived'. I found it hard to disagree. And, again, Elvis began so well, if a little incongruously, with 'Hound Dog'. More in that vein followed and I even sang along to a few songs. There was no response from Mum but maybe she could still hear. When we got into Elvis's gospel songs, though, the mood began to change and singing along became too much of a struggle with 'Take My Hand Precious Lord', especially the part where he sang about the Lord taking him home.

I turned off the music then, preferring the sound of Mum's breathing. It was late and dark on Sunday, the room was cold, although Mum felt boiling hot, and I hadn't seen anyone apart from her since Michael and my uncle had left. The nurses now had nothing to do for my Mum since I had told them to stop moving her and there were no longer any feeding tubes to administer. Just the morphine. It seemed that everyone had already forgotten about her.

Sometimes she struggled for breath but then calmed down and sometimes there was a little noise in her throat. She was also making peculiar movements with her hands on the blankets, almost as though she was picking bits of fluff off them.

By 8pm, I had decided that I couldn't leave her alone all night in that room at the end of the corridor. I could have added, 'To see if she was all right' but of course she wasn't going to be all right, now was she?

I sat in the plastic chair, not sleeping but holding Mum's hand, and I listened to her untroubled breathing. It sounded as though she was having a deep sleep and

I told myself that, actually, she really was going to be better. Listen to her! So calm!

I said as much to the nurse, who came in at 6am, and she looked at me with profound pity but also as though I was stupid.

By then, my back was so sore that I could hardly walk but I reeked of hospital so went back to the hotel to change, leaving Mum for just an hour.

Her brothers and sister arrived but we all had little to say by that stage. You can hardly make plans for future family occasions, can you? My father's former carer came and pointed out that people often 'picked' at their bedclothes as they slipped away. I asked her too why Mum was making that funny noise in her throat and she told me that meant it wouldn't be long.

I didn't believe her for a second. I had been sitting with Mum pretty much continuously for five days and she seemed determined to hang on. Surely she was going to make a miraculous recovery? She's my Mum, after all! Come on, everyone! Keep the faith!

But as the hours crawled by, and she didn't show any signs of consciousness, all I could do was hold her hand. If she had to go, I would not let her go alone.

Mum's breathing became more laboured, especially once Dad's carer left. The air in the room had become thick and I could hardly see as my eyes were swollen from so much crying.

At about 7.15 that evening, I had to leave to get some air. I rang Michael from the pavement outside the hospital. He could hear the defeat in my voice through the sobs even when I said, 'She's still here. She doesn't want to go. I know she doesn't. This could go on for weeks.'

It was cold and damp so I only stayed outside for ten minutes, just enough to inhale some air that wasn't stale, before I dragged my body back up to Mum's room. Each step took an age, as though my feet didn't want to get the rest of my body back too quickly.

Somehow I reached the corridor and as I got closer, I could hear *Coronation Street*'s theme tune blaring from the room next to Mum's, and I thought how much she would have loved to watch it. I walked in quietly and slowly.

I realised then. She had waited for me to go out.

I knelt by her, put my forehead on the blanket and held her hand for a moment. Then I stood at the end of the bed to say *The Lord's Prayer*: it was the only thing I could think of.

And then I just kept saying, 'Oh Mummy, oh Mummy, I'm so sorry' over and over again.

Blearily, I told a nurse what had happened and said I didn't know what to do now.

'She died when I went outside,' I said.

'She was waiting for you to leave,' she said. 'But you've been with her the whole time. She knew that. You mustn't feel guilty *at all*.'

She was the nurse who said how privileged I had been to spend those last few days with my mother.

She was right.

* * *

For months afterwards, every night at 6pm – that time was sacrosanct even though it might be only one of the daily phone calls – I cried. A few times, alone at home, I doubled over in pain from the grief as though I had been punched in the stomach. Sometimes, I would go outside to scream.

Part of my reaction was the shock I felt at Mum's death. Michael opined that I was suffering from post-traumatic stress disorder. But part of it was also the shock at the strength of my feelings. I had simply been unprepared for the loss. My grief was somehow compounded, too, by the overwhelmingness of 'too much to do' because she had left me so much to sort out. Of course, there were all the usual formalities to complete, including the dreaded funeral, but there were mountains of rubbish to climb and everything had to be gone through with a fine toothcomb to make sure I didn't miss an important bit of paper – such as her will, for example (which was never found).

My brother, though, was less assiduous with Mum's belongings. He preferred to bundle everything and anything into black bin bags, which were then transported to the garage. That was soon full to the roof but he wanted the house empty as quickly as possible and arranged for a house clearance company to empty the garage so he could refill it. There would have been items in those bin bags that could have been vital and we did have a couple of tense shouting matches, but the very last thing on earth I wanted to do was to fall out with him. *This was not about me.*

However, after a couple more weeks of that, I often went to Mum and Dad's house on my own, to work painstakingly through everything. I approached it as though it was a crime scene: I had to look inside everything (including empty bubble bath bottles, of which there were over 50, and matchboxes totalling over 200) as well as underneath everything.

There were millions and millions of pieces of paper as Mum had kept every shopping list she had written for the past 40 years as well as the accompanying receipts. There were also pay and display parking tickets by the thousand. And thousands of times I looked heavenwards and asked, 'Why?'

Then there were the piles of opened letters that had been put back in their envelopes with the date received and her initials on them. *JMS 3.7.98* etc.

When I eventually burrowed my way to her wardrobe – which she hadn't been able to get to for the past eight years and which was full of clothes covered in thick dust and cobwebs – I discovered several hundred letters she had written and never sent: to her brothers, sisters, friends, me, my brother, my husband, to Sylvia and Robin. (Not a clue who they were.) The letters showed a side to her that I had only occasionally seen, or more likely hadn't bothered to pay much attention to: insightful, funny, political, intelligent, desperate. As I found and read more of the letters, I realised she was using them as therapy to try to deal with her anxieties, of which there were a multitude.

The letters began in early 1980 but really hit their peak in the mid-80s, shortly after she had a deep-vein thrombosis and was prescribed warfarin. In many of the letters she writes, 'I should never have been prescribed it in the first place. I had blurred vision for a considerable length of time, was supposed to rest, which I loathe, and am left with the peculiar electric shocks in my head. Since then, I have not taken anything medical whatsoever.'

This incident might explain her subsequent mistrust of doctors and pharmaceuticals.

There was a recurring theme to her letters that would often begin: 'You will not recognise this handwriting as it's that of one who writes letters that are never sent. Actually starts letters and, due to too many interruptions, abandons to the pile of "unfinished letters".'

In one, to my godmother, she wrote, 'I start letters with intentions of actually completing and sending them, but too many interruptions and distractions and I fail and my unfinished letters compete with the ironing mountains (almost ceiling height!).'

She frequently reminded her correspondents that 'I wouldn't be able to compete on Mastermind. I've started so I'll finish. I start but I don't finish, specialist subject gardening, general knowledge too slow and I hate nights out.'

One of my favourite letters, which I discovered in her wardrobe, was to a friend of my brother's.

'Welcome to my dirty house! Believe it or not I used to be very house proud. I still am but don't have the same energy. I'm trying to catch up after awful effects of taking Warfarin three years ago, why the hell people take other drugs defeats me... However, forgive this sloth, it's not like me at all, perhaps it's the change (!) And I wonder what I'll change into. I could do with some male hormones, had that treatment once and felt marvellous, didn't grow a beard but it's preferable to buying Tampax.'

Funny and ever so slightly mad. Yes, that was my mother.

And I found many letters to me, again never sent. In one, she wrote: 'We realise that you are under a great deal of pressure from everyone wanting your attention and energy because of your absolute dedication, utmost competence and loyalty towards the success of others in their achievements. We can understand all this and the sheer hard work involved and consequences of same in exhaustion of taking too much on, being unable to delegate as everyone wants you, is an accolade of your extreme efficiency and competence and professionalism but not at the detriment to your health and personal happiness.

Daddy and I have great admiration for your dedication and seriousness to your work, in the stamina that you have employed, the stamina in working under pressure but work also has to be fun and enjoyable, to take time off to laugh and have fun. Life is for living, it's here and now. Ian Botham's recently retired, I wouldn't say he was the most intelligent man in the universe but his philosophy, when he was asked, life – live it.'

Funnily enough, I think I did follow Both's advice and I dearly wish my mum had.

As well as the heaps of letters, there were also the countless notes such as one dated 3/12/14:

'7.44am look for Morrison's receipt for Mon 1/12.'

Later, she wrote,

'Found. Was in my pocket.

8.03am turned washing machine off.'

In a crossover example of notes and letters, on a letter written on A4 card to an unnamed recipient, on the back of the card she wrote,

'Transfer this note as my letter on back.'

So, yes, there were plenty of crazy notes but also letters with thoughts on AIDS, gardening, drugs, politics, poetry and more, all of which overwhelmed me, and I left each visit to my parents' house feeling exhausted as well as frustrated that I was making very little progress sorting through the mounds of paper. After each trip I returned home with boxes of belongings and bundles of paper, adding further to my sense of chaos as well as loss.

Mum may have used her hoarding to fill some unidentifiable space in her life but none of it was filling the gap I felt.

I was an orphaned adult and I found the grief almost impossible to bear.

Until, again, cricket came to my rescue.

* * *

Three weeks after Mum died and a week after her funeral, I received an e-mail from the World Cup Cricketeers, the organisation charged with finding volunteers (called Cricketeers) for the 2019 Cricket World Cup, which I had applied to earlier in the year:

'Congratulations! You're in! We are delighted to offer you a role as a Broadcast and Media Team member at the Hampshire Bowl, Southampton.'

I read to the bottom of the e-mail and cried. It had become my new hobby. The first person I wanted to call was my Mum. Mind you, months before when I had rung to tell her I was applying to be a Cricketeer, her response had been, 'Why do you want to do that? You do too much.'

I disagreed with her. My approach to life had always been to do as much as possible: apart from drugs (never done them); watching *Love Island* (never seen it); or eating oysters (just why?).

I answered Mum then by saying that cricket had given me so much and it was a great chance for me to give something back to the game. I didn't realise then that cricket would reciprocate a thousand times over.

And, as it turned out, I would need cricket more than ever because the universe, in its wisdom, was busying itself to lob another bombshell in my direction.

The Curveball

Two weeks before my first World Cup match, I met up with my brother for a visit to the theatre in Chichester. Nothing unusual in that. As siblings go, we were very close. We often went to plays in London together and each summer we would go to Test matches at Lord's and The Oval. On those occasions, we drank copiously, ate well, laughed liberally and talked non-stop. There was no reason to suppose that day in Chichester would be any different other than the thought that it might be even more celebratory than usual as his first book *Lunch With the Wild Frontiers: A History of Britpop and Excess in 13½ Chapters* was going to be published (and to great critical acclaim) at the end of the month. I felt even more proud of him than usual.

He ordered a good bottle of wine and said he had something to tell me. I looked up at him from the menu, still undecided whether to have fishcakes or steak and, if it was the fishcakes, with or without an egg. These things seemed important.

'Please don't let him be ill,' my internal voice said as my stomach did a peculiar flip.

The waiter appeared with the wine and sloshed some into my glass. He had barely finished pouring it before I took a large glug, which instantly went to my head.

'Cheers!' I clinked my brother's glass even though I had already drunk something. Wasn't that supposed to be bad luck?

There was no run-up. 'I'm transitioning.'

I was midway through another worthy slug from my glass, tried hard not to choke and concentrated on rearranging my face. What did he mean exactly?

And then, in a matter of seconds, the sense of loss I had been carrying around like a yoke for months seemed to get even heavier. It was the strangest feeling, as though my entire family had just been obliterated. Even odder, I had a vision of my parents looking at us, their two children, sitting together at the restaurant table and knew that I owed it to them to show compassion to their youngest child. *This isn't about me.*

We talked for the next two hours about how he had felt in the wrong body for most of, if not all, his life. None of this was made any easier by the fact that he had a wife and two young children and I felt sad and confused for them as well as for myself. And we talked about the process of him becoming female.

I said all the right things: how much I loved him and wanted him to be happy. All of that was true but inside I was reeling.

Thank God I could sit in the darkness of the theatre for a couple of hours and not have to talk. Nothing was making any sense.

We went backstage after the play to meet my brother's friend (they had been at school together), who was starring in the play, but nothing was mentioned and I didn't speak much. All I really wanted was to talk to my parents and for them to hug me.

My brother (I was going to take a while to call him my sister) had told me not to tell my husband but that wasn't going to happen, was it? Michael was taken aback and floundered even more by not knowing how to comfort me.

'I have lost my whole family in just over five years,' I wept. 'I don't even know how to begin to get over this.'

Michael tried to reassure me that I had not lost my family and that my brother was still the person I loved. He would just look different from the outside. I didn't sleep at all that night, going over and over scenes from our childhoods. My brother had always been androgynous, which had suited his career in the music business; he had often worn make-up and frequently at cricket matches or in restaurants would be greeted as 'Madam'. I never thought anything of it. That was just him.

Except, of course, it wasn't.

* * *

A few weeks after my mother's death, friends recommended a therapist to me as they were concerned that I was struggling to cope. They were right. I was lashing out at everyone, angry as hell with Michael and with the world even before my brother's announcement.

With the therapist's help – as well as watching replays of Test matches on a loop – I found a way forward in my new reality as an orphaned adult and a confused sibling. The therapist, 'J', was the first person I turned to after my brother told me of his transition.

There has been a scarcity in research on how gender transition affects an adult sibling and hours of Googling didn't return much. One paper I found suggested that the grief I was experiencing was comparable to that which siblings of disabled or terminally ill people felt, while the Family Research Council in Washington said, 'It's as though someone murders your loved one and then the murderer gets extremely angry if you won't let them take the victim's place in your family.' That was not at all helpful, as you might agree.

My inner turmoil only increased with the struggle I felt: I was no longer a daughter and I had lost my brother.

When someone, anyone, transitions the very nature of the process means it has to be all about them. How could it not be? No wonder that, with my mantra *this is not about me* as the soundtrack, I found myself more bereft and confused than ever because I was also trying to deny having any feelings about what my brother had embarked upon.

There was the additional stress of getting ready to sell my parents' house, which eventually resulted in four aborted transactions. My brother wanted the house sold quickly and I was continuing to deal with that pressure. Meanwhile, he regularly sent me photos of his new appearance seeking reassurance, which I hopefully provided.

'J' helped me to pilot a way through it all, guiding me with language I could use to convey reassurance to my sister. 'J' gave me permission to feel the shock and the sadness and said I was allowed to stay a bit in the past, encouraging me to look at family photographs even if they made me cry. I was allowed to feel my distress, however uncomfortable that made me. Photographs and memories would help me to say to myself that my brother had been my sibling forever and I had *always* thought my sibling was fantastic. All my friends knew how proud of him I was and that couldn't be taken away from me.

So from then on, I had a sister.

'J' also said I could say to my sister that I wasn't very good at dealing with the change right now and was still processing it, *but* I 'am really happy for you that you are doing this; it is just taking me some time to come up to speed'.

All the while, I could validate my sister's feelings – as well as my own – acknowledge her process and show her that the love was still there.

So now I have a sister who makes me laugh as much as she ever did and is as sparky as she ever was. We have in-depth conversations about cricket and will go to many more Test matches together to eat well, drink copiously and laugh liberally at absurd conversations around us. I am proud of her for many reasons, not least her courage. And I hope beyond anything that she is happy.

You see, some things never change.

* * *

It was clear that cricket was going to have to step up to the plate like never before. While I was still dealing with having a new sister as well as a new phase of life as an orphaned adult – and continuing to struggle with, as Michael called it, the longest menopause in history that was, by then, entering its 12th glorious year – there was a lot of pressure on the sport. But it had risen to the challenge before.

After all, cricket is not just a distraction from real life. It *is* real life. It is all there on the hallowed turf of Lord's, Trent Bridge, the Antigua Recreation Ground,

Newlands, the WACA, the Gaddafi Stadium, Eden Park, the Rajiv Gandhi Stadium, the Galle Stadium or whichever ground floats your boat. I throw down now the challenge for you to watch any cricket match and not find a metaphor for life contained within it.

My new chapter began at the far-from-glamorous Hampshire Bowl in Southampton, but I had to start somewhere. My first World Cup shift saw me leave home at sparrow's fart, dressed in a fetching blue and green polyester tracksuit that, unsurprisingly, didn't do much to alleviate hot flushes. The bright cricketeers' uniform was designed to make sure that we stood out from the crowd and with the extraordinarily high synthetic content, there was a sporting chance that we could spontaneously combust at any moment, which would surely meet that objective.

The volunteer 'army' for the Cricket World Cup was loosely modelled on the successful London Olympics template. E-mails leading up to the event emphasised how much fun we were all going to have, the plethora of exclamation marks in each message only adding to the frenzy, so by my first shift on 5 June for South Africa v India, I was well and truly hyped even if rather clammy.

Southampton had become a suburb of Mumbai for the early stages of the World Cup and there seemed to be five million India fans outside the ground, many of whom were without tickets and keen to show that they were ready to pay whatever it took to get in. Security was intense, however, and ticket-less supporters had no chance.

Luckily, I was going to have a bird's eye view from the superb press box but that was only after moving tables, chairs and beds (yes, beds) to make the journalists' lives more comfortable. The Hampshire Bowl has a hotel at one end of the ground and top-floor bedrooms and balconies had been commandeered by the World Cup to serve as extra facilities for the media. Security was also part of the cricketeers' remit and part of our job was to stop attempts by fans posing as members of the press from making forays into the area. We weren't always successful and at least one interloper was frogmarched out of the box.

I had been banking on watching every ball of the game but, after only a couple of hours, that seemed to be a forlorn hope as the tasks piled up. A brief moment of respite saw me standing alongside three male cricketeers in the press box and I snuck a glance at the field where every move, even if it was only a batted eyelash, by an India player was loudly applauded and cheered. At that moment, a journalist approached our little cricketeers cabal and asked me to get him a coffee. I stared at him for a moment while and looked at my male colleagues then back at the journalist. But no. In the words of Lionel Richie, it was me he was looking for. I thought, then, that things seemed not to have changed much in the world of cricket. Perhaps I should have refused his request but that would have been impolite and, heaven forbid I could ever be that, so I did get his precious coffee and didn't even spill it all over his invaluable notes when I plonked it in front of him. I made a point, though, of disappearing every time he stood up again just in case he had me marked as his drinks monitor. Who was more pathetic? Me? Or him?

India never seemed to be in trouble in the match even when their captain Virat Kohli was out for 18, an event that provoked the only moment of silence in the game, and they won by six wickets with two and a half overs to spare.

One of the main responsibilities of the media cricketers was staging the after-match press conferences, which included escorting the journalists from their desks on the other side of the ground to the pavilion, where the players would be interrogated. Trying to corral 50 or so unbiddable reporters through a sea of India supporters was a challenge made more precarious by the thousands of fans lying in wait, in this instance, for Virat Kohli, whose appearance always incited mass hysteria. I was a big fan of Virat and mentioned this to one of the journalists from India. He replied, looking at me as though I didn't know the first thing about the game, that Virat was one of the most arrogant men on the planet and none of his colleagues liked him. That's me told, then, but I did want to say, 'And you would know, sir.'

Having survived the hurly-burly of the walk to the press conference, we then enjoyed the added frisson of teeing up the reporters who wanted to ask the questions and handing them the microphone without appearing in camera shot. Not easy when you were wearing blue and green polyester, which sparked with static every time you moved. Cricketeers also risked an icy stare from one of the International Cricket Council officials if they got it wrong.

This match had been only the eighth game of the World Cup round robin games and already cricket fever was high in the country. Before that game, England had won the opener against New Zealand by 104 runs at The Oval; West Indies had thrashed Pakistan by seven wickets at Trent Bridge and Bangladesh had beaten South Africa by 21 runs. With their defeat by India at Southampton, South Africa looked in deep trouble already.

Glad to have my first match under my belt and with my Fitbit in meltdown, I drove home feeling pumped up from the game but with the by now familiar sense of something missing. That would be Dad again. He would have loved hearing every little detail and my heart ached that nobody would ever again fulfil the role of unconditional listener.

Still sad when I arrived home as well as sweaty, I poured a large glass of something cold and had a stern word with myself. Either I was going to surrender to my grief over my parents and my sister or I was going to concentrate on the World Cup. This time, unlike many other times in my life, cricket *had* to triumph. Sometimes distraction therapy is the only therapy that works. And it's free (depending on the price of your ticket).

It had been years since I had flown solo at a cricket match and it was only fitting that my next game as a spectator was at the Hampshire Bowl for England v West Indies. It felt self-indulgent to make lunch for one and pack it in a small cool bag for the day. No squashed pork products for me.

I took my seat in the middle of a stand rammed with England supporters and, not for the first time, sat on my hands for much of the match as the West Indies were thoroughly outplayed and lost by eight wickets. Joe Root scored a sublime century for England, who never looked in any trouble. I had my headphones on to listen to *Test Match Special* and didn't have to speak to a soul, just concentrate on every ball. Bliss. Well, apart from the result.

As well as a packed schedule of World Cup volunteering duties and my annual (well, when we are lucky enough to get tickets) trip to Glastonbury at the end of June with my youngest daughter, I took in Lord's for England v Australia with my cricket-mad friend Tim, sharing a monumental lunch and a great deal of wine. I left Tim briefly for a wander around the ground and ran into a lift just as its doors were shutting to find one of England's greatest-ever players standing there, as smartly dressed as he could be considering the excess weight he was carrying, which probably contributed to him sweating from every pore.

He smiled as his eyes travelled slowly up and down my body and I wondered if he recognised me since I had interviewed him many times in my past life. He stared lasciviously but I decided not to say anything. Instead, I looked him up and down, my eyes pausing at the straining fifth button on his moist shirt, and turned my back. I got out on the next floor, feeling unsettled and grubby. The same could be said of the England team, who were beaten by 64 runs.

Tim and I sighed as the last England wicket of Adil Rashid fell. We looked at each other and, in unison, said, 'Well, we're not going to win the World Cup if we play like *that*.'

How to Speak Cricket

Don't say: 'It's a bit cloudy. I was looking forward to some sun today.'

Do say: 'If we win the toss, we should definitely bowl in these conditions, don't you think? The cloud cover will make the ball swing more.'

Don't say: 'This stop-start rain is a real nuisance.'

Do say: 'I'm so excited about working out the Duckworth-Lewis method for this game.' Note: only say this at a one-day game as it doesn't apply to Test cricket.

[The Duckworth-Lewis (D/L) method is a mathematical formulation to calculate the target score for the team batting second in a one-day or T20 cricket match interrupted by the weather or another circumstance. Thus it attempts to predict what would have happened if the game had been able to reach its natural conclusion so that a result can always be achieved in a reduced-overs match. The method was devised by two English statisticians, Frank Duckworth and Tony Lewis. We are forever in their debt.]

Don't say: 'Why are all those fielders crouching so close together?'

Do say: 'Isn't it fantastic to see an old-fashioned slip cordon?'

Don't say: 'Bloody hell. He could have taken the batsman's head off with that ball.'

Do say: 'What a brilliant bouncer.'

Don't say: 'C'mon ref. Do you need glasses?'

Do say: 'Looked to me as though that was too high and missing the off stump.'

Don't say: 'What a shame he dropped that. Still, there will be other chances.'

Do say: 'Catches win matches. And that was a really bad miss.'

Don't say: 'Jimmy Anderson is looking a bit old, isn't he?'

Do say: 'I reckon Jimmy will still be bowling when he's 60. He's superhuman.'

Don't say: 'Joe Root looks about 12.'

Do say: 'Thank God for Rooty's experience.'

Don't say: 'Why is everyone shuffling from one foot to another now the score is on 111?'

Do: Stand up and shuffle from one foot to the other. [The score 111 is called Nelson and also its multiples – e.g. 222, which is a double Nelson – and is considered unlucky. Umpire David Shepherd famously lifted his legs to cheers from the crowd whenever the score was on 111.]

Don't say: 'What on earth are they singing over there?'

Do: Join in with

We are the army, the Barmy Army

Oh we are mental, and we are mad

We are the loyalest cricket supporters

That the world has ever had

Don't say: 'Mine's a half please.'

Do say: 'What's everyone having?'

Don't say: 'God, this is so boring.'

Do say: 'This is what I love about Test cricket. The ebb and flow, the light and shade, the quick scoring then the knuckling down. It's like a great game of chess, isn't it?'

Don't say: 'I think I'll head home after tea.'

Do say: 'Oh, I'm not going anywhere. I'll be here until the umpires call "stumps".'

Chapter Nine

Get In The Car.
The World Cup Final 2019

Poleaxed yet again by the grief that keeps on giving, I bent over and put my hands on my knees, trying to get my breath back after running from Lord's, and to compose myself. As I did, someone put the palm of their hand on the middle of my lower back to check if I was okay.

It felt so warm it might have been a hot water bottle.

'That's kind,' I thought and I stood up ready to thank them.

But there was no one there nor within 50 yards of me.

I knew who it was, though.

IT'S 6AM, Sunday, 14 July 2019. I am sitting at the kitchen table refreshing the ICC's World Cup ticket site for the thousandth time. I briefly leave my station to refresh my orange juice instead and stare wistfully at the collection of delicacies I had bought, just in case for a World Cup Final lunch in front of the television. I sigh loudly but really want to weep then return to my chair where, for the next two hours, I keep refreshing the website every 20 seconds. The amount I had initially decided I would pay is increasing by the minute but still nothing comes up. My shoulders are slumping lower and lower and my eyes are getting drier. Yet I still refuse to believe I am not going. Apart from my brief sojourn at Glastonbury, I have watched every ball of this World Cup, either in a ground or on TV. I *have* to be there.

I decide to do some visualisation (it worked for Brian Lara against Australia in 1999, after all) and picture myself sitting close to the boundary at Lord's. It feels right to me that this summer, of all summers, I should be at that match. It would help me draw a line under my grief and give me hope. Please God, or whoever is supposed to be in charge, hear my prayer.

By 9am, it is looking hopeless.

'Oh well, never mind,' said Michael.

'Oh well, never mind?!' I want to shout at him. But I don't.

He doesn't seem to realise at all how important it is and what it means to me. To be fair, though, how could he? And, anyway, is it fair of me to pile such a burden on to a mere cricket match? I mean, it's hardly the responsibility of the International Cricket Council to help my life to turn a corner, is it? Pathetic.

'We'll watch it together on TV,' he adds, and I know that what he really means is that he will get to enjoy, for this day only, the usually forbidden high fat foods he has spotted in the fridge.

I harrumph about a bit, in full victim mode, still in my threadbare dressing gown and sigh even more heavily.

My mobile rings; it is very loud. Michael gives me a cross look. This man more suited to life in the 19th century is not a fan of noise. (I have sometimes wondered whether he might be on the spectrum, but I will let you be the judge.)

My screen says 'Richard Mobile calling'.

Richard, one of our oldest friends, is wildly enthusiastic about everything, not just cricket, but his voice is uncharacteristically calm. Almost subdued, you might say, which is definitely odd for him.

'Get in the car. Now,' he commands, slowly and quietly. His words echoed those of my father, when he would drive round the village looking for me, years ago.

My words come out in one big fast slur *whatyouhaven'tnoreally?*

'I have. Get up here. Now. I am in the ground. Friend of mine can't go. I have got his ticket.'

I wondered what calamity had befallen his friend, looked down at my dressing gown and can you believe it? In that one second, I hesitate!

In that second, I try to work out how to break it to Michael that there will be no lunch with me during which I would have explained the complexities of the match, and that I am indeed going to leave him for the day. But, for that one second, there was only one question: was life going to get in the way of cricket again? Oh, come *on*!

Michael interjected, 'You obviously must go.'

I realise I have the best husband in the world.

In 20 minutes, I am on a train to Waterloo. It is packed, but not with people heading for a cricket match. No cool bags and no MCC egg-and-bacon ties to give them away.

I race through the underground, almost vault the turnstiles at St John's Wood before remembering that my dodgy hips wouldn't allow it and run to the Grace Gates, where Richard is yelling at me. There are thousands of India fans, some standing on other people's shoulders, all with their faces pressed to the railings. They eye me enviously as Richard, overseen by a steward, passes the ticket to me. *My* ticket. And if my name wasn't actually written on that, it was written in the stars.

I miss only the first few overs and I am there for that day, that match and those tears, a lot of which are mine and not just for an England victory.

* * *

Lord's was very unLord's-like that day. It was nothing like the 1983 World Cup Final but it was still a riot of colour, full of noise and irreverence: just the way I like it. I raced to my seat in the Tavern Stand, three rows from the boundary, just as I had visualised earlier that morning. Jonny Bairstow was patrolling the ropes and exchanging banter with the crowd. The excitement was already off the scale; it was as though the whole crowd had swallowed amphetamines. I wedged myself between two middle-aged, award-winning man-spreaders, who made it clear that they were not going to change their ingrained postures for a woman; after all, what on earth was *she* doing here? However nothing, not even two boorish poshos, was going to spoil my day and I just made myself small to fit on to the uncomfortable seat.

By the time I arrived, New Zealand were 24 without loss, seemingly waiting for me before losing their first wicket in the seventh over when Martin Guptill fell lbw to Chris Woakes, making the score 29/1.

Bairstow was busy on the boundary and, between overs, continued to engage with spectators. His relatives seemed to be in the stand too and various messages were passed to and fro. He put on a sensational fielding performance that day, highlighted by a full-length dive along the grass to stop a Kane Williamson boundary.

Meanwhile, all around me, snakes of beer gathered pace and length as they weaved their way from the bar, and the crowd got louder. The two are often connected.

I looked up to the Edrich Stand and pictured my father and I sitting there at the 1983 World Cup Final, smiled with the knowledge that he would have loved this and somehow knew that he was watching with me. And he would have been well into his sandwiches and sausage rolls by now.

The Kiwis continued to move along nicely and we had to wait until the 23rd over for the next wicket. But what a wicket! The mighty Williamson was given out after an England review, caught by Jos Buttler off Liam Plunkett for 30 and New Zealand were 103/2.

As one, the crowd let out a grateful sigh, which turned into loud cheers four overs later when Henry Nicholls was bowled by Plunkett for 55, making them 118/3. England fans were becoming more raucous, but I heard my father's voice telling me not to get too over-excited yet. 'Calm down, sweetheart. Early days.'

As usual, he was right and New Zealand knuckled down, closing their innings after 50 overs on 241/8, an interesting target, though I was sure they would have been happier with 270-plus on the board. But they had been helped along the way by England donating 30 extras, including 17 wides. I knew exactly what Dad would have had to say about that. 'You can't give away free runs.'

As the players walked off for lunch I sprinted to the Rose Garden, where Richard and Sandy were waiting with sandwiches and champagne. Champagne! I imagined Michael would be relishing his picnic at home without me but I knew I was the lucky one, so we'll drink to that. Cheers. Have one yourself.

Richard, Sandy and I agreed that New Zealand were in the driving seat and we all felt exceptionally nervous about how England would respond. And by the 24th over, when England captain Eoin Morgan was out for nine, making the score 86/4, it seemed our nerves were well founded.

But still.

We had reckoned without Ben Stokes. There are very occasionally matches in any sport when you might be lucky enough to witness a player so deeply in the 'zone' that it sends shivers down your spine and you hug yourself at your good fortune that you are there.

So it seemed that day at Lord's. Stokes reminded me of Bob Willis during the famous 1981 Headingley Ashes Test, a match in which the Warwickshire fast bowler hadn't taken a wicket in Australia's first innings but returned figures of 8-43 in the second after bowling in what seemed to be a Zen state. Watch it now and you will see he was in a trance.

Stokes was operating at a similar level. It's easy to say that with hindsight, of course, and for most of the afternoon all of us at Lord's could only watch through our fingers, unaware that Stokes was predestined for glory.

On the other side, too, New Zealand's captain Williamson was operating at a higher level, not just a Zen master but a Grand Master of chess. Some of his field placings were breathtakingly clever while his apparent calmness permeated through his team. Even better, he was such a decent man. After the match, he was named the player of the series but appeared to say, 'Who? Me?' before making his way to the rostrum, seeming to forget that he had scored 578 runs in the tournament as well as playing with outstanding sportsmanship.

In the post-match press conference, Williamson was asked by a journalist whether he thought 'everyone should be a gentleman like you?' He responded by saying, 'Everybody is allowed to be themselves. Everybody should be a bit different too.'

The difference that day was Stokes, scoring 84 not out in England's innings with two sixes and five fours, although our memories since may have kidded us that he hit boundaries off every ball.

The turning point came in England's final over when, needing 15 runs to win, Stokes was on strike with two wickets remaining. There was no score off the first two balls of the over, so England still needed 15 off four balls, and the crowd was mostly struggling to watch. I wanted to hide under my seat, although I am sure the man-spreaders would have had something to say about that.

Then Stokes heaved the third ball for six, leaving nine runs needed off the last three balls.

With the next ball, a full toss from Trent Boult, Stokes hit to midwicket, where Martin Guptill was fielding. Stokes and his batting partner Adil Rashid ran for two with Stokes pelting to the wicket for the second, throwing himself into a dive for the crease when the ball struck the tip of his bat and raced towards and over the boundary.

It was ridiculous. But, looking back on it now, of course, it seems predetermined. How else could you explain such a bizarre incident?

It is cricket convention that if the ball hits a batsman's bat in those situations, the batsmen shouldn't run and the England batsmen didn't. But once the ball passed the boundary, the umpire had to signal six runs (two runs plus four overthrows). Stokes held his hands up in apology and appeared to ask the umpires not to let it count while the crowd went ballistic.

Three runs were needed off two balls.

Stokes hit the next ball to long-on and Adil Rashid was run out at the bowler's end as he set off for a second run. But as he had completed one run, that left two needed from the last to win. Stokes hit that to long-on, reckoning that he could just about get two runs. New Zealand's Jimmy Neesham threw the ball and Mark Wood was stranded and out going for the second run. England had taken one, the scores were level, the match tied and we were facing a 'super over' for the first time in a World Cup Final.

By this stage, there was pandemonium and the crowd, never mind the players, were exhausted. Somehow, even then, every single spectator, including the members in the traditionally staid atmosphere of the pavilion, was on their feet singing 'Sweet Caroline'. Everyone belted out 'Good times never felt so good. So good! So good!' and while it was mostly out of tune, I had never heard anything like it at Lord's and probably never will again. I was trying to listen to Jonathan Agnew on my headphones and couldn't hear him over the noise, but I thought I heard him saying something about his elevated heart rate. His and 30,000 others in the ground.

Stokes, his eyes declaring that he was still in a Zen state even though his body looked in tatters, came out for the 'super over' with Jos Buttler and New Zealand's Trent Boult bowled again. England hit 15 off the over, setting New Zealand a difficult but do-able target.

My man-spreading 'friends' had left before the 'super over' – perhaps they thought England had lost – but the young chap who had moved into the seat next to me asked me who I thought should bowl England's over. Before I had time to reply 'Chris Woakes', word spread through the crowd that it would be Jofra Archer, a comparative newbie and not someone I would have bet on to take it. He had only taken one wicket in New Zealand's innings. As Archer's first ball was a wide, it seemed that my doubts were justified, although I joined in with the boos directed towards the umpire who had awarded the extra. 'That's not a wide, no way,' we all yelled in unison.

Neesham scored two then heaved a six. 'Game over,' we all thought and covered our eyes with our hands. They got two from the following ball, which was misfielded, then two more and New Zealand needed three runs off two balls. They got one from the fifth ball (which was actually the sixth due to Archer's wide), leaving them needing two from the last one to win the cup.

If they scored one run and the match was tied, England would win by virtue of having scored more boundaries in the match prior to the 'super over'. I know: cricket laws (they are not referred to as rules), eh?

The collective heart rate around Lord's reached critical point as Archer prepared to bowl the last ball and I would have taken Valium right then if it had been offered. The noise was deafening as Guptill hit the ball to midwicket, where Jason Roy scooped it up and threw it to wicketkeeper Jos Buttler, who took it cleanly and dived for the stumps with Guptill a yard out. England were world champions.

My phone buzzing with dozens of texts and my heart pounding, I ran to meet Richard and one of his twins, Joe, to celebrate as fireworks and champagne corks exploded around Lord's. Strangers were hugging each other and wherever I looked, everyone was in tears.

After the match, England's Chris Woakes said, 'Everything that happened today was destiny.' From the moment Richard rang me with news that I had got a ticket, to Ben Stokes's fluky six, I couldn't disagree.

I could have hung around and joined in the beer-sodden hugathon that looked as though it would continue for hours, but I was exhausted and wanted to get home. I ran out of the Grace Gates and started running towards Baker Street Tube station, thinking that would be less busy. After ten minutes, though, I stopped and wept. It wasn't just for the joy of witnessing one of the most dramatic games of cricket I would ever see but for the despair of not being able to share it with my father.

Poleaxed yet again by the grief that keeps on giving, as well as from running, I bent over and put my hands on my knees, trying to get my breath back and to compose myself. As I did, someone put the palm of their hand on the middle of my lower back to check that I was okay and it felt so warm that it could have been a hot water bottle.

'That's kind,' I thought and I stood up ready to thank them for their concern. The thing was there was no one there nor, in fact, anyone within 50 yards of me.

I knew who it was, though.

* * *

In the days that followed England's World Cup victory, nothing could dent the euphoria in my house or across the country. Not even, or especially, the naysayers who protested that England hadn't actually won at all because of mistakes made by the umpires. The controversy mostly, but not exclusively, centred on those overthrows in the final over of England's innings. Former umpire Simon Taufel, a five-times winner of ICC's umpire of the year award, said the on-field umpires at the final had made a 'clear mistake' by awarding England one run extra after the ball had deflected off Ben Stokes's diving bat when, in fact, the batsmen had not crossed for a second run. This contravened Law 19.8.

However, Kumar Dharmasena, the umpire who awarded the six runs while admitting he made an error, said he didn't have the benefit of TV replays that could have shown that the batsmen had not crossed. He did, though, consult the square-leg umpire, Marais Erasmus, at the time as well as the other match officials who, according to Dharmasena, confirmed that the batsmen completed the second run.

In an effort to close down the controversy, the ICC said it was against their policy to react on decisions taken by umpires and England's director of cricket, Ashley Giles, said, 'We are world champions, we have got the trophy and we intend to keep it.'

But the controversy didn't end there. Cricket followers all around the world criticised the ICC for the rule that decided the result on which team, in the event of a tied 'super over', scored the most boundaries in the match. The Twitter echo chamber was burning with tweeters slamming the governing body for such a ridiculous rule. But everyone knew the rule before the final, indeed before the tournament even started, which might have been the right time to question it and to do something about it. I had no truck with the complainers.

Needless to say, many international media outlets also poured scorn on England's win. *Gulf News* said the match 'sank into the abysmal depths of spectacular farce' and was 'devoid of moral legitimacy and sporting spirit'. You might think they didn't like England much. I just added them to the lengthy list of those who always hanker for 'anyone but England' to win at anything. I mean, I am guilty of that but only when England play the West Indies.

Meanwhile, I could continue to bask in the knowledge that I had been at Lord's to see my second team win the trophy as well as get used to the unexpected feeling that, while my grief had not miraculously and permanently disappeared, I might have put the worst behind me. For the first time in many months, I felt alive and hopeful. I had not done all this myself, of course; cricket had done that for me with numerous games that summer showing me that, if you just hang in there, you can emerge unvanquished.

And just to make sure I had really got the message, cricket had another card up its sleeve that summer, a card that again had Ben Stokes's face on it and one that I have replayed many times since.

A month after the World Cup's dramatic conclusion, England began a five-match Ashes Test series. The first Test at Edgbaston saw Australia post a resounding victory by 251 runs and the second was drawn at Lord's. There was a lot to play for – with many in the media saying that Joe Root was playing for his captaincy – as the players gathered at Headingley in Leeds on 22 August. England won the toss and elected to field, a decision that looked to be the right one as Australia were bowled out for 179, Marnus Labuschagne hitting 74 and Jofra Archer taking 6-45 runs. But, oh; wait. England's first innings saw them all out for 67. That's 67, with only Joe Denly reaching the dizzy heights of double figures with 12. Australia's Josh Hazlewood took 5-30 in 12.5 overs and it began to look as though we were in for an Ashes drubbing of the most humiliating kind, particularly when Australia scored 246 in their second innings, that man Labuschagne scoring 80.

England, then, were set 359 to win, which would have been their highest successful chase in Test history. Not a chance! As the third day came to a close, England had reached 156/3, captain Joe Root on 75 not out and Ben Stokes on two. Most England fans were preparing themselves for the worst while simultaneously praying for the captain to get a century.

The fourth day, a Sunday of a long Bank Holiday weekend, dawned hot and sunny, which in itself was uncanny, and it seemed the weather gods would not help the Test to be rained off and therefore assist England in their quest to avoid ignominy.

Meanwhile, I had a very long list of gardening jobs to do and merely hoped the match would last long enough for the radio commentary to keep me company while I laboured.

England began determinedly; the first four overs were maidens and Stokes was hit on his helmet, resulting in parts of it flying around his head and the wicket. It took 20 minutes until the first run of the day was scored by Root, the crowd indulging in ironic cheers.

Then disaster struck as Root was caught by the diving Warner off Lyon's bowling for 77.

Oh well. It was fun while it lasted.

But by lunch, England had reached 238/4 with Bairstow on 34 and Stokes on 32. There was a definite buzz around the ground as well as in my garden, where the radio was on full blast. I was getting text messages along the lines of, 'They can't. Can they?'

England's batsmen had been playing patiently, hitting bad balls around the ground and otherwise digging in. But we've been here before, haven't we? This is England we are talking about, after all; we all know it's not going to end well.

But still.

Sure enough, after lunch, Bairstow was caught by Labuschagne off Hazlewood for 36 and my heart took another lurch. I tried to find some positives and perhaps all was not lost as Jos Buttler was the next man in and he was not too shabby. But Stokes, on strike, called Buttler for a run and then sent him back. Too late: Buttler's stumps were hit by a brilliant diving throw from Travis Head at midwicket and he was out for one. England were 253/6. Urgh.

A few balls later, England reached 259/6; exactly 100 to win and the crowd roared again. There were more cheers as Stokes brought up his half-century. It seemed everyone in the crowd (apart from the few Aussies) was in love with the man.

But the next over saw Chris Woakes caught by Wade off Hazlewood for one, making the score 261/7, and it seemed as though that really was that. I wonder how many, wanting to spare themselves the sight of England in their death throes, picked up their cool bags and left the ground then?

Jofra Archer was the next batsman in and he had a very simple job. He just had to *stay* in. Archer, however, looked nervy to say the least but played some good defensive shots before hitting a couple of boundaries. And then he was out, caught by Head off Lyon's bowling for 15. And that really was that, wasn't it?

There was absolutely no way England could come back from 286/8. I mean, Stuart Broad was the next man in. A fellow Nottingham Forest supporter and Nottingham-born, I adore Stuart Broad but I feared his innings would not last long. I was carrying my radio around and the television was on in the kitchen, so that every time I walked past the window I could cast a glance at it. I couldn't bear to watch it, though.

Sure enough, Broad was out lbw second ball to Pattinson for nought. As was Broad's habit, he asked for a review. And, funnily enough, it was still out. England were 286 /9, still 72 runs behind, and then out came the bespectacled Jack Leach.

For non-cricket speakers, let's just say there is a reason he is a number 11 batsman. A month previously, he had scored 92 as a nightwatchman at Lord's in a one-off Test against Ireland but that innings was regarded by many as a glorious aberration. This was a crucial Ashes contest; don't let that Lord's innings turn your head.

But still.

Stokes whacked a six over long-off and got a single off the last ball of the over, so he kept the strike in the next, a pattern he managed to repeat several times.

But still.

With each ball, Stokes appeared to grow taller and wider; with each over, he assumed the size of a tithe barn door that just kept getting bigger. A cricket ball became the size of a marble next to him. He was a Colossus. And Leach, at the other end, took the role of the anti-hero whippersnapper.

Stokes hit another six off Lyon over long-off and four balls later did it again with a six from a breathtaking reverse slog sweep – or some such shot you may not find in a coaching manual – into the stands. By the end of that over, England were 310/9 and needed less than 50 to win. Needless to say, the crowd was going crazy and I was under the garden table with the radio. I daren't go and actually watch as I would definitely jinx it. That's something to do with quantum physics, apparently.

And let's just calm down, anyway. Australia needed only one wicket to win and in the next over Leach had to face Pattinson. Did anyone apart from Leach and his family actually watch those balls? Between each ball he faced, Leach took off his steamed-up glasses and cleaned them. Joe Root said after the match, 'The fact that he had the ability to take his glasses off and clean them between balls shows he was in the moment.'

And Leach survived.

But still.

There was another six from Stokes in the next over, then two more runs and England needed less than 40. Stokes and Leach crossed for a single so that Stokes could stay on strike.

But still.

Hazlewood came on to bowl, replacing Pattinson, and Stokes hit his first ball for four to bring up his century, which he didn't seem remotely interested in celebrating. That milestone was not the point of his innings. What focus that man has. He hit the second ball for six and the third for another, bringing up the 50 partnership after just 6.1 overs between him and Leach, who was *still* on nought. Stokes nonchalantly poked the penultimate ball of the next over for one and Leach just had to see out the last ball of the over.

He survived. We all survived. Deep breaths now.

England were 341/9. The target of 359 still seemed a long way off.

There was only one run from the next over and then Stokes was dropped by Marcus Harris off Cummins's bowling with the first ball of the next over, before hitting successive fours. With the fourth ball of the over, Stokes hit one to leave Leach facing two. Stokes squatted on his haunches not able to watch and he was not the only one. The first ball to Leach went flying over his head as he ducked. With the last ball of the over, Cummins appealed for lbw against Leach, which was given not out. Cummins reviewed. It was still not out. Australia had used up all their reviews, a fact that soon became very relevant.

Leach survived, England were 351/9, eight runs still needed, and Stokes was on strike on 125.

But still.

Stokes hit a six off the third ball of the next over and England needed two to win. Two balls later, there was a missed run-out when Leach began to sprint down the wicket, was miles out of his crease, but Lyon dropped the ball. There was no run-out in this script.

With the next delivery, Lyon hit Stokes on the pad but umpire Joel Wilson ruled him not out. Australia had no reviews left but the replays clearly show that Stokes should have been given out.

But still.

England were 357 for nine and Leach was facing Cummins, who bowled a bouncer that whizzed over Leach's head. No run. The next ball was delivered at 85mph to Leach, who pushed it away. No run. Leach prodded the next ball past short leg and they darted for a run, Leach's first, or as former England captain Michael Vaughan called it, 'the greatest one of all time', and the scores were level.

More importantly, and hallelujah, Stokes was on strike.

The noise in my garden at that moment might have been louder than at Headingley. The radio was full blast and I had gone inside to turn up the sound on the television in the kitchen so that I could almost imagine being there, despite the fact that I still could not watch. I curled up on the ground outside.

Stokes prepared to face Cummins's next ball, struck it handsomely through the covers for four and threw his head back, his arms wide, and let out a bellowing, leonine roar. He was the king of the jungle.

* * *

Stokes had cemented his place in the pantheon of national heroes but life had thrown several curveballs at him, as it does to us all. A year before his heroics at the World Cup and at Headingley, he (and batsman Alex Hales) had been cleared of affray at Bristol Crown Court after an incident in September 2017 following a one-day international between England and the West Indies. Stokes was stripped of the England vice-captaincy, stood down from the Ashes tour and later fined for bringing the game into disrepute. Many commentators talked of Stokes's redemption but the man himself said redemption was 'not a word I'll ever use'. Instead, he laid his success that summer firmly at the door of hard work, demonstrating just what is required to not allow life to get in the way of cricket. Sure, the sport can be your teacher but only if you put the hours in.

But as much as I have found solace in cricket, there are many players who, tragically, have suffered from depression. This is not merely a modern curse. David Frith wrote a study of cricket suicides, *By His Own Hand,* first published in 1990, which documented heartbreaking stories going back to the 1880s. And in 2001, Frith wrote in *Silence of the Heart* that English cricketers were almost twice as likely to die by suicide compared to the average English male. Mike Brearley, however, said he was not sure that cricket was to blame. 'It is not cricket which causes suicide: people kill themselves for reasons that are internal to themselves and their histories.'[19]

Almost two years after his triumphant performance at Headingley, Stokes announced that he would be taking an indefinite break from cricket to recover from a finger injury and to prioritise his mental wellbeing. Stokes's father had died just a few months earlier and I could understand how bereavement and grief could affect even the strongest.

More than a decade before Stokes's break, in February 2006, Somerset and England player Marcus Trescothick suddenly left England's tour of India and returned home for personal reasons. It transpired that Trescothick had been suffering from depression and in his remarkable, award-winning autobiography *Coming Back to Me*,[20] he revealed that he had been affected by anxiety attacks since he was a young boy.

He has spoken extensively about the mix of anxiety and depression that has plagued him. 'It's a constant feeling of being on edge, and uncomfortableness, and generally unhappy – there is no hiding place from it,' said Trescothick,[21] adding that 'it's a lack of sleep, constant tremors and a shaking feeling'.

While Trescothick continued to play domestic cricket, which meant he was always able to get home to

---

19 *The Guardian*, 22 April 2001.

20 *Coming Back to Me*, Marcus Trescothick 2009

21 *Huffington Post*, Head in the Game series, 7 February 2020.

his family, international tours were off his agenda. But in March 2021, Trescothick was appointed England batting coach and announced that he was continuing to make good progress in dealing with his travel-related anxiety.

Stokes, Trescothick and others who play my beloved sport have taught me that if you fall down, you can get back up again. And each time you get up, your legs get stronger.

My Fantasy XI

1. Gordon Greenidge (Barbados)
2. Desmond Haynes (Barbados)
3. Viv Richards (Antigua)
4. Larry Gomes (Trinidad and Tobago)
5. Gus Logie (Trinidad and Tobago)
6. Clive Lloyd (Guyana) (captain)
7. Jeff Dujon (Jamaica) (wicketkeeper)
8. Malcolm Marshall (Barbados)
9. Andy Roberts (Antigua)
10. Michael Holding (Jamaica)
11. Joel Garner (Barbados)

Cricket aficionados will have spotted that while this is indeed a dream of a team, this XI was an actual side. Can you believe it? In the 1982/83 season, this West Indies team beat India by ten wickets in Barbados in the fourth Test of the series between the two sides.

In the home side's first innings, Greenidge made 57, Haynes 92, Richards 80, Logie 130 and Lloyd 50. That is how to set up an innings right there. Andy Roberts took eight wickets in the match. The pace quartet of Marshall, Roberts, Holding and Garner only played in six Test matches together. The West Indies, in fact, fielded 37 different pace quartets between 1979 and 1994; seven played five or more Tests together. The comparative rarity of the Marshall/Roberts/Holding/Garner combo makes my 'fantasy' team even more exceptional. Malcolm Marshall, who surely *has* to be in everyone's fantasy XI, played 14 Tests with Curtly Ambrose, Courtney Walsh and Patrick Patterson, and that quartet only lost three out of the 14 Tests they played.

The fourth Test in Barbados brought forth complaints of intimidation from the Indian tour manager and also from the captain Mohinder Amarnath, who was the only India batsman to make a mark in the match, scoring 91 in the first innings and 80 in the second. But Amarnath was part of the international batting elite who knew that the West Indies pace quartet was, in fact, the ultimate test. The late West Indies cricket commentator, the great Tony Cozier, once told me, 'The class batsmen had no problems.'

My dream team is captained by Clive Lloyd, the mastermind of the four-pronged pace attack, and an inspirational leader of his men. After the nightmare 5-1 defeat in the 1975/76 series between Australia and the West Indies, Lloyd pulled his team from the depths of despair, developed his analytical approach and encouraged freedom of expression on and off the field. John Arlott said, 'Lloyd's captaincy has been marked by dignity; firm, unfussy discipline; and cool, realistic strategy.'

Lloyd captained West Indies from 1974 to 1985 and, apart from that series rout in Australia, his side didn't lose a Test series under his leadership.

As Fantasy XIs go, this one seems hard to beat and great to watch.

Chapter Ten

The Corridor of Uncertainty[22]

'Does any game have as much resonance as a Test match or as much lyricism? We become totally absorbed and swept along as the story unfolds, in all the moments of despair as well as exhilaration,' I explained to my tutee, the Cricket Guinea Pig.

'Ah, but that might mean that cricket is just a distraction from real life, not a metaphor for life,' he argued.

'Well *of course* it's a bloody distraction too! And, God knows, we need that sometimes,' I countered.

A COUPLE of weeks before my mother's first birthday, and apparently unbeknown to her, England's cricketers were embarking on the first day of the fifth Test against South Africa in Durban.

---

22 In cricket terms, the corridor of uncertainty is a small area of the wicket just outside the batsman's off stump where the bowler can aim to deliver a ball to confuse the batsman as to whether he should play forward, back, or leave it alone. It is also a metaphor for life. Well, it has been for mine.

The match began on 3 March 1939 and finished on 14 March, the longest and last of the timeless Tests (there had been 99 in total) and much beloved of cricket statisticians. The Test featured two Sunday rest days plus a day lost to rain and only finished on the tenth day as England's cricketers had to travel to Cape Town to catch the boat home. England had begun the last day on 496/3 needing 200 runs to win and, as the rain came down again, they were 654/5 and in reasonable sight of victory. There was a brief discussion about extending the match into another day but, miffed as they were, England's players had to leave and the match, after 5,463 balls bowled, was declared a draw. That fact alone might baffle non-cricket speakers.

There were many notable feats in the protracted match, one of them being the England Test debut of 28-year-old Reg Perks, a fast-medium bowler from Worcestershire who took five wickets for 100 runs in the first innings. He played his second Test in August the same year against the West Indies at The Oval, where he took 6-156 in 30.5 overs. Then came the Second World War which, according to John Arlott, made Perks 'one of the most unlucky [cricketers] in playing few Tests'. By the time cricket resumed in 1946, Perks had missed his prime years and although he played for Worcestershire until 1955 (and took more than 2,000 wickets for the county), he never troubled the Test selectors again.

I am quite sure that my mother was unconcerned by Perks's despair at missing more than six cricket-playing years due to the war. She would have been paying far more attention to my Auntie Eunice, who would frequently tell the terrified child, 'You don't need to worry your little head about that wicked Hitler man.' I wish Auntie Eunice could have offered the same reassurance to Peter O'Toole who, in his childhood, was similarly terrified and later wrote that he came to believe 'Hitler was a tyrant of insane bestiality who would, if let, torture and kill us all.'[23] Perhaps Eunice could have comforted Reg Perks too and told him not to worry.

However, Eunice, renowned for her maxims, might only have added to his despondency with one of my favourites of hers, which was liberally and frequently delivered. 'Tis later than you think,' she would say in her rich, rolling Somerset dialect. Her warning, even with a twinkle in her eye as she said it, was irrefutable and I thought of it often as my mother lay dying and as the timeless Test of grief reared its head.

* * *

I should not have been surprised that death got in the way of cricket; after all, life had got in the way too. But I was unprepared for the reality that grief was such hard work. It might be a bit bleak to live our lives preparing

---

23 Peter O'Toole, *Loitering With Intent*, 1992.

for the inevitable but having now experienced it twice, the knowledge that I may have to confront it again is perhaps always somewhere in my subconscious. Maybe, next time, I will know what to do even if I will not want to do it.

I am hardly a world expert on grief but I do know now that none of us can get through it alone, although I did try (and failed, naturally). Whether it is a concerned GP prescribing Valium ('yes, please, only for a couple of weeks, definitely no more, thank you'), a friend bringing comfort food that *must* include plenty of potatoes in whatever form, your partner walking through the door with your favourite bottle of wine or your children offering unconditional hugs, it seems to be a good idea to accept all the help that's offered. A good therapist too is literally a life-saver. Oh, and three million cheers for HRT.

I unexpectedly found comfort in comedy, the more absurd the better. A few days after my father's rain-sodden funeral, my sister and I saw *Eat, Pray, Laugh!*, the farewell show of Barry Humphries (with Sir Les Patterson, Sandy Stone and Dame Edna Everage, of course) in London, which was completely daft. Sometimes daft is all the distraction we need.

Music is obviously consoling, although when you are in the emotionally incontinent phase of grief it is best to choose carefully. It is probably better to turn off REM's 'Everybody Hurts', for example. I started listening to a lot of rap as well as electronic music and the night before Dad's funeral, as I was writing his eulogy, I played Chase and Status's 'I Feel So Alive' at a very high volume because, perversely, I felt just that.

Weird.

But in my case, and luckily for me, I also had the West Indies, the team that keeps on giving (to me, at least), in my corner to help me deal with my bereavement.

Even they, however, hadn't been able to offer me comfort in the early stages after Mum died. I didn't have the energy to pay much attention but was vaguely appreciative of the West Indies' 2-1 series victory over England in the Caribbean at the beginning of 2019. They won the first two Tests by 381 runs and by ten wickets respectively, so not inconsequential. England won the last Test by 232 runs but it was still the West Indies' first series win against England since 2009.

While Michael thought that I was probably suffering from some degree of post-traumatic stress disorder brought on by the suddenness of my mother's demise, I thought it just as likely that I was suffering from shock at my stupidity at not having been remotely mentally prepared for it. And, in our privileged Western society, we are less exposed to death and its consequences than our ancestors.

I started to veer between extremes of thinking that everyone I knew was about to die but a second later would absolutely know that we were all going to live forever. (I adopted a similar mindset at the beginning of Covid.) Needless to say, with that kind of thought pattern I was exhausted but wasn't sleeping much, although there was nothing unusual there. I could get by quite easily without sleep. I wasn't paying much attention to anyone else in the family and that was new.

I had taken seriously my responsibilities (and privileges) as a daughter and therefore it probably comes as no surprise to learn that I had applied the same dedication to my endeavours as a mother. I had been ill-equipped and under-prepared, though, for the limitless variety and quantity of problems that being both a daughter and a mother present.

Perhaps I would have found it easier, and reaped greater monetary rewards, to have run a multi-national company or two than to deal simultaneously with the heart-rending issues presented by children with eating disorders/abusive partners/drug problems and similarly agonising difficulties presented by parents with dementia/hoarding disorder/copious health issues/ financial hardship. There wasn't a league table for these difficulties: the 24/7 problems often ran concurrently and the opportunity to put my chair on my desk on a Friday afternoon and head for a Club Tropicana weekend, where all the drinks were free, didn't present itself. The chief of a multi-national company might have delegated some of his workload and he (it is still likely to be a 'he') would certainly make sure that he wouldn't miss a cricket match for which he had a ticket. Even if he hadn't paid for it himself.

I don't begrudge him a pound or the ticket. If you take mothering seriously, you sign up not for the richer rewards that you might sometimes receive (always remembering that you don't give to get).

As my mother lay dying (such an active expression for a passive, unbidden act), it dawned on me that the meaning of life was pretty simple. I experienced, among the conveyor belt of sadness and the motorway pile-up of regrets, a flash of absolute clarity. 'This is what life means,' I thought. 'This is what it is all about.'

It was so straightforward. The message, whether it had been delivered from a divine source or not, was transparent: life was only about love. Nothing else. If we are lucky, it is all we come into the world with, all we travel with and all that we leave with. The realisation didn't help my heartbreak or the feeling of isolation but, at least for the first few days after Mum's death, I felt reassured that, in my (our) endless quest for life's meaning, I had finally found it. If only it was that easy.

Needless to say, it didn't take long for the micro-stresses of mundane everyday life to return and often the feeling of clarity I had experienced would dissipate in as quick a flash as it had arrived. But I still try every day, even now, to live in remembrance of that clarity and the axiom that life is about love.

What was more tricky was the actual process of grieving. There was no prescribed timeline to refer to, no advent calendar to count down the days to the last window and a breezy trumpet fanfare of 'Ta-da! It's over! Now you can move on!'

For several weeks after my mother's death, I turned inward. I didn't answer my phone, I ignored messages and the only trips I made were to my parents' freezing, cheerless, cluttered, rodent-infested house and to supermarkets. Supermarkets were, more than usual, a special form of hell. Choosing food to buy that I wasn't interested in cooking or eating and overhearing couples debate whether they should buy a pack of four toilet rolls or a pack of nine ('How much does that work out per roll?') offended me with their banality. It didn't help that I was crying all the time and sometimes breaking into werewolf howls, which must have been embarrassing for everyone, apart from me because that was my new normal. 'Nothing to see here!' my tear-stained face would say.

I abstained from social media for months, knowing I couldn't cope with seeing any vapid memes or, worse, vitriol (that would be Twitter). I also felt I couldn't talk to anyone about how I was feeling because no one seemed to understand, not even Michael, who had already lost both his parents but carried on living and working perfectly normally. I couldn't work out how anyone carried on at all after their parents, spouse, child, friend, or anyone close to them, had died. What on earth was the point? Nor could I speak to my sister about it as she was dealing with her own process on many levels.

It is obvious now but I didn't realise it at the time: I was going through all the conventional stages of grief – although as Eric Morecambe might have said, 'not necessarily in the right order'.[24]

Denial was my first port of call and I dreamed every night that my mother was getting better in hospital. Some nights she would appear yelling at me for taking all her clothes away because, now that she was ready to go home, she had nothing to wear. Then when I did get her home, she would be standing up, completely healthy, in her spotless house with my father in the pristine kitchen, making a cup of tea. I would wake up in a cold sweat, which certainly felt different to the hot sweats that, unsurprisingly, had become turbo-charged.

Then I began to blame myself for my mother's death. Surely I should have fought harder for the hospital to treat her for the multifarious health problems she had? They could have saved her. I went over and over the time she was in hospital, analysing every word from the nurses, specialists and the palliative care nurse.

---

24 In the *Morecambe and Wise* 1971 Christmas special, the pianist and composer Andre Previn told Eric Morecambe that he was playing 'all the wrong notes' on the piano. Morecambe grabbed Previn (or 'Preview' as he called him) by the lapels and growled, 'I'm playing all the right notes, but not necessarily in the right order.'

For several days I believed that the hospital had, in fact, killed her. That much was obvious. Her fear of being murdered by morphine had been realised, I thought, and I started to make notes on how I would begin legal action. Through all of this, Michael endeavoured to calm me down, patiently explaining that my mother had been extremely ill and there was nothing anyone could have done.

I stayed in the guilt phase for a few weeks. Not content with blaming myself for her death, I relived scenes in my head, remembering all the times during my life when I had been unkind to her, especially when I was a vile teenager, as well as the shameful occasions I had been impatient, particularly in her last few years. Again, Michael reminded me of how much I had done for both my parents and the thousands of journeys I had made. I didn't listen, though: I had a catalogue of guilt to work through, thank you very much. One of the ways I dealt with that was to take great care of the myriad belongings, even the rubbish, left in the house. At least I could treat that with respect and patience. And I took a lot home with me, which was not really the point of sorting things out. In fact, all I was doing was moving rubbish at speed, like a mobile skip, along the A303.

I didn't know then that it was time to move into the next phase and to get angry. Which I did with great aplomb with myself and everyone else, including my mother. Why hadn't she looked after herself? Why had she declined medical interventions that would have made her better? Why had she kept every single sodding bit of paper for 40 years? Why hadn't she let me help? Why had she continued to live in a house that she could no longer cope with?

Why hadn't my sister done more to help me? Why hadn't Michael ever cooked us a meal when I returned exhausted from my parents' house? Why was he being so effing useless about literally everything? Why, in God's name, didn't *anybody* understand what I was going through?

My pinball machine brain pinged unanswerable questions all day and all night.

For the first time in my life, I felt angry with my father too, and then I felt guilty for feeling that. Why had he let her get away with it? Why didn't he stand up to her? Why didn't he insist on them moving house to be closer to me? Why did he let her walk all over him?

And how *could* Geoff bloody Boycott have run out Derek Randall at Trent Bridge in 1977?

And why was I crying so much? I just want to ring my Mum.

I was pretty sure I was going mad. I was snatching a few hours of sleep a night so was knackered the whole time. I didn't want to see anybody, talk to anyone and I didn't want to eat. I could manage red wine as that didn't need any cooking (my favourite wine? Screwtop) and it seemed to numb the pain to give me some temporary respite from thinking about 'things', but even I realised that it wasn't a long-term solution. My moods were violent one minute and utterly benign the next and Michael had no idea which version of me would be in the house.

I would normally spend a lot of time talking to Lucy and Sisi on the phone or on WhatsApp every day, but I couldn't even concentrate on that. So then I could beat myself up for being a terrible mother too.

From a distance, it is so easy to see what was going on. It was 'just' grief, with an unhealthy dash of depression. I had been acquainted with depression so many times in my life that at least I could recognise that. Alarmed by my behaviour in the midst of my angry phase, Richard and Sandy had recommended a therapist and, at the same time, I started to devour books on grief. The most helpful by far was *The Orphaned Adult* by Alexander Levy and I realised that everything I was feeling was completely normal and I didn't need to think about killing myself. There was a point to my life. Slowly, I started to be kinder to myself and to the ones closest to me.

I realised that my grief was not going to disappear and that it might, indeed, be a lifelong partner, but it didn't have to dominate me. Nor did it mean I would wallow in it. Rabbi Earl A. Grollman wrote, 'Grief is love not wanting to let go'. And, honestly, who would really want to let go of love?

When there is a sudden, seemingly inexplicable, rush of tears and a piercing pain in my chest as I am doing something as innocuous as making gravy, I have to accept it because it reminds me of my mother and all the times I watched her making it. One morning, more than a year after her death, I put on Mum's gardening gloves, which I kept by the back door, and howled and howled. That was love, too.

One of the reasons I found it difficult to talk to some people about my bereavement was because, sometimes, I felt I had been entered unwittingly into a Grief Olympics. Someone might ask me how I was and, as I began to reply, they would interrupt me to tell me how they either hadn't felt anything at all when a loved one had died or conversely that they had fallen apart. It was often the former, which would then leave me feeling inadequate for not 'getting over it'. One person told me that their life really began the day their mother died. Perhaps they had been trying to offer comfort but it really didn't work for me.

Having thought that the experience of grief was universal, I began to appreciate that a bereavement was entirely personal and 'like a fingerprint, each person's grief was unique'[25]. It doesn't matter whether it lasts a minute, a month or a lifetime. The only thing I could do was try to get through it and, if I couldn't ever get

---

25 *The Orphaned Adult* by Alexander Levy, Da Capo Press, 2000.

all the way through it, I would have to learn to accept it. And I have. I carry my parents with me every day in the words I speak, the actions I take and the look, more often than I ever expect, in the mirror of both my parents staring back at me. I hadn't lost them at all, except in the physical sense.

There was an unexpected bonus from grief, which only dawned on me fairly late in the process. Grief made me – and virtually everyone I know who has been through it too – a kinder person and one with more humility. The death of a loved one stops you in your tracks and makes you confront the essence of what it is to be human. The philosopher Plato was spot on when he said,

'Be kind, for everyone you meet is facing a harder battle.'

After the death of my last parent, that became my go-to daily mantra.

The questions I had asked myself when I was newly bereaved – 'Who was I and what was I supposed to do?' – had been answered. I was an orphaned adult daughter and my life had had to take on new meaning and purpose. Perhaps we only really grow up when our parents die.

* * *

I had been back to the beginning, not realising at first that 'where there is ruin, there is hope for treasure'[26] and, among the detritus that I painfully waded through in my parents' home, I had been lucky enough to find it.

'So that is who I was,' I thought as I unearthed my long-hidden cricket mementoes. With each photo of Viv Richards, every yellowing press cutting from Test match reports and old match programmes, my head filled and my heart softened with the memories of how cricket had ignited a passion in me and had sustained me through so much of my life. I knew I had to get back to that girl who was somewhere inside me still and to put my faith in the game again.

Around that time, I tried to explain to a non-cricket speaker how Test cricket, in particular, can provide a metaphor for life, but he looked at me as though I was a few balls short of an over. I refused to give up and, determined to persuade him, began to describe how cricket can be our guide.

'First, a coin is tossed. Heads or tails?' I asked him.

'Heads,' he replied.

'Bad luck. It's tails. The winner of the toss gets to choose whether to bat or bowl first.'

The CGP (cricket guinea pig) interrupted. 'So you're saying that because of some arbitrary coin toss, my team's performance is already likely to be affected

---

26 Rumi.

through something out of my control and down to luck?'

'Uh huh. That's right – but that's life, isn't it? It's called Test cricket for a reason; it is the ultimate test of physical ability, mental stamina and resilience in the face of setbacks. And it takes five days, weather permitting.'

'Five days?' The CGP was incredulous.

I wondered how on earth anyone could *not* know that a Test match was five days long. Wait until I tell him about the longest timeless Test!

'Yes, and the matches are part of, traditionally, a series of five Tests over a couple of months or so,' I explained.

'*Months?*'

It was my turn to roll my eyes.

'And how long are the days?' he asked.

'Play starts at 11am and finishes around 6pm'.

'*What?*'

'You have lunch and tea during that time, of course. And drinks breaks.'

'*God!*'

'Maybe it's best if I give you an example of a great Test match and then you might understand better. I don't know how I can choose just one, though.'

CGP was looking bored now. 'Well, just try. If you must,' he muttered.

I thought about the Headingley Test in the 1981 England v Australia Test series, the formative experience for so many of my generation, but ruled that out on the grounds that everyone knew about it, or would at least have heard about Ian Botham's role in it, even CGP. I didn't ask him, though, as I would have been thoroughly despondent if he hadn't. I could also have told him about the Test, again against Australia and again at Headingley, in 2019 when Ben Stokes played one of the greatest innings of all time to see England to victory. Too recent, I thought. And, of course, I could have chosen any Test innings from Viv Richards. But that would have been too obvious. To me, at any rate.

Instead, I chose the third Test between the West Indies and Australia in Barbados in 1999, a match I have probably watched a hundred times or more and one I wish I had been present at.

CGP didn't look remotely enthusiastic when I mentioned it and I knew I had a difficult task on my hands to try to explain why this match encapsulated so much of what I love about Test cricket.

'I'll have to put it into context first. West Indies had been in South Africa from November 1998 until February 1999 and had a shocking series. They lost all five Tests,' I began.

'It was their first Test tour of South Africa and most of the players were in dispute with the West Indies Cricket Board over pay and security to the extent that they went on strike. Nelson Mandela even wrote to

West Indies captain Brian Lara to try to salvage the situation. Eventually, the tour went ahead but the team was an utter shambles and became the first West Indies side to lose every match of a five-Test series.'

'Golly,' said CGP, stifling a yawn. 'That all sounds a bit dramatic.'

'Well, yes, it was. After that disaster, the last team you would want to play against would be Australia, who began their tour to the West Indies in late February 1999. The Aussies had some great players in their side – Ricky Ponting, Steve Waugh, Glenn McGrath, Jason Gillespie, Shane Warne.'

'Oh, I've heard of him,' CGP interrupted. 'Didn't he go out with Liz Hurley?'

I sighed. 'Indeed. But the point is that West Indies were pretty down and Australia had, as seems to be the case most of the time, their tails up. Especially as they had just beaten England 3-1 in the Ashes.'

'I've heard of that too.'

'Well, that's something, I suppose,' I said. 'Lara had been appointed captain for just the first two Tests in the four-match series because the board were, to put it politely, *disappointed* by what had happened in South Africa.'

'Hold on,' CGP interrupted. 'Why were there only four Tests in the series?'

'That's just the way it is sometimes. There would have been commercial reasons, probably,' I said flippantly, as

I had no idea. 'The point is the board didn't have much confidence in their captain.'

'Didn't he feel a bit pissed off by that?' CGP asked, reasonably.

'I'm quite sure he did. And that's life, too, isn't it? Sometimes things just don't go your way and you have to prove yourself. In the first Test, in Trinidad, West Indies were bowled out in less than 20 overs in their second innings for 51. Australia won by 312 runs, a whopping victory for them. It looked as though Windies would be thoroughly routed in the series, don't you agree?'

'It certainly looks that way.' CGP still seemed less than engaged.

'But in the second Test in Jamaica, West Indies bowled out Australia for 256 in the first innings and scored 431 in their first. In the second, West Indies ran through Australia to bowl them out for 177 and so needed only three runs to win, which they got, of course.'

'Okay, I understand that.'

'And Lara was appointed for the rest of the series. He had risen to the challenge and showed the board what he was made of when it really mattered. There's a lesson there too, of course. So now we get to the third Test in Barbados. Australia won the toss and chose to bat, scoring 490.'

'If they got that many, you would say it was a good decision to choose to bat there,' said CGP, now seeming to warm to the subject, even if only slightly.

I smiled at my tutee. 'You would think so, based on that first innings, wouldn't you? Especially, when I tell you that, at one stage, West Indies were 64/4 in their first innings and eventually all out for 329, meaning they trailed Australia by 161 runs. That looked like a mountainous lead already so the Windies bowlers had to come up with something. And Courtney Walsh, a mainstay of the side, did just that. He took five Aussie wickets for 39 runs. The Aussies were all out for 146.

'But you'd probably still make them favourites, wouldn't you? They had built up a lead of 307 runs and the Windies seemed fragile. What would you do at that point?'

'Give up?' said CGP.

'Really? I don't think you would. Really? Is that what we do? In life, I mean?' I asked. 'Or would we find some inner strength to carry on?'

'Some of us give up and some of us don't,' CGP countered. 'Not everyone has got inner strength. That's life too.'

'I have never seen a single cricketer ever give up in a match, however hopeless the situation seems. I've seen some who have been pretty bloody hopeless but they haven't given up. How could they do that to their team-mates? Or, off the pitch if you like, how could we do that to our family or to our friends? Our own teams? Surely we would keep fighting? Still, I will concede that it did look as though West Indies had no chance. In their second innings, they lost three wickets having scored 78 runs and still needed 230 to win. Then Lara came in.'

I pressed play on the recording of the match.

We watched mostly in silence, apart from when I would exclaim, 'What a shot! Did you see that? Look at what Lara did there!'

And Lara did so much there. He was powerful; cutting and hooking, hitting the ball for miles, thumping it over the stands to reach his 50, swatting balls away with disdain. His boundary that won the match was the signal not so much for the crowd to invade the pitch but for it to cascade out of the stands, a tsunami of joy flowing over the ground.

At one point, the West Indies had been 105/5 but Lara scored 153 to propel them to an astonishing victory. Even the Australian Steve Waugh said he had never played in a better match.

Lara had batted for nearly six hours as if he was a man possessed and it turns out that he had been using visualisation techniques for the last two Tests, during which he had scored 213 and 153 runs respectively. You could say the technique worked.

CGP even seemed enthralled by what he had seen.

'OK, I will give you that. It was an exciting match and he looks a great player. And I can see how you could view it as a metaphor for life: not giving up when the chips are down, blah, blah, blah. But lots of things could provide that metaphor, couldn't they? Football? Golf? And just about any sport you could name, really.'

'But do *any* of them have as much resonance as a Test match or as much lyricism? Maybe it is because they often last for five days and develop their story slowly, like a symphony, culminating in a dramatic – sometimes – finale. We can become totally absorbed and swept along as the story unfolds, in all the moments of tragedy as well as exhilaration.'

'Ah, but that might mean that cricket is just a distraction from life, not a metaphor for life,' argued CGP.

'Well *of course* it's a bloody distraction too! And, God knows, we need that sometimes,' I countered. 'But I'm going to stick with my idea of cricket as a metaphor for life, thank you. Oh, and I'll take its role as distraction therapy, too.'

'Good. Actually, I did quite enjoy watching that and I *might* watch some more. Where do you think I should start?'

He might just become a cricket fan. Hallelujah. We must never, ever stop trying to convert the non-speakers.

* * *

Thanks in large part to the World Cup and the Ashes, my heart had begun to heal in 2019 and, at the end of the year, I joined Surrey as a county and England member for the 2020 season. I began to understand that I was allowed to feel some relief from the agonies of dealing with my parents and, instead, began to look forward to carefree, happy, sunny days at The Oval, with lashings of soggy sandwiches and warm wine, especially as the West Indies were touring England that summer.

But in March that year, as the Covid pandemic began to unfold, England's tour of Sri Lanka was abandoned after 12 days and the UK went into lockdown. Carefree days became careworn. Cricket was the last thing on anyone's minds – apart from the England and Wales Cricket Board (the ECB). Behind the scenes, the ECB worked out a bio-secure plan to allow the West Indies to make the tour (slightly delayed) to England and it is to the huge credit of the tourists that they agreed to it when so many of them were worried about leaving their loved ones in the Caribbean. Becoming the first touring side to endure bio-secure cricket was no small feat and after the series, which England won 2-1, Stuart Broad said the West Indies had been the heroes of the summer.

The first Test began on 8 July; the third and last finished on 28 July. The series didn't seem long enough but at least I got my West Indies fix and, for most cricket fans, our mental health was salvaged by *Test Match Special.* And cricket kept on giving with a three-Test series against Pakistan in August, which England won 1-0. The last Test, at Southampton, was notable for England's Zak Crawley's epic innings of 267 and for

James Anderson taking his 600th Test wicket, which at least gave the nation something to rejoice about in a relentlessly bleak year.

The new year began in similar vein but as we all tried to navigate our way through a strange Covid world, I focused on looking forward to getting back to The Oval for the 2021 season. Despite my initial apprehension at being in a non-socially distanced crowd, it didn't take long for the joy of being at a Test – which India won spectacularly by 157 runs – to kick in. Marvelling at the thousands of pints drunk, listening to the dozens of songs played by the Barmy Army and the Bharat Army – and the Salami Army throwing food around in the Galadari stand – lifted my soul. And that was even before play started. It was the first time I had been to a match with my sister for two years and if felt like a lifetime.

'I've missed this so much,' I said as we took our seats on the first morning. And I didn't just mean the cricket. The atmosphere was joyful: the men around us were babbling on about lawnmowers and problems with wives, cool bags were full to bursting, but not for long, and the beer snakes became longer and more elaborate as the day went on. We eavesdropped all day to the men who thought they knew everything about the game but didn't, as well as to those who had an encyclopaedic knowledge and shut everyone else up.

I regaled my sister with tales of our wonderful father befriending fellow spectators at The Oval and reminded her of our childhood jaunts to Trent Bridge, many of which she had forgotten in the mists of time. Of the many blessings that Test cricket, more than any other sport, bestows, it is the time between overs that affords an indulgence for nostalgia as well as for conversations that lead nowhere but make a joyful journey.

The advent of The Hundred, for all its qualities, will never give such benediction and nor is it intended to but I hope the sport's new converts will begin to fall in love too with Test cricket, the pinnacle of the most beautiful of all ball games. I hope future generations will relish the natural pauses between overs to chew over life's complexities and to find solace or distraction in what is happening out in the middle.

It is impossible, though, for me to ignore the fact that, for the past few years, there has been someone missing in the seat next to me. The man who introduced me to the game, and to Viv Richards and thus West Indies cricket, is irreplaceable. I have made the journey from despair and heartbreak at my father's loss to a feeling of abundant gratitude that we enjoyed so many hours together, sometimes in silence, often eating and drinking, watching sporting giants show us the way forward. Cricket bestowed us those days together as only cricket could.

I still feel my Dad's absence so deeply but I also sense him at every game with me, however many years have passed.

At every match, wherever it is being played, I take my seat in the stands yet I can still see my 12-year-old self sprawling on a sunny outfield in Somerset with Dad, who is wearing a version of one of his many plaid shirts, lying prone on the grass next to me. He is trying to ease his chronic back pain as we chat aimlessly about cricket and about life. I see the sun burst from behind a grey cloud and feel the frisson of excitement as I have my first sighting of a West Indies cricket god who changed my life and opened my eyes in ways he would never know.

And then my father stands up, rubs the small of his back as is his habit, and I watch him walk towards the pavilion.

Acknowledgements

I OWE huge gratitude to those who stood on the shore and urged me on through some very choppy waters.

For having faith in me and then keeping it: my brilliant agent Melanie Michael-Greer.

For life support when I most needed it: Trevor and Eve Weeks, Christine and David Ackary, Kenneth and Susan Weeks, Peggy and Dennis Jones, Marion Allard, John and Christine Savidge.

For allowing me to stand on their shoulders: my *Evening Standard* colleagues, in particular Emma Wilkinson, Mick Dennis, Michael Herd, Manny Robinson, Evan Samuel and Michael Weinstein.

For helping me to (literally) put one front in foot of the other: Dr Jennifer Hudson, Dr Rob Baylis, Peter Black of BodyWorks, Dr Susan Horsewood-Lee, Marisa Peer, Lucy Clare, Rachel Ballard.

For lifelong love: 'Miss' Caroline Brown, Sandy and Richard Dale, Rhona and Christopher Day, the Johnson family, Rachel and Vincent Kelly, Jane and Chris

Goodger, Jo Hill, Ruth and James Ramsden, Gillian Sims, the Footballers' Wives and their husbands: Sara and Richard Brown, Nicki and Grant Elliott, and Susie and Charles Glaisher.

For reading, feedback and more: Tim Andrews, Aidan Caruana, Sandy Dale, Rhona Day, Nicki Elliott, Daryl Johnson, Michael Johnson, Lucy Johnson, Sisi Savidge, Jane Savidge.

For his immense kindness and help: Nigel Anthony in Antigua.

For the guiding light: Sir Vivian Richards.

For the delight (and even the despair): all West Indies cricketers, past, present and future.

Special cheers to my sister Jane Savidge who, despite being immersed in her own writing and much else, gave me advice, reassurance, much laughter and kept me going through the dark days.

It is 25 years since my last book was published, mainly for three very good reasons:

Lucy Johnson, the original chuckly buckly, who brings the sunshine in, DFILU.

Sisi Savidge, who brings such joy and keeps me on my toes, DFILU.

And thank you, Michael, my one and only, for being my loudest and most loving cheerleader. 'If not for you, I'd be nowhere at all.'

Selected Bibliography

C.L.R. James, *Beyond A Boundary*, Stanley Paul & Co, 1963

Ruth Miller, *Careers For Girls*, Penguin, 1973

Norman Mailer, *The Fight*, Little Brown and Company, 1975

John Arlott and David Rayvern Allen, *Arlott on Cricket – His Writings on the Game*, Harper Collins Willow, 1984

David Foot, *Sunshine, Sixes and Cider*, David & Charles, 1986

Malcolm Marshall, *Marshall Arts: The Autobiography*, Queen Anne Press, 1987

Michael Manley, *A History of West Indies Cricket*, André Deutsch, 1988

Hilary McD Beckles, *The Development of West Indies Cricket, Vol 1, The Age of Nationalism*, The Press University of the West Indies, 1988

Viv Richards, *Hitting Across The Line*, Headline Book Publishing, 1991

David Frith, *By His Own Hand*, Hutchinson, 1991

Peter O'Toole, *Loitering With Intent: The Child*, Macmillan, 1992

Tony Francis, *The Zen of Cricket*, Stanley Paul & Co, 1992

Mike Marqusee, *Anyone But England: Cricket Race and Class*, Verso Books, 1994

Hilary McD Beckles and Brian Stoddart, *Liberation Cricket*, Manchester University Press, 1995

Michéle Savidge and Alastair McLellan, *Real Quick: A Celebration of the West Indies Pace Quartets*, Cassell Blandford Press, 1995

Nothing Sacred: The New Cricket Culture, Two Heads Publishing, 1996

Peter O'Toole, *Loitering With Intent: The Apprentice*, Macmillan, 1996

Hilary McD Beckles, *The Development of West Indies Cricket, Vol 2, The Age of Globalisation*, The Press University of the West Indies 1998

Alexander Levy, *The Orphaned Adult*, Da Capo Press, 1999

Rob Steen, Alastair McLellan *500-1 – The Miracle of Headingley '81*, BBC Books, 2001

Andrew Collins, *Where Did It All Go Right?* Ebury Press, 2003

Marcus Trescothick *Coming Back To Me*, Harper Sport, 2009

Edited by Stewart Brown and Ian McDonald, *The Bowling Was Superfine: West Indian Writing and West Indian Cricket*, Peepal Tree Books, 2012

Ashley Gray, *The Unforgiven: Mercenaries or Missionaries?* Pitch Publishing, 2020

Michael Holding, *Why We Kneel, How We Rise*, Simon & Schuster UK, 2020

Michéle Savidge began her career as a sports journalist on *The Cricketer* magazine before becoming deputy editor on Imran Khan's *Cricket Life*. After that magazine's spectacular financial collapse, she became the first female sports subeditor on the *Evening Standard*. She is the co-author (with Alastair McLellan) of *Real Quick: A Celebration of the West Indies Pace Quartets*.